RESPECT

THE POETRY OF DETROIT MUSIC

Edited by Jim Daniels and M.L. Liebler

RESPECT

Michigan State University Press | *East Lansing*

♾ The paper used in this publication meets the minimum requirements
of ANSI/NISO Z39.48-1992 (R 1997) (Permanence of Paper).

Michigan State University Press
East Lansing, Michigan 48823-5245

Printed and bound in the United States of America.

29 28 27 26 25 24 23 22 21 20   1 2 3 4 5 6 7 8 9 10

Library of Congress Cataloging-in-Publication Data
Names: Daniels, Jim, 1956– editor. | Liebler, M. L., editor.
Title: R E S P E C T : the poetry of Detroit music / edited by Jim Daniels and M. L. Liebler.
Other titles: Respect : the poetry of Detroit music | Poetry of Detroit music
Description: East Lansing : Michigan State University Press, [2019]
Identifiers: LCCN 2018059545 | ISBN 9781611863369 (pbk. : alk. paper)
Subjects: LCSH: Music—Poetry. | Detroit (Mich.)—Poetry.
Classification: LCC PS595.M684 R47 2019 | DDC 782.42164026/8—
dc23 LC record available at https://lccn.loc.gov/2018059545

Book design by Charlie Sharp, Sharp Designs, East Lansing, Michigan
Cover design by Erin Kirk New
Cover art: Monument to Joe Louis

Michigan State University Press is a member of the Green Press Initiative and is
committed to developing and encouraging ecologically responsible publishing
practices. For more information about the Green Press Initiative and the use of
recycled paper in book publishing, please visit *www.greenpressinitiative.org.*

Visit Michigan State University Press at *www.msupress.org*

Contents

II. Detroit Blues. Hastings Street Opera

III. Northern Soul. Dancing in the Streets

IV. Detroit Rocks. Kick Out the Jams

Duke Fakir

Foreword

We are The Tops and we want you to know,
We will swing if the band will just blow.
We'll sing you songs, some fast, some slow,
We're ready to bring you our show.

We'll sing you songs, some fast, some slow,
New tunes, old tunes, some you won't know,
Take you places you'd like to go.
We're rearing to bring you the show.
We're The Tops, and we want you to know.

I wrote that song years ago. We used it a couple times—way back in the day. This was in the fifties to open our shows. That's when we sang some good old standards and then some blues because we didn't have a record deal back then. We did that for like ten years before we came to Motown.

However, Motown is the real story, and it has a very poetic theme to it for sure. A lot of the story of Detroit's contemporary music scene started in the late 1950s, first with Little Willie John, John Lee Hooker, Jackie Wilson and then with The Motown Story. I am happy to say that The Four Tops played a significant role in this Motown/Hitsville; I now look at the Hitsville house on West Grand Blvd as the place where the The Four Tops were truly born. Hitsville is where The Tops became serious recording artists with major hit records like "Reach Out—I'll Be There," "I Can't Help Myself (Sugar Pie, Honey Bunch)," "Bernadette," "Loving You Is Sweeter Than Ever," "Wake Me Shake Me," and of course "Standing in the Shadows of Love," and many more number ones. I look at Hitsville as our home, our birthplace, and the place where we grew up with the rest of our siblings: The Temptations, Smokey &

The Miracles, Supremes, Marvin Gaye, Martha and the Vandellas, and many others. We had such fun. I mean, that house was full of love, excitement and most importantly music. We ate together, we played together, and we all worked very well together. The one common denominator at Hitsville was love. And that's why when they say Motown was a family, that's not just a cliché. That's because all of us respected each other, and we all sincerely loved what we were doing. We always helped each other out and supported each other. So, when I drive by today, I often pull over to the curb to take a few minutes to remember that house as the place where The Four Tops once lived, grew, thrived, and came into their own. The story of Hitsville and Motown is an absolutely amazing story that people all over the world know and enjoy to this day. Wonderful folks from all over the world, especially in England, have helped to keep the Motown music flame burning. It is now often referred to as "Northern Soul" in England, Europe, and Japan, but it is still the "Sound of Young America."

I believe The Four Tops are a real Detroit story. Ours is a story of how working-class kids form lasting friendships, cultivate and nurture each other's talents, and give the world some of the most memorable music ever created on planet earth. Levi Stubbs, Lawrence Payton, Obie Benson, and I never forgot where we came from and who we were. All four of The Tops remained in Detroit for our entire career. We didn't move to the West Coast. We stayed here and did our work. The Four Tops went from high school friends who loved to sing together and believed in ourselves to the experienced group that Berry Gordy signed to his new fledgling record label, now known as Motown. From a house with a garage made into a studio ("The Snake Pit") and the wonderfully talented Funk Brothers and support system of brothers and sisters who cared and truly loved each other, we all went on to be one of the remembered Motown artists. From singing on the school bus to singing in a [now iconic] garage at a house on West Grand, we soldiered on as four friends who eventually ended up forever remembered in The Rock Hall of Fame in Cleveland.

While I still lead and perform with The Four Tops all over the US and the world, Levi, Obie, and Lawrence have since passed on. What started in Detroit in the 50s with four young guys eventually became one of the cornerstones in The Motown Story. We were always very happy to be "Standing in the Shadows of Love."

M. L. Liebler and Jim Daniels

Introduction

Some people say a city can't have a soul. Those people are not from Detroit. A lot of music and a lot of poetry come out of Detroit. It's the nature of the beast. The beast of Detroit is not tameable. The poems in this anthology reflect the feelings and the rich history of Detroit music as clearly shown throughout the moving funeral for our queen, Aretha Franklin. These poems, divided by musical genres jazz, blues, soul, rock, techno, and hip-hop, all celebrate the heart, soul, and spirit of the recognizable sounds that were born and nurtured right here in the Motor City. The poems we have selected offer readers fresh insights, important historical memories, and a new understanding and appreciation for the major role Detroit music has played, and continues to play, in our daily lives and in lives around the world—Detroit music rising up from the (313) and out to the world with a beat.

We compiled this anthology with very few resources beyond our love for the music of our city—how the music represents the unique complexity and diversity of our community and our sense of pride and identity. We have long connected poetry to music in diverse ways in our own careers, so we felt it natural to bring together the poetry and music of others into one collection that exhibits the spirit and heart of the Motor City.

We started our research for this book by scouring journals, books, the internet, and our memories, looking for the best poems about all genres of Detroit music. We next set out to track down, beg, cajole, and grovel for permissions from poets, lyricist, and writers to let us use their work in this book. We looked for a wide representation of voices from across the country who had written poems about Detroit music and asked poets we knew (many nationally known, some regionally known, and others young and up-and-coming) who we thought might want to write a brand-new poem expressing their love of and connection to the music of our beloved city. Many of the poets wrote new poems for the collection—some real gems and new classics. Among the poets and writers in this book who wrote original pieces are Lolita Hernandez, Heather Bourbeau, Andrei Codrescu, Desiree Cooper, W. D. Ehrhart, Robert Fanning, Diane DeCillis, Hayan Charara, Brian Gilmore, Brooke Horvath, David James, John Jeffire, James Kenyon, Gerry Lafemina, John D. Lamb, Richard Peabody, Jack White, and Michael Zadoorian. Of course, we both wanted to include a few of the known classic voices of Detroit poetry like Mark James Andrews, Melba Joyce Boyd, John Sinclair, George Tysh, Chris Tysh, Kim Hunter, Jim Gustafson, Bill Harris, Robert Hayden, Robin Eichele, Linda Nemec Foster, Philip Levine, Lawrence Joseph, Toi Derricotte, Rayfield Waller, Tyrone Williams, three of the MC5—Fred Smith, Rob Tyner, and Wayne Kramer—and others. We also wanted to include some young poets we knew to be writing poems about Detroit music. A great example of this are the poems by the wonderful, young Detroit poet Nandi Comer and her talented InsideOut and Detroit public high school students involved in the Detroit Techno-Poetry project.

We are grateful to the many poets and songwriters in this anthology who allowed us to use their work for little or no money in order to support our greater goal of preserving poems about Detroit music in the pages of this beautiful book. Now, thanks to all of them, these poems and lyrics will live on forever. In addition to all of the wonderful poets, there are and have been many great musicians who have been inspired by our city to write songs as a homage to Detroit. Songwriters who fit the bill for this book, and who were very generous with their work, include folks like Billy Bragg, Ginny Carr, Fats Domino, Don Duprie, Joe Henry, Tino Gross, Champtown, Jan Krist, Robert Jones, Gordon Lightfoot, Art Lyzak, Marshall Mathers (Eminem), Paul Simon, Carolyn Striho, and others. The whole editing process has turned out to be quite an incredible ride for us. Here, readers will find great poems and lyrics covering it all: Detroit jazz and blues, doo-wop, Detroit soul, Motown, classic rock, the "Kick Out the Jams" 1960s, punk rock, alternative, avant-garde, hip-hop and techno.

Detroit has always been an incubator for innovation in music and in all of the arts. Through our blood, sweat, tears, we have created a unique, earthy style of music, art, poetry. Detroit's status as a hotbed of musical talent is exemplified by the years 1962 to 1967 when there were well over four hundred record companies in Detroit, and there were scores of legendary places before like Joe Von Battle's JVB Records on Hastings Street, Fortune Records, Clix Records, and other rare gospel labels. Many of these legendary studios were located very close to M. L.'s office at Wayne State University. Within a mile-and-a-half walk is Hitsville U.S.A.—the house that combined the music of Detroit's best jazz musicians, now known as The Funk Brothers, with fine young singers to give the world The Four Tops, Smokey Robinson, The Supremes, The Temptations, Stevie Wonder, and Marvin Gaye. Marvin's legendary album *What's Going On* was recorded and first mixed in that house located at 2648 West Grand Boulevard. Just thinking of that gives us a chill and a sense of pride in our history. Within five blocks, The MC5 rehearsed and recorded. Four blocks over on Third Street was Fortune Records, and on the north end of campus is the Granddaddy of all the Detroit recording studios, United Sound. The building still stands as an iconic structure on the corner of Second Street and Antoinette. George Clinton, in his red tennis shoes and multicolored dreads, recorded and rehearsed there daily. The Rolling Stones recorded there in the late 80s, and an excited WSU *South End* staff photographer captured them hanging out on the corner of Second Street.

As young, suburban kids, we attended concerts throughout the Detroit area. M. L remembers taking the bus downtown to see WABX's Free Concerts featuring Detroit's best-known rock bands like Third Power, The Amboy Dukes, Brownsville Station, The MC5, and others either on the lawn of the Detroit Public Library or down West Warren at what was once known as WSU's Tartar Football Field. Jim remembers going to noon-to-midnight rock and roll revivals at the State Fairgrounds, where he saw Bob Seger and Mitch Ryder and Detroit on the same bill, along with Frut, Mutzie, Teagarden and Van Winkle, and other Detroit bands.

For all the national heat taken and the various autopsies of Detroit that have been performed over the decades, it is still the city that gave (and continues to give) the world some of its best music across all of the genres. In *Respect* we have made an honest attempt to be inclusive of musical genres and to feature the rich diversity of America's poetic voices. We tried to represent the incredibly rich musical legacy of this city as best we could, given the various challenges of obtaining rights and permissions. We tried to highlight and pay tribute to diverse styles of music, diverse styles of poetry, and the magic that happens when these two art forms come together. The 45 rpm of "Instant Karma" by John Lennon and Yoko Ono says PLAY LOUD on one side and PLAY SOFT on the other, and perhaps if we have a bias here, it might be toward the PLAY LOUD side. We apologize for any omissions, knowing that inevitably we will have missed some work that we wished we had discovered and included. After all, the Detroit music and the Detroit poetry never stop.

Rather than provide extensive footnotes, we encourage you, if you are unfamiliar with some of the songs, bands, singers, and musicians in any of these poems and lyrics, to look them up, find out more about them, and give their music a listen; to use our list of reading recommendations at the end of the book; and perhaps even purchase some music to keep the industry vital. We also encourage you to buy the books of the poets included here. We thank Michigan State University Press editor extraordinaire Julie Loehr, who believed in this project from the beginning. M. L. is grateful to his Wayne State University intern Miranda Shell and his Motown class peer mentors and teaching assistants Kara Frank and Aaron Proudfoot who all offered their services to research, run down emails leads, and much more out of a love for poetry and Motor City music.

We are proud of this collection that we have pulled together, and deeply honored by all of these writers who have graciously offered their work in the spirit of preserving the words for future generations to appreciate, discover, and rediscover Detroit's vast musical history. Our music comes from a gritty, working-class, DIY ethic and attitude. Economic, manufacturing, and housing challenges have tried to pin Detroit down, but we keep getting up and reinventing ourselves in our music, literature, and art. These poems will get you rockin' in the same way our music does. This anthology you hold in your hands rocks, shakes, and shimmies to the sounds of Detroit. What Detroit stands for is uniquely American. We hope that when you finish this collection, your ears are buzzing a little or a lot.

We offer readers this book to riff on the song Sister Aretha made famous:

What you want,

Detroit's got it
What you need
You know we got it?
All we're askin'
Is for a little respect . . .
(just a little bit).

Kenny Cox

Eddie Jefferson

Alice Coltrane

Marcus Belgrave

Strata Gallery

Contemporary Jazz Quartet

Yusef Lateef

Charles Moore

Blackbottom

Paradise Valley

Hastings Street

Baker's Keyboard Lounge

Pepper Adams

Ray McKinney

Griot Galaxy

Faruq Z. Bey

Harold McKinney

Ron English

Robert Hayden

RJ Spangler

Danny Spencer

Art Tatum

I.

DETROIT JAZZ

Paradise Valley Days

Mark James Andrews

Shot 3 Silenced the Singer: The Murder

Eddie Jefferson is on the marquee in Detroit
Baker's Keyboard Lounge
May 9, 1979
1:35 in the a.m.

When the music's over, step out into quiet night
1, 2, 3, 4, exit
Baker's on Livernois Avenue
into the Motor City street.

The Patriarch Lyric Composer of Jazz Vocalese
Griot Poet who busted rhymes
on the solos of the Jazz Giants
for the World Stage
is now hustling back to his road home
the Leland House Hotel
with friends Cheryl Francis,
Leonard Paul Harrell & Valerie Chalk.

Eddie Jefferson shut down the gig EARLY
some snide audience heckling
ripping the pick-up band
& his hard post-bopping Alto player Richie Cole
an attack from an Avant-Garde aficionado faction
or maybe an unspoken fear or premonition
that his ticket would be punched on the Night Train
by a Grim Reaper in a chugging Midnight Special.

EJ had spidey sense & threw a safety net over Cole

3

told him to lay out of his party
stay put with his Flame
actress Brenda Vaccarro
who was hanging in D Town
with The Alto Madness Man.

Eddie Jefferson hit the Street.

Cheryl Francis painted a gothic tableau:
We heard a loud bang.
I saw smoke.
It was a green Lincoln.
I saw fire shoot out of the passenger side
Just a big burst of fire came out the window.
I kept asking, Where is Eddie?

Leonard Paul Harrell followed Eddie out of the club,
53, of Detroit, a dancer
& old running buddy of EJ.
He viewed the green & chrome
Lincoln of Death
pull around a Checker Cab & stop.

2 shots close together rang out
I SAW THE BARREL OF THE SHOTGUN
OUT THE WINDOW FIRING.
THE 3RD SHOT HIT EDDIE.
HE SAID "HUP," like that.

I guess the force of the shot turned him to the right
& he started running.
I looked up to the 4th shot coming to ME.
I could only see the barrel of the gun & the person
that was holding—

the shadow of the person holding the gun
It was a green Lincoln Town Car
Light green or dark green?
Green like the green in a flower
green like a leaf
that green
Green like the St. Patrick's day hats?
Not that bright. Not that bright. A green leaf.
Like a green leaf?
Green leaf.
That's all.

BANG BANG BANG BANG
Paul hit the bricks yelled
"Get down!"

The Lincoln made a U-Turn.
The killer made good his escape.

The artist who put words to Eddie Harris'
Freedom Jazz Dance
took flight
made Last Dance steps
35 feet down an alley
made THE BIG JUMP
Vamping, Looping, Riffing
a funky gurgling New Vocalese
fresh for the yank
by The Sandman with the Shepherd's Crook.

I said, Shotgun
4 blasts from the DRIVER
Lincoln Continental
Late model / Leaf green.

I said, Shot 3
silenced the SINGER
put him Out, Baby
Off the spinning Earth
Hey!

Glen Armstrong

The Last DJ

for Ed Love & The Famous Coachman

There was a vaguely Japanese-sounding rag
   and then the last DJ's voice.

There was a keepsake inscribed
   by Robert Johnson:

  Stop Breaking Down

And then his voice, calm, almost apologetic,
   aware that he'd entered our bedrooms.

There was a saxophone player
   who filled a chordal bell tower
   with flutter-mouse melodies

   who had been the best man
   at the last DJ's second best wedding.

     In the Still of the Night.
     Misterioso.
     Bitter Suite in the Ozone.

When he told us about his famous friend,
   I thought I heard him coughing.

He worked that almost secret shift
   between trouble and sunrise,

between memory and dementia,
between the blinking red light
and the accident cleared from his throat.

Each time he approached the microphone,
he seemed to lose something irreplaceable.

Without his advent candle of a broadcast,
the smoky clubs,
the sharkskin suits,
the bad blood in the rhythm section,

would never have been forgotten.

Like him, I wanted to distill my every fiber
down to a voice

that could protect those naked bodies
from the shadows beyond their sheets,

that would nurture insomnia
until the uncertainties of daylight
replaced the certainties of jazz,

and like his other desperate listeners,
I wanted to be loved
for hearing things that might not be there.

Peter Balakian

Joe Louis's Fist

1.

After the sun rose into rust between gravel and horizon,
after the scent of you oxidized the steel of my car going
into the lidocaine of the morning air as the highway slid

into northeast Detroit past Chill & Mingle,
I did a double-take and took a wrong turn at Rim Repair.
(Long ago my father said I should see the fist).

No one spoke Swahili on 12th Street, still rubble
after the blind pigs folded up.
It was a cliché of the image of itself but it was, it was

like nothing, the vacant burned-out bungalows, car parts, metal scraps,
arson jobs, abandoned homes, barbed wire playgrounds,
shacks pummeled along Six Mile Road—derelict since '67.

2.

My father said when Louis won, the radio static was a wave
of sound that stayed all night like the riots blocks away in Harlem,
as the scent of lilac and gin wafted down Broadway to his window

across from the Columbia gates where the sounds of
Fletcher Henderson and Dizzy buzzed the air,
where the mock Nazi salutes were shadows over the

granite lions and snake-dancing, and car horns
banged the tar and busted windshields,
even coffee shops south of 116th were looted.

3.

It came back in fragments—through the gauze
of the summer of love, through Lucy in the Sky
and other amnesias; streets of burnt-out buildings,

paratroopers bivouacked in high schools with gas and bayonets.
By 6 a.m. July 23 national guards were walking
in the rain of black cinder and pillars of smoke—

a black body hanging from a fence of an auto-part yard,
whisky-faced boys shooting through the fire
as torn bags of loot trailed the streets.

Prostitutes used pool cues to defend themselves.
Booze and cartridge smoke ate their skin.
One trooper said it looked like Berlin in '45.

4.

Samson, David, and Elijah in one left hook
my father said, (6/22/38) upbraided Neville Chamberlain
liberated Austria and Sudetenland

knocked the lights out in Berlin—
sent Polish Jews into the boulevards
for one night of phantasmal liberation.

Because Hitler banned jazz, because Black Moses led
crowds and crowds to the marvelous, inscrutable, overwhelming
balked dreams of revenge, millions seeped out of doorways, alleys,
tenements—

dreaming of the diamond pots, of Chrysler heaven,
the golden girls of Hollywood and Shirley Temple
who rubbed some salt into his hands for luck.

Untermensch from Alabama—
sucker for the right hand—the other side of Hailee Salisee
black men howled to him from their electric chairs.

5.

When I drove past Berry Gordy Jr. Boulevard
and the Hitsville USA sign on the studio-house,
the lights were out and I could only

imagine the snake pit where Smokey Robinson
spun into vinyl, where "Heat Wave"
came as sweet blackmail in the beach air of '64,

where the Funk Brothers and Martha Reeves
took the mini opera and dumped it on its head.

By the time I hit Jefferson and Woodward
the sun was glaring on the high windows,
and then it hit me—spinning the light—

horizontal two-foot arm smashing the blue
through the empty pyramid holding it up
in the glare of skyscraper glass: molten

bronze-hand, hypotenuse of history,
displaced knuckles—

the smooth-casting over the gouged-out wounds—
the naked, beloved, half-known forms.

Melba Joyce Boyd

A Mingus Among Us and a Walden Within Us

for Donald Walden (1938–2008)

Dexter Gordon
glanced back,
saw Donald Walden
taking Giant Steps.

So, Dexter held the gate,
makin' the jazz greats wait—
Monk, Bird, Coltrane,
the contentious Miles,
the tumultuous Lateef
and the sultry Billie—
makin' a wake
for the sax man
from Detroit
by way of
St. Louie,
representin' bebop
breaking fixed notes,
traversing linear scales,
and all repressive
constrictions impaled
on music sheets,
resisting the
inconvenience
of mortal skin
when spirit enchants
song and rules of

Earth bound
dominions
diminish.

In the "D"
he was called
"the bebop police,"
who styled in
razor sharp
GQ slacks
as distinctive
as his tenor sax,
articulating
transformative
sets marking
planets.

Yeah,
there is a
Mingus
among us,
but there is
a Donald Walden
within us.

Melba Joyce Boyd

Blow Marcus Blow

for Marcus Belgrave (1936–2015)

There's jazz around the corner
Just beyond the golden gate,
Halleluiah jazz.
                              —Art Paul Schlosser

Marcus blows away
our Detroit blues,
I said,
Marcus Belgrave
blows away our
never-ending blues.
he breaks off
circuitous sounds
inside the city's
contentious womb.

Motown lyrics swing,
as bebop registers
iconic scales
that make
spirits soar
even when
winter comes
and locks
in the cold.

We shiver with
uncertainty within
shifting winds—
this end of an era
we mourn with the
passing of a true
Renaissance man,
and then celebrate
his reunion with
Dizzy, Miles,
and Satchmo,
kicking it with
Cox,
McKinney
and Walden
inside timelessness—
the freedom zone
of eternal jazz.

So, blow Gabriel.
Go blow your horn
cause jazz is
round the corner,
"Halleluiah jazz,"
and Marcus Belgrave
is joinin' your band
in the Promised Land.

Blow Marcus Blow!
Blow Marcus Blow!

Melba Joyce Boyd

The Bass Is Woman

for Marion Hayden

At a left—
                    angled tilt,
                    adjacent to
her throat,
Marion mind—
melds with this
magnificent
instrument.

Lithe, swift
fingers
         restringing
eighth notes
in cut time
against
bare-knuckle
restraints
releasing stress
from neck
past breasts
through a
navel leading
into a womb
gifting violet
riffs like sweet
rose water
brimming inside

uninhibited
thick hips
that swing
and sway,
dancing on
ripples of
unreachable
prayers.

Her brown
curves ground
earth tones
at the base
of rhythm—
the back-
bone of song.

The bass
is woman.

Melba Joyce Boyd

Working It Out

for Kenny Cox (1940–2008)

A lot of people have died for this music.
                                    —*Dizzy Gillespie*

black keys
conversing
with ivory
like oblique
irony in
unrhymed
psalms

Chopin sonatas
confer with
Strayhorn
symphonics
Monk disrupts
with tempos
linked like dominoes

this dialogue occurs
with Kenn Cox
composing suites
on piano
without primacy
in Multidirection
or as Guerrilla Jams
engaging a

dystrophic
democracy

on dim streets
blue notes
stud starlight
at high altitudes

Kenn Cox
at the keys
channeling ebony
freely through
the integrity
of well-honed ivory

Writer L. Bush

A Love Supreme

> *Inspired by the compositions of John Coltrane and the music of Motown*

Boom-**boom**-boom-**boom**.
A love supreme.
Boom-**boom**-boom-**boom**.
A love supreme.
Boom-**boom**-boom-**boom**.

This is not The Primettes mixed with Holland-Dozier;
This is not a Ballard ballad, boosting us out of the Brewster projects;
Nor will it **Stop** In The Name Of Love,
For it is **truly** A Love Supreme!

Hugging us with black and blue strung-out arms,
While all about us, the **Equinox** shrieks
And Pierces each of the Night's Thousand Eyes,
Creating a thousand drug-addled, climactic sighs.

Blow, 'Trane, **blow!**
Blow Black blood through that ax!
Swing that golden sax!
Brass-magic-tenor-arms / Roped-off with-strings,
Blow-us-a-few-of-your-favorite-things . . .

Your spit valves open,
And drip in the dust;
Hold **still** your muddy music,
And rub it on us,
Until we hear if we do not see

The Yazoo river,
The Delta of The Mississippi.

Boom-**boom**-boom-**boom.**
A love supreme.
Boom-**boom**-boom-**boom.**
A love supreme.

A Love Supreme has four parts:
Acknowledgement, Pursuance, Resolution and Psalm.
We acknowledged drinking and drugs as we pursued them,
But we found in them
No resolution
And **no** psalm.

So we died, **BLARING!**
Repeating the history of Billie, Miles and Bird.
Echoing into the emptiness,
Notes never before heard.
Treated like lords all over the world
Only to come back and have the **shit** beaten out of us
On the streets that **WE love!**

Yes, we came back out of love.
We endure out of love.
Our art was **birthed** out of love.
We tarry out of love.
A **supreme** love!

Keep sacred this music called Jazz;
Our only original art form.
Shapely and fertile;
house her in your ear.
Her bosom: Black;

Her eyes: Kind Of Blue.
She is our true
American Dream!
A love supreme.
A love supreme.

And we did love supremely, once—Before they divided us again and again like mitosis.
Our own jealousy killing us off quicker than cirrhosis!
What's happenin,' *bro'?*
What up, **blood?**
My ace **boon coon;**
What's going on—what it is—what it *be's* like?
It's all love, cat.
Once we spoke like that;
We **Spoke** . . . with love.

A love supreme.
A love supreme.

Riding the Blue Train to infinity—Echoing across the universe as notes
We will float—Divinely and **supremely** loved
We will no longer fear the night's many White eyes
Because the soul needs but **one**

Can you . . .
Dig what I mean?
And we will no longer need needles
Offering placebos
Of what can only be found in A Love Supreme.

A love supreme.

A love supreme.
A love supreme.
A love supreme.
Boom,
Boom,
Boom,
Boom . . . boom.

Ginny Carr

He Was The Cat (A Tribute to Eddie Jefferson)

from the recording, "Vocal Madness" by Uptown
Vocal Jazz Quartet, featuring Richie Cole

There was a fellow named Jefferson who
Would tear it up with the band.
A vocalizin' phenomenon who they used to call the "Main Man."
He would think like a sage, sing like a horn,
And there on the stage somethin' special was born.
He would swing, "dit n' doo dat."
He was The Cat.

He sang with Moody in '57.
He put a lyric to bop.
When little Benny came down from Heaven,
He put it over the top.
Jazz was hot in the East, cool in the West,
But his vocalese, it was simply the best
Because man, couldn't he scat.
He was The Cat.

Eddie was hip but wise as an old man,
Takin' that trip to celebrate Coleman,
Lettin' it rip on "Body and Soul," man,
And oh what he'd do, the poetry flew.
A founding father was Jefferson but
He never got the acclaim.
We're here to tell you that he's the one that
Put vocalese in the game.
He would dig sittin' in, blowin' the hit,

And then he would spin out a story to fit,
He was some acrobat.
He was The Cat.

There was a time when there was jazz cookin' up on every corner.
Everybody would sit and listen as they blew,
Tellin' stories they knew in each his own way,
Tellin' the news, bop to blues,
Set the moods any way they'd want to.
Innovation was always there
Electrifyin' the air everywhere you'd be,
Let me tell ya.
All around you'd hear the sound of life abounding free
Comin' out of a horn, bein' born a new way.
Never knew what you'd hear.
First we heard from The Bean
Then the word on the scene was so choice:
Eddie Jefferson's voice, what a beautiful noise.
Master of a lyric and what an inventor,
Singin' with the spirit of jazz at the center,
Anyone who'd hear it knew that he was a mentor:
Enter for the love of the sound.
You found the rhythm town where you can marry vocabulary
To every melody that you'd hear.
For when Eddie would sing, the story was king.
He'd talk about a thing, then be sockin' it like the swing of a bat,
He sang it like that!

He would embrace his lyrical zen to
Tickle those phrases like he was meant to
Take us to places nobody'd been to,
An Everest climb, the cleverest kind!
When Charlie Parker and Moody played it,
There was a hush in the crowd.

And then when Eddie would elevate it,
The jazz community bowed.
He'd evoke what we heard on the soloin' rides
And make every word tell a story besides,
And we're all tippin' our hat!
He Was The Cat.

Esperanza Cintrón

Music -3 The African World Festival

on John R. at Warren in Detroit

Streets narrowed by white
tents, vendors tight on both sides,
like a third-world street market
Browsing brown folk
stroll to the smell of incense
barbeque and fish frying
Speakers creak and crackle
beneath the strained falsettos
of an R&B quartet dressed
in sharkskin and doing a Motown
dip and strut across the grand stage,
the lone keyboard resolute
as the sun struck band takes
a break, guitars and drums idle
Drooping parents sit on folding
chairs or curbs, feet splayed
Toddlers lick cones and sticky fingered
caramel corn in waxed paper bags
near booths packed with
wooden sculptures from
Mali, metal via Ghana
and vibrant bolts of cloth
amid the musical voices of dark
men bartering with smiles
and straight white teeth
as evening begins to tip in
and the blessed air cools

David Cope

River Rouge

after Charles Sheeler

FACES IN SHADOW
toxic clouds roil & pass above—
        specks land
               in the unseen housewife's
fluttering washlines,
in the nostrils of the workers—

here, the machine itself, "functional
        architecture" half-distorted barns,
             half featureless rectangles—
the river, reflecting this
        ochre & brown geometry,
            the treeless land—

yet *nowhere* in this landscape do we see
the armies of workers marching
        thru the doors at dawn,
            chatter & coffee & taking in
        the enveloping roar of the machines,
          leviathan

eating them alive, the
mad labor of the assembly line, the men
sweating, pulling, turning,
        teasing out parts and forms
        forcing out Ford's cars
robotic in

dizzying line, ears

gone deaf in the noise,
                    bosses above
counting down every movement,
                    measuring time,
measuring the men themselves to see what more
they could squeeze
                    from blood & bone.

BEYOND THE SHADOW
My dad grew up in the D,
                    his dad a mechanical engineer
                                   redesigning high speed

          pipe turns at Con Ed,
his childhood neighborhood
                    raising three to be trans—

                              national corporate officers—
          by day a wild flight of kids
jumping off roofs, racing

          thru back alleys—by night,
                    families cowering in basements
          as Feds & the Purple Gang

shot it out a block away.
          he'd dream back dancing
                    whole groups of friends

          swinging at the Grande to
the Duke & Goodman,
          & there was the

              "Battle of the Overpass,"
         where Ford's goons battered
Walter Reuther until

         his skull bled, the workers
                    "sticking to the union
         'til the day they'd die"—

& as a young married man
         he'd lock my mother in
                    braving machine guns

         at intersections to get
to his job working on
         bell housings of Sherman tanks

                    during the race riots of
         '43—Hitler still rampant,
first islands pacific after blood & fire.

THE SCYTHE
My grandma died at Eloise Asylum
now a phantom ruin—still standing,

empty halls, paint peeling,
a fading stone in the cemetery.

I was born at Women's Hospital
& saw Ted Williams hit one into

the center field upper deck at
Briggs, Kaline hitless that day.

Later Janis Joplin played the Grande,

the Stones drove 'em crazy at Olympia—

Motown rose with muscle cars
on the Reuther, the riots of '67—then

burned out years & neighborhoods,
ruined homes & blocks, the Rouge itself

become a relic of another time—
ghost world of shades chewed up

in the scythe, Time itself become
a tale buried in the lost villages

of Anishinaabeg & voyageurs
filled with the light of the forest,

who fell in love with this land of waters.
& I come back & dream my grandfather

toiling in his garden, my dad a boy
again, his dream of the D & those men

who sang these streets & turned
lathes & worked the lines, hopeful.

Diane DeCillis

The Girl from Ipanema Visits Detroit, 1964

Slender, exotic—a jazz singer with smooth dark hair,
Ava arrived from Malone, New York, where she
and my mother grew up. Here to perform at Baker's

she never knew her brief stay was enough that I, at 13,
would shelve the Motown sounds of Junior Walker,
and Gladys Knight for all that jazz. The only

jazz I'd listened to was Getz and Gilberto
because The Girl from Ipanema was # 5 on the charts.
After Ava left, I stood at the mirror, singing

tall and tan and young and lovely . . . bought
Brubeck's Take 5, Montgomery's guitar riffs,
hoping Ava's sleek sophistication would glide

through me like the silky notes of Smokey
Robinson and Marvin Gaye. I eyed the cool loungy
demeanor that, for her, came easy as Ella

though I had no clue what I'd do with it. What I knew
was even in black stirrups, turtleneck, and curly hair
smoothed slick, my reflection rang dissonant as those

jazz instrumentals I tried so hard to like—I didn't exude
the aloof, bossa nova vibe of *when she passes*
each one she passes goes aaaah. Like other girls

in my neighborhood, I wasn't groomed to follow
my passions or even know what they were, needed
lyrics with r-e-s-p-e-c-t to tell me what to want.

Soon, jazz just didn't jive. It lacked the soul
of My Girl, the cool new beat of Dancing in the Street
and I'd had enough syncopated improvisation,

collecting bits and pieces of others to collage myself
whole. Back then, if Ava had asked what I want,
I would have said the wonder of Stevie, the marvel

of Marvelettes, the Dee-troit strut of Temps and Tops—
voices that would drown out Gilberto's ethereal
whispers in a song that was never about the girl

but about a lonely guy who could only watch
this ephemeral image *swing so cool and sway so gently*—
a girl, unattainable, even to herself

Toi Derricotte

Blackbottom

When relatives came from out of town,
we would drive down to Blackbottom,
drive slowly down the congested main streets
      —Beaubien and Hastings—
trapped in the mesh of Saturday night.
Freshly escaped, black middle class,
we snickered, and were proud;
the louder the streets, the prouder.
We laughed at the bright clothes of a prostitute,
a man sitting on a curb with a bottle in his hand.
We smelled barbecue cooking in dented washtubs,
      and our mouths watered.
As much as we wanted it we couldn't take the chance.

Rhythm and blues came from the windows, the throaty voice of
      a woman lost in the bass, in the drums, in the dirty down
      and out, the grind.
"I love to see a funeral, then I know it ain't mine."
We rolled our windows down so that the waves rolled over us
      like blood.
We hoped to pass invisibly, knowing on Monday we would
      return safely to our jobs, the post office and classroom.
We wanted our sufferings to be offered up as tender meat,
and our triumphs to be belted out in raucous song.
We had lost our voice in the suburbs, in Conant Gardens,
      where each brick house delineated a fence of silence;
we had lost the right to sing in the street and damn creation.

We returned to wash our hands of them,
to smell them
whose very existence
tore us down to the human.

Bob "Detroit Count" White

Hastings Street Opera (Part One)

Boys it's all down Hastings Street
Hendrie and Hastings
The corner bar,
It's the only place you can walk in
Get yourself a bottle of beer
Turn your head
And somebody's drinking it.
Boy that's a bad joint.

Well, down the line, down Hastings street
Palmer, Ferry, Kirby, Frederick
Golden Bar across the street,
The only place you can walk in
And shovel the sawdust off the floor
To buy yourself a drink

Hastings Street Opera
Way on down Hastings Street
Warfield Theater
Sleeping Hours til 6 O'Clock
Yes-Yes anything can happen on Hastings Street

Still on Hastings
The Silver Grill
That's the only place you can walk in
And have to make the bar tender and owner drunk
To even get a drink. Yeeees!

Warren & Hastings Streets, Hancock

Bell Smith's joint
Walk in with a bottle of beer
Walk out the side door with a hamburger

Forest and Hastings—Sunnie Wilson's
The longest bar in town
The onliest place you walk in to gettin a bottle of beer
And gotta walk a mile after you get in the joint to get it.

Across the street is Jake's Bar,
He got all the something someone want
Garfield and Hastings
Mary Farm got 101 (inaudible)
That's the only bar
You fight all you wanna fight
Ain't nobody run out.

Canfield and Hastings
Last Stop!

Willis & Hastings—The Willis Theater
That's the only picture show in town;
If you missed it fifty years ago
You can still see it at The Willis Theater
Right now showing Rudolph Valentino
In *The Lost World*

Malone ain't hide nobody
He's the bartender, he's the porter and all of everything

George's Taproom—Old Folks Home
The only bar in town where the ladies can walk in
Buy a bottle of beer and he'll give them a dip of snuff

Goin down Hastings Street now
(Inaudible) bar, one way out. I ain't never goin in that joint

Leland and Hastings! Leland Bar.
That's the only place in town
Where the bartenders carry pistols
And when they set you up
They say "You got any money?" You say "Yes."
They say "will you please pay then?"

Miss Rice's Fish House
You smell that fish cleanin
They just got up on ya boy.
All down the line.
That's the only place you buy a steak sandwich
And it tastes like fish. They cook everything
At Miss Rice's in the same grease.

Raymond Head's fillin station
25 cent a gallon minus some tax
Joe's Record Shop
He got everybody in there
'Cept a T-bone steak.

Down on Hastings Street!
Eliot! Benson! Hastings Street Bar,
That's the only place where
Bartenders shoot everybody after two o'clock.

Aurora Harris

So Beautiful

9/5/2016 5:45 a.m.

The music in this city.
This City of Geniuses
Detroit, Michigan.
From sun up to sundown
With doo wops at bus stops
Pure squeaks and squawks
Walking bass thumps and
Brushing snares / crashing cymbals and
Djembe drums!
Music imitating machines!—

Memorable lyrics / rhymes / harmonies / beats
And way out tones / settling in bones
So beautiful! So beautiful!
This homegrown and transplanted
Colorful quilt of sound
Motown / Blues / Jazz / Soul
Gospel / Rock/ Techno / and Rap
Wrapping our souls up
Clearing heads from troubles
Being backdrop music in
Human rights struggles. Music
Wailing and strolling deep in places
Making us sigh / cry / dance / laugh
Tap feet / snap fingers 'til we're tired
Collapsed in a heap of
Joy / and happiness / and good memories!
So beautiful! So beautiful! The music in this city!

Bill Harris

Ron Carter: The Pulse in Autumn

> "The first thing I learned,
> was how important it was
> for the bass
> to play the pulse . . ."

Is, &
was there
when it was,

& is
now, still, stalwart,
moderate of manner, but
steadfast in support, was

& is
the pulse, punch,
beat,

whether at a strummed saunter
or full throttle charge
is
in charge.

Is ever gracious
as a gift bouquet, elegant
as a silk pocket square
of blazing oak leaf resplendence,

is sturdy
as the tree clinging to it
with all its might.

Kaleema Hasan

Lost Bird: Take 2

Written as a tribute to Bird-Trane-Sco-NOW and performed with the band in 1987 at the Red Door Unitarian Church as a celebration of the life of Ali Muhammad Jackson, the bassist.

and this is how we lost you
looking for the ruptured memory
aching for the corrupted feeling to be still

we lost, you, Bird, in a series of mistakes
forgotten
defacto-cultural genocide

(after a while)
we stopped looking
for (your) names on marquees
we took down portraits

(oft repeated rumors of betrayal
of carefree oppression
yet encompassing beautiful tone on
saxophone
equated to cultural-apathy).

we stopped talking.

we did not tell our children
we did not forget (however)

we came to all Bird's funerals
in fur tattered rags   ruptured memories   and all. . . .

kim d. hunter

the sound before

for faruq z. bey

jimi hendrix quipped
you can't call home
a long distance public saxophone
or was it you can't go home
except long distance

the saxophone player asked me why
hendrix sounded like he did
i mentioned the stratocaster's
harp like transparence
even through a wall of electrical charges
even in mountains of over amplification
there was the sound of light

and it dawned on me
how they both rose in the same generation
shared a brotherly otherness

one with steel gut strings
the other a dark tall stranger than most
breathing life
into a question mark shaped
like a horn of plenty

faruq skidded hard on a two wheeled rocket
thank god he had his helmet
a book of theory

to answer the question of
why home seemed such a distance
measured in coltranes
mapped in volcanic whispers
dislocated in oceans of now

what happens when
the outlaw becomes the law
and nothing is law without jazz

if there is a criminal element
i am of it

             *   *   *

faruq learned the music of sound
as a child before childhood
before the eye separated
from the tongue and the ear
or how sirens call from cities
where ambulances scurry
like rats on a drowning ship

measured in coltranes
the blue reed of his horn
slick with black ice
beneath a two wheeled rocket
bell of the horn tolling for thee
its keys valves for steam
released in the birth process
circular as breath

in the century of my birth
a building had been leveled and cleared
on a city block

there was almost no one else to stand
with the child john coltrane birthed from charlie parker
even in the municipality with the largest
percentage of africans in the united states
so faruq took up the call of the volcanic whisper
wailed for us like it was dinner time
and the final call at that

he wailed
come out dark citizens
and citizens of the dark
we're going to jerk the twist
like junkie the bird
wave albert ayler's cleveland cataclysm vibrato
found in a foreign river
drowned and drawn
from the map in his head

there was almost no one else to stand
so he gathered guerrillas and misfits
and wailed on detroit's leveled city block
bell of the horn
open as sun

i like to think i was present
slapping my forward in applause
howling at the alternate moon
the horn was just another
way to breathe

George Kalamaras

Every Note You Play is a Blue Note

for Johnny O'Neal

Let's say the kindness of the heart mated with a riverbed
of gravel. The offspring, of course, would be

your voice. *Old School*, Johnny. The term, invented
for you. We were born the same year. You in Detroit.

Me in Chicago. How can the only 281 miles between
our birth-beds along I-94 have created such space?

You're older than me by galaxies. You are the age
of the oldest love. You move through clusters of stars

at the piano with your Milky Way hands, your fingers
kneading bread. Baking it. Smoothing butter and honey across crisp

slabs of toast. It is the warmth of every stage of our most basic food
that you feed us. You were meant to caress the keys

inside the soft places we show no one. How'd you know
you were the one born to reach in? Lucky you, when at thirteen

you first heard your pianist father play Erskine Hawkins' "After Hours,"
and he warned you never to embellish a melody. I'm listening

tonight to your gig at Smalls. The gorgeous
"I'm Born Again." And I *am*. Just in hearing

all eight minutes four seconds. Somehow you get me to taste what I thought
I could not. A snowslide of stars pouring down a quiver of silk. Sorry

if I mix my metaphors, but you confuse both my happy
and my sad. Now I want to cry, four minutes fifty-six seconds in.

And you grunt out—Mingus-like—fifteen seconds later, an animal
sound I know I was and buried and bathed and would have loved

to have asked the world to accept. Slowly,
you bring me to myself. The way starlight dissolves

into night and back again. And back. And I'm here in Indiana and there
at Smalls and back in Detroit—all in the same instant—thanking the
    midwife

as she coaxes you from the starlight safe of your mother's belly
so you might one day bring that peace out into the world. How can I say

I love you, Johnny, when your piano runs already say
there are no words for love except the silence you stir

from blowing snowfields of the inner ear? And I'm *small* this evening,
hearing you at Smalls as if all your years of Blue Note and Blakey

and Clark Terry and Oscar and Diz were there
only to give you—tonight—to me. For you to praise,

without word this night, how great the star-sounds
from which we all somehow fell.

James E. Kenyon

Autumn Leaves

People who debate whether Detroit is a baseball town or a hockey town are missing the obvious because deep in its bones Detroit is really a bowling town.

Bowling: a proletarian pastime without glamour or steroids or fist fights or corporate sponsors, just 16-pound balls, rented shoes, the holy grail of the 300 game and beer, no need for a field of dreams, or ice or skates, the lanes look as slick as ice anyway. No need for a team, either, you can bowl alone, the ball comes back automatically, machines do that now, not like when pin boys sat on little ledges above the pins, their job to clear away the fallen wood whether strike or spare, then shove your ball back down the return chute for you to roll again, but not before assembling a pyramid of ten white pins; over and over again they did that, the same routine by those sons of Sisyphus, all of them gone now, unlike bowling, which still thrives in Detroit, a bowling town.

My father bowled.

He slung steel at Ford's, helped raise four kids, ran the numbers on the side and still had enough energy to bowl on the weekends. A lefty, he bowled on countless leagues, "UAW Local 600" sewn on the back of his short-sleeve bowling shirts, cool shirts, every year a different color, and never tucked inside his slacks.

Then as now he drank 100-proof Old Grand Dad Kentucky bourbon. Some bowling nights he drank so much it must have affected his hearing because he came home and played his albums loud enough for passing motorists to hear. The music woke up us kids or drowned the sound of the picture tube if we were allowed to be up late, but sleep could wait and TV, too, because Daddy is downstairs throwing strikes.

He owned enough jazz on vinyl to keep the neighbors up for weeks without repeating himself but he knew that at some point the bourbon was going to put him down and he couldn't or wouldn't allow that without hearing "Autumn Leaves," the first cut from the album "Somethin' Else." Miles is on it, yes, and Hank Jones and Sam Jones and Art Blakey and they play as only they can play, but it is the leader, Julian "Cannonball" Adderley on alto sax, who my father needs to hear to make the night complete.

The tempo is medium/slow for the now-familiar five-note vamp by Hank on piano and Sam on bass, with brush work by Blakey. Miles lays down the melody with casual elegance, but with my father at the controls the master's muted trumpet is at decibels that could put a hole in your chest, it's like sucking on a mentholated cigarette six months after you quit. Two seconds exist between the moment that Miles silences his horn and Cannonball steps in, and my father uses that instant to turn the volume up two or three or four more clicks. Now Cannonball is next to you, he's kicking over the furniture as he launches into a 64-bar solo that is bluesy, sassy, a little bit nasty and replete with the flourishes that are his signature sound. Halfway in he unleashes six screaming notes, each one more urgent than the last, and thankfully my father has been caught up, he can't move, you'd have to strike him to get his attention because nothing else will reach him now. He can only smile and listen, eyes closed, as Cannonball buries himself in the pocket of "Autumn Leaves."

Michael Lauchlan

Raptor

for Marion Hayden

Cruising thermals over wooded hills
over a quick scurry in the ferns
over rattlers sunning on rocks
over road and thistled beach,
the beautiful hunger of hawks sails
on wings shaped for nothing else,
fitting a corner of sky as though
inked into being, then gone,
dropping to a necessary feast
of torn fur and flesh. You glide
from brief repose into a song's
ordered moment and meet
a desolate ear, meet souls
calling on God in a town
living and dying on a beat,
each head bobbing to your struck
string (shaped for nothing else),
each granite heart split open,
each gig just one more descent
from Basin Street and Highland Park,
from Mingus and Marcus Belgrave
and all the voracious angels
to the macadam where we wait.

Philip Levine

I Remember Clifford*

Wakening in a small room,
the walls high and blue, one high window
through which the morning enters,
I turn to the table beside me painted a think white. There instead
of a clock is a tumbler of water,
clear and cold, that wasn't there
last night. Someone quietly entered, and now I see the white door
slightly ajar and around three sides
the light on fire. I remember once
twenty-seven years ago walking
the darkened streets
of my home town when up ahead
on Joy Road at the Bluebird of Happiness
I heard over the rumble of my own head
for the first time the high clear trumpet
of Clifford Brown calling us all
to the dance he shared with us
such a short time. My heart quickened
and in my long coat, breathless
and stumbling, I ran
through the swirling snow
to the familiar sequined door
knowing it would open on something new.

---

*The Great Trumpeter Clifford Brown influenced Detroit's Kresge Eminent Artist Marcus Belgrave.

Philip Levine

The Wrong Turn

There are those who will tell you
that the shortest way to get
to NYC is by way of Buffalo,
but back in 1949 if you left
Detroit at 2 a.m. when the clubs
were closing down, and the car—a '48
Studebaker that looked as though
it were going in two directions
at the same time—was owned by
Frenchman Jack, who along with
Pepper Adams was about to be
drafted, then why not misread
all the road signs and go by way
of Columbus, Ohio? Pepper was not
yet the greatest baritone saxophonist
—he was 21—but he was good,
so on a Saturday night he was working.
and he was tired. The Frenchman
had been out all day scrounging
money and supplies, so he was tired.

I, the driver, had been recovering
from a week of polishing plumbing parts,
which meant sleeping in until noon,
then clearing the debris out of my room,
which meant sweeping the rug with
precision and intensity so the reds
glowed like fire in the afternoon
and the Persian blues settled in.

Oh, how a man can love a rug
when it warms his only floor!
Thirty-five years ago, so I've forgotten
why I went to NYC and even
how I got back, I've forgotten
who I stayed with and whether
or not I walked the streets at night
wondering that so many lives
behind glass were not mine or if
I filtered through the bookstores
on Third searching for words that could
become mine so that I might say
what I did not yet have to say. I
recall that night I stood in the rain
for almost an hour, too shy even
to speak to the girl who waited
beside me for the bus. I recall
that I arrived too late to hear
even a single number. The bar
was closed, so I watched Pepper
remove the mouthpiece and wipe
it carefully with a handkerchief
and stow the huge sax meticulously
in its garnet plush-lined case
which I carried out to the car
while he said goodbye to Kenny,
Elvin, and Tommy. In the dark
The Frenchman gave me a swig
of something hot and vile and I
almost gagged. They settled down
in the back, we decided to go
by the way of Toledo, and they
talked and smoked and snoozed by turns
until there was silence. After

Toledo it was all two-lane,
no cars and no lights. The wet
fields of Ohio rushed by, rich
and autumnal, looming with presences
I couldn't imagine. I remember
the first sign that read "Columbus 45,"
and the next that said "Columbus 14,"
and I pulled over on the shoulder
of the road and turned on the map light.
Out of the back Pepper asked, "Where
are we?" and I answered, "Columbus"
because I thought that was where
we were. When Jack awakened
Pepper told him "Columbus."

Philip Levine

Above Jazz

> *A friend told me*
> *He'd risen above jazz.*
> *I leave him there.*
> > —*Michael Harper*

There is that music that the hammer
makes when it hits the nail squarely
and the wood opens with a sigh. There is
the music of the bones growing, of
teeth biting into bread, of the baker
making bread, slapping the dusted loaf
as though it were a breathing stone.
There has always been the music
of the stars, soundless and glittering
in the winter air, and the moon's
full songs, loon-like and heard only
by someone far from home who glances
up to the southern sky for help and finds
the unfamiliar cross and for a moment
wonders if he or the heavens
have lost their way. Most perfect
is the music heard in sleep—the breath
suspends itself above the body, the soul
returns to the room having gone in dreams
to some far shore and entered water
only to rise and fall again and rise
a final time dressed in the rags of time
and made the long trip home to the body,
cast-off and senseless, because it is

the only instrument it has. Listen, stop
talking, stop breathing. That is music,
whatever you hear, even if it's
only the simple pulse, the tides
of blood tugging towards the heart
and back on the long voyage that must
always take them home. Even if you
hear nothing, the breathless earth
asleep, the oceans at last at rest,
the sun frozen before dawn and the peaks
of the eastern mountains upright, cold,
and silent. All that you do not hear
and never can is music, and in the dark
creation dances around the single center
that would be listening if it could.

Philip Levine

On The Corner

Standing on the corner
until Tatum passed
blind as the sea,
heavy, tottering
on the arm of the young
bass player, and they
both talking
Jackie Robinson.
It was cold, late,
and the Flame Show Bar
was crashing
for the night, even
Johnny Ray
calling it quits.
Tatum said, Can't
believe how fast
he is to first. Wait'll
you see Mays,
the bass player said.
Women in white furs
spilled out of the bars
and trickled toward
the parking lot. Now
it could rain, coming
straight down. The man
in the brown hat
never turned his head up.
The gutters swirled
their heavy waters,

the streets reflected
the sky, which was
nothing. Tatum
stamped on toward
the Bland hotel, a wet
newspaper stuck
to his shoe, his mouth
open, his vest
drawn and darkening.
I can't hardly wait, he said.

M. L. Liebler

The Jazz

for Faruq Z. Bey (Collaborator and Friend)

The touch is soft
And meaningful
And fast
Like jazz uptown
In sweat
In hard driving notes
That break our opportunities
High
High
The jazz
The jazz
Can dig what's happening here?
The blowing future barking
Is back to the dog houses
Of our present lamp,
And the jazz—jazz
Beats and polishes
Everything
Every damn thing
Right down to the bone.
So, let us talk soft
And slow
And then say no words—
And just listen
Just listen to the jazz—
To that magic poetry jazz
Jazz.

Sonya Marie Pouncy

Musing I: Her Inspiration

for Alice Coltrane

you, night sky,
secreting fire
from your pores—
tendrils to tickle earth

in foreplay. somehow
complete & full of holes,
are you vaporous truth
to be taken as breath?

are you primordial
womb? dyastema
in the smile of time?
this hour, connecting

your beauty marks,
i find a labyrinth
of spirit worm holes,
amniotic iron ore

to fall & become holy, or
maybe your stars are racing
spindles to weave this:
us.

what did she, the a-trane,
find in your face?

what did you whisper
in her ear? was it you

who taught her to transcend
vinyl, to leave man's
harp and pluck instead
rays of light reaching
for what—me?—through
this dark matter?
did you teach her
the string theory

of the comet's plume?
what was it caused her
to pull down fire, wrap it
'round wood and find song?

if i offer my body
as instrument, will i sing?
will i, too, be a burning melody?

Eugene B. Redmond

Kwansaba: Rolling Late Sixties–Style Ntu Motor City

We stopped in love's name on the
In-skirts of Motown after driving (with
Kindred drivin wheels) outta East Saint Love.
Treaded tracks of Smokey's tears & pools
Behind Jackson 5's ears. Rolled ntu Broadside
Press, anxious to claim just-issued *For
Malcolm* & palaver with Poet Dudley Randall.

John G. Rodwan Jr.

JC on the Set

for James Carter

"Who is this kid?"
I wondered.
(I considered all jazz musicians my age
to be kids, and at the time, we were,
nearly.)

Never having heard of
this fellow Detroiter,
I was unprepared
that afternoon in Hart Plaza,
for the soaring saxophonic assault,
for the sudden shift from
firmly grounded rhythmic blues
to almost uncontainable blasts,
for the Ellingtonian suavity
mixed with nasty funk,
for the reincarnation of
the 5,000-pound man,
Rahsaan Roland Kirk,
in a natty suit.

One thing I did know:
JC had leapt in.

John Sinclair

"bags' groove"

for philip & milton hale

the sound of detroit
ever pulsates, from the streets
of the motor city
after the 2nd world war

when the arsenal
of democracy
carved out the freeways
& built up the suburbs

& started moving
all the white people
& the tax base
out—

but the cars
kept rolling
off the assembly lines
& the peoples

all had jobs
& paychecks
& cars
& homes of their own for a while

& the schools
taught music & art

to the children
of the working class

& the pulsation
of the music
grew ever stronger
& more powerful

& the city grew huge
with the artistry
& brilliance
of its great musicians—

teddy wilson,
j.c. heard,
lucky thompson,
yusef lateef,

milt jackson,
hank jones,
thad jones,
elvin jones,

wardell gray,
billy mitchell,
tommy flanagan,
donald byrd,

paul chambers,
doug watkins,
curtis fuller,
pepper adams,

louis hayes,

roy brooks,
alice mcleod,
kenny "pancho" hagood,

betty carter,
barry harris,
ali muhammad,
sir roland hanna,

sonny redd,
louis smith,
herbie williams,
wilbur harden,

abe woodley,
joe brazil,
hugh lawson,
ernie farrow,

art mardigan,
frank isola,
frank morelli,
frank rosolino,

bernard mckinney,
ray mckinney,
earl mckinnney,
harold mckinney,

terry pollard,
dorothy ashby,
jimmy wilkins,
miller brisker,

todd rhodes,
maurice king,
thomas "beans" bowles,
donald townes,

lamonte hamilton,
claire rocquemore,
moon mullins,
in & out of the penitentiary,

willie wells,
melvin mccray,
boo boo turner,
willie metcalf,

& in the modern era:
sam sanders,
kenny cox,
wendell harrison,

marcus belgrave,
donald walden,
george bohannon,
bennie maupin,

teddy harris,
charles boles,
bess bonnier,
jack brokensha,

kirk lightsey,
cecil mcbee,
freddie waits,
phil lasley,

joe henderson,
leon henderson,
ernie rodgers,
marvin "doc" holliday,

bud spangler,
roderick hicks,
george davidson,
ralphe armstrong,

charles moore,
danny spencer,
phil ranelin,
ralph "buzzy" jones,

lyman woodard,
ron english,
larry smith,
leonard king,

allen barnes,
robert lowe,
norma jean bell,
regina carter,

marion hayden,
eileen orr,
gaye lynn mckinney,
jeribu shahid,

reginald "shoo-be-doo" fields,
rodney whitaker,
tani tabbal,
faruq z. bey,

geri allen,
kenny garrett,
james carter,
james "blood" ulmer—

working their motor city magic
on the ineluctable,
on the irreducible,
on the irrefutable,

on the eternal,
non-stop,
24-hour-a-day groove
laid down by bags

& the men & women
who came after him
out of northwestern high school
& miller

& cass tech
& northern high
& wayne state university
& all over the city,

reaching out from detroit
to the ends of the earth—
this is the music
that made the motor city great

> —*jazz loft*
> *greektown*
> *detroit*
> *july 30, 2007 > april 14 > 21, 2008/*

amsterdam espresso

2nd & forest

detroit

august 28, 2007/

eastern market

detroit

april 20–21 > october 8, 2008

Keith Taylor

Detroit Dancing, 1948

in memoriam: Leo Golus

Everyone home from the war with stories
to tell. Except me, of course. Just a bit
too young to know the horrors of Iwo,
Normandy, the Bulge, I spent the duration
peddling popcorn outside a theater on
Gratiot; later, groceries at the Market.
No woman would be wowed by any yarn
I could spin. And I'd never win a turkey
with my looks. You see, everyone needs
an angle. At the Polish National Alliance
in Hamtramck the women gathered dutifully
around their returning heroes, wide-eyed
in the presence of such courage. But when
they danced, they danced alone, their arms
circling the smoke from a hundred cigarettes.
With luck one might find another woman
anxious to show her grace. Think of it,
years spent watching two women, nineteen
or twenty, sway each other over
the stained floor. So I taught myself dancing,
downstairs, at home, in the old neighborhood,
humming "Moonlight Serenade" for rhythm,
waltzing the broom, my partner, from coal bin
to canning jars, learning to finish
with a flourish (dipping its bristled head
gently toward the cement), until I could
walk into any club anywhere in the city,

pick out any woman, turn her once
across the floor, and, if I didn't sweep
her off her feet, I hear at least
(and this was almost enough, then)
that I was certainly light on mine.

Chris Tysh

By any means necessary

And suddenly shouts lit up the silence
We had attacked, we the slaves, we the dung underfoot
We the animals with patient hooves,
We were running like madmen; shots rang out
We were striking . . . and the flames flickered
Sweetly on our cheeks

Dear Fay:
I have not been a model prisoner and the slant of my reading and
intellectual interest is oriented toward the best interests and survival
of my class.
The point is, because I have not rushed to please all concerned,
I am doing natural life for second-degree robbery.
I'm looking forward to seeing you.
Sincerely,
George

The dope was so bad in Detroit—it was like Philly Joe used to say
about some dope, "You could have bought a Hershey bar and saved your
money"—because it was cut so much. And so that gradually makes your
tolerance for it go away; shooting it wasn't doing nothing for me
except putting more holes in my arms. I was only doing it for that
fucking feeling you get sticking a needle in your arm. And then all
of a sudden I didn't want to put no more holes in my arms, so I stopped.

Without that struggle, without that knowledge of the practice of

action, there's nothing but a fancy-dress parade and the blare of
trumpets

We hate you white people. We hate you white people. The next time,
one of you jive-ass paddies comes accusing me of hating you because
of the color of your skin, I will kick you in your ass.

They want us to say uh uh, bossman, that's not what it means. Later
for you, honky.

We already had our riot and we're here to show you how it's done.

Motown, if you don't come around, we are going to burn you down.

I have folded my sorrows into the mantle of summer night.

What is tomorrow
that it cannot come
today?

ACKNOWLEDGEMENTS FOR "BY ANY MEANS NECESSARY"

Aimé Césaire, *Les Armes Miraculeuses,* cited in *The Wretched of the Earth* (Fanon 88)
George Jackson, *Soledad Brother: The Prison Letters of George Jackson.* (New York: Bantam, 1970), p. 149. Reprinted
  by permission of Jonathon Jackson.
Miles Davis, *Miles: The Autobiography.* Miles Davis with Quincy Troupe. (New York: Simon & Schuster, 1989) p.
  173. © 1989 Estate of Miles Davis. Reprinted by permission/ All rights reserved.
Frantz Fanon, *The Wretched of the Earth.* (New York: Grove Press, 1968), p. 147. Reprinted by permission of Grove/
  Atlantic, Inc.
Bobby Seale, Excerpt from "Fillmore East Speech," The Dial-a-Poem Poets. Giorno Poetry System Records. 1972.
  Used by permission of Giorno Poetry System Records.

Stokely Carmichael, unidentified member of the SNCC, Rap Brown in *American Odyssey,* by Robert Conot (Detroit: Wayne State University Press, 1986), p. 529. Reprinted by permission of William Morrow & Co., Inc.

Bob Kaufman, *Solitudes Crowded with Loneliness.* (New York: New Directions, 1965) p. 3. © 1965 New Directions Publishing Corp. Reprinted by permission of New Directions.

Amiri Baraka, *The Dead Lecturer.* (New York: Grove Press, 1964) p. 78. © 1964 by Amiri Baraka. Reprinted by permission of Sterling Lord Literistic, Inc.

George Tysh

JAZZ

jazz leads us

rock leads us

boogie leads us

poems lead us

sexy ways lead us

detroit drives us

Barry Wallenstein

Julian

Lyrics from Music of Pepper Adams

Within the beat he drove his sound
from the cannon out to the stars.
He never knew fangs of fame.
For they played Mercy Mercy under his spell;
they played it well.

Within his heart he struck a match,
lit the wick, preserving the flame,
and Cannonball became his name.
Never was the end in sight. It never came;
he flew so high he never died.

And the music is now, now burnished bright.
Note follows note to be reborn.
The sounds in time do a free fall
into the folds, the folds of time.

Oh, shine on gold and silver horns,
stay true beyond all remorse.
Your inner breath beats so true.
Now untamed to the lonely soul,
too wild to lose, or to live without.

Rayfield A. Waller

This is Faruq Bey on His Bike

This is Faruq Bey on his bike. This is Faruq on his bike being the Detroit that used to deserve our love. This is Faruq being the Detroit that used to deserve our love when Faruq was young and so were we. This Faruq Bey is the one on his bike being the Detroit that used to deserve our love when he was young and so were we and we were unafraid of what anybody thought of us. Faruq is here in this version of himself on his bike being the Detroit that used to deserve our love when he was young and so were we and we were unafraid of what anybody thought of us and we were princes, kings, and queens of the city and we HAD a city. Faruq Bey here on his bike is being the Detroit that used to deserve our love when he was young and so were we and we were unafraid of what anybody thought of us and we were princes, kings, and queens of the city and we HAD a city and everywhere we went the funk was sure to go. This is Faruq Bey on his bike being the Detroit that used to deserve our love when he was young and so were we and we were unafraid of what anybody thought of us and we were princes, kings, and queens of the city and we HAD a city and everywhere we went the funk was sure to go and we loved one another and we loved ourselves.

So tell the children that this is Faruq on his bike.

Tyrone Williams

How Like An Angel

for Miles Davis who lived in Detroit and played The Bluebird Inn in 1953

1.

Blow   blowing
  winging
    winged by blow by
      blow
was all   was all
  you ever
    and ever
      wanted
that   and a
  horse
    to ride until
      you woke to find yourself
back in E. Slo-Mo
  a horse strapped to your back
      hooves cracking ribs
        hard
to blow   out an Eve
  much less the bitches
    that kept you
      hard
greedily eating   the ribbed back
    of your hand
      laying out
        cold cash
for to   blow
  and how

howl—
        ike
how   like
    howlike
        an
            an—

    2.
gel
        which is what
        with Miles around the wonder

the wonderful
                world of Dizzy
                B. Bird Prez Monk

grew
        a mongrel
        mutt muttering

whispers
            blues per blooper
            over the drawn-in in—

the warning track out—
                field of All-Stars
                What a piece of work

is how
        like an angel
        virgin as a frontier

prior to predication
                predator
                a crooked man and he went a crooked mile

a miss
    is as good
    as a mile of warm sea-scented beach

in Paris
    Juliette in a taxi with Bird
    throwing down fried chicken

a fried blonde
      at his crotch
      in the blare squawk bleep of traffic

3.

That blinding blankness of your back
tunes drums exactly shaping
shapely. Cross-eyed

inverted commas cross t's
remarkably, indifferently blurring
colors way inside way outside

the lines—thrown in relief—a lineage
curving away like the back of a world
for miles and miles and miles

down that moonlight mile, a junkie
junket, one small step for a giant
leapfrog over all the angels

who can't get down to it, here,
where the sky is not a box of glass
in some church or institute of art.

4.

Is it not like the king.	Play what isn't there. Then
It not king is like.	The play above that
Like the king.	It is not the exact pitch of a hinge
Not the king is like.	Dooring and walling
The it is not king.	Like the play is the thing
King the like.	Not it is in apprehension

5.

Every mile is two in winter
    twice five miles of Kubla Khan
and miles to X the KKK
    to lap the miles

noble in reason infinite in faculty in form and moving

how express and admirable in action how like a

law length rule

bulk volume size

standard dimension data

depth breadth extent

pattern rest criterion

and many miles to
and miles to go before

6.

How like Hollywood to cast down—
pours in films about jazz, jazz

in movies about whoring. A schizoid Gemini
behind bars when Bird died,

you never brown-bagged your trump
card or drifted in from the cats

and dogs to play My Funny Valentine.
If anything you would have drifted

by, driftwood at the mercy of merciless
surges, surging cross-purposes—

Frances, Irene, Cicily, etc.
How like an angel, a bolt of lightning

sheathed in ice? How like a simile,
simulacrum, similar else, as

7.

though it were the case
that a torch hovers,
haunting the gate to
the five hundred acre
estate your grandfather
thought was his, and how like
an avenging angel you
gunned the horses of your blue
demon, backing away from
Julliard to Minton's and then
floored it, plowing right through the flames,

brakes failing, wrapping it around
a needle, wandering from bump shops
to junkyards for all the parts you would
never find, still learning how to listen
around corners for the future paragon
of animals black beauty of the world

Willie Williams

The Baron

for Harold McKinney

Musical griot,
who pounds the piano
with percussive force
like unto drum beats
flying fingers over ivory
dropping down and
striking swiftly
squeezing sounds from and
making the ivories cry
of far away shores
of times long ago
echoing drum beats and cries.

Musical griot, who noteworthily alits
pain and joy on paper.
A symphonic synthesis
of east and west,
of traditional and modern
fusing two classical forms
recording the continuum
that we are a part of
The Baron sing and play
your songs of praise.

Al Young

Detroit 1958

Only parts of the pain of living
May be captured in a poem or
Tale or song or in the image seen.

Even in life we only halfway feel
The tears of a brother or sister
Mass disenchantment in cities,
Our discovery of love's meagerness,
The slow rise and fall of the sun.

Sadness is the theme of existence;
Joy its variations. Pain is only a portion
Of sadness, and efforts to escape it
Can lead to self destruction,
One aspect of pain lived imaginatively.

It is in life that we celebrate pain;
It is in art that we imitate it,

Beauty is saddening, or, as the man sings,
"The butter not makes the song so sweet."

Al Young

Who I am in Twilight

Like John Lee Hooker, like Lightnin' Hopkins
Like the blues himself, the trickster sonnet,
Hoedown, the tango, the cante jondo
Like blessed spirituals and ragas custom-made,
Like sagas, like stories, like slick, slow,
Sly soliloquies sliding into dramas,
Like crime and punishment, like death and birth,
Canal street, New Orleans, like the easy,
Erasable, troubled voices in a whirling,
Ceiling fan makes in deep summer nights in
Hot, unheavenly hotels—Oklahoma, Arkansas,
Tennessee—like the Mississippi River
So deep and wide you couldn't get a letter
To the other side like Yosemite National Park, like beans &
Cornbread, like rest and recreation, like love
And like, I know we last. I know our bleeding stops.

Calvin Frazier
Joe Von Battle
Thornetta Davis
JVB Records
Johnnie Bassett

The Rev. Robert B. Jones
Elmwood Cemetery

Famous Coachman
Alberta Adams

Joe Louis' Fist
Detroit Count
The Butler Twins
Son House

The Rev. C. L. Franklin

Robert Jr. Whitall & Sugar Mae

Blind Arthur Blake
John Lee Hooker
Big Maceo
Mr. B

Uncle Jesse White
Big City Blues

Eddie "Guitar" Burns
John Sinclair

Little Sony

Bobo Jenkins

The Blues Scholars

II.
DETROIT BLUES
Hastings Street Opera

Arthur "Blind" Blake

Detroit Bound

I'm goin' to Detroit, get myself a good job
I'm goin' to Detroit, get myself a good job
Tried to stay around here with the starvation mob

I'm goin' to get a job, up there in Mr. Ford's place
I'm goin' to get a job, up there in Mr. Ford's place
Stop these eatless days from starin' me in the face

When I start to makin' money, she don't need to come around
When I start to makin' money, she don't need to come around
'Cause I don't want her now, Lord. I'm Detroit bound

Because they got wild women in Detroit
That's all I want to see
Because they got wild women in Detroit
That's all I want to see
Wild women and bad whisky would make a fool out of me

Fats Domino

Detroit City Blues

Detroit City
It was the finest in this world
Yes, Detroit City
It was the finest in this world
I'm crazy 'bout that city
And I love its pretty girls

When you leave that city
And you feel this kind of love
When you leave that city
And you feel this kind of love
Just one goes out hasty
And you find a good place to go

You don't need a lot of money
To have a real good time
You don't need a lot of money
To have a real good time
Just be a real good sport
And everything will turn out fine

28 December 1965

the hold George Garnett, musician,
entered
garners
the man
"of the most gentle
I've known"

thrown
fate accompli, fate diabolique

thrown
as the color of his skin

thrown to on black
man walk
gait
the gated death
flying and falling

play.

I asked of death that music
but my day talks on
in endless silence

from the cellar
the bridge of what final
moment
of what face

bound in the last second

I still see light over the expressway
and will not know the radical
of that memory

witness scores pale in my ears
while the brain enlarges
the horn in my heart

      fated sounds

    where arms and lips grip
    invisible
    torn into
    paper

     all paper
     out cut angles
     bit to form by the wind

wind brings "George"
as it took
"your"
   silent brass and steel
   left behind

Robin Eichele

Blues Scholars at Work

for John Sinclair and Charles Moore

A couple of guys
      gettin down
            down on the blues train
                  goin on downtown

brothers in the blues screamin bout their dues
      bout the currency of musical union
            that's all paid up
                all made up in
                      the union of musical skins

bout Coltrane on the spirit express
bout where the breath comes in
bout where the music comes out
bout images of rattlesnakes dressing us up in our dreams
      and being blessed with a talent and a
            whole lotta love
bout the bridge over muddy waters
      and the woodshed and the years and the tears
            in the big horn of the spirit
bout the "scholarly endeavor" of footnoting our lives
      making meat-memory melodies . . . melodious improvisations
            improvised histories
     the talent you're born with
            can't be given to
            or away

bout another day on the glory train
        Motown to New Orleans to L.A.
bout that simple geography
        and the enormous memories
           in between

Bryn Fortey

Hey There Blues

Hypnotic baritone
Droning guitar
Tapping foot
Mighty mighty boogie-man
Hey there: John

From primal blues to hit parade
From plugged in electric to acoustic folk
Hey there: John Lee

Smooth mover
Smart operator
Never out of fashion
Master to all those white boy pretenders

Hey there: John Lee Hooker

Robert Hayden

Homage to the Empress of the Blues

Because there was a man somewhere in a candystripe silk shirt
facile and dangerous as a jaguar and because a woman moaned
for him in sixty-watt gloom and mourned him Faithless Love
Two timing Love Oh Love Oh Careless Aggravating Love,

>   She came out on stage in yards of pearls, emerging like
>   a favorite scenic view, flashed her golden smile and sang

Because grey laths began somewhere to show from underneath
torn hurdygurdy lithographs of dollfaced in heaven;
and because there were those who feared alarming fists of snow
on the door and those who feared the riot squad of statistics,

>   She came out on stage in ostrich feathers, beaded satin,
>   and shone that smile on us and sang.

Robert Hayden

Mourning Poem for the Queen of Sunday

Lord's lost Him His mockingbird,
　　His fancy warbler;
　　Satan sweet-talked her,
　　four bullets hushed her.
　　Who would have thought
　　she'd end that way?

Four bullets hushed her. And the world a-clang with evil.
Who's going to make old hardened sinner men tremble now
and the righteous rock?
Oh who and oh who will sing Jesus down
to help with struggling and doing without and being colored
all through blue Monday?
Till way next Sunday?

　　All those angels
　　in their cretonne clouds and finery
　　the true believer saw
　　when she rared back her head and sang,
　　all those angels are surely weeping.
　　Who would have thought
　　she'd end that way?

Four holes in her heart. The gold works wrecked.
But she looks so natural in her big bronze coffin
among the Broken Hearts and Gates-Ajar,
it's as if any moment she'd lift her head
from its pillow of chill gardenias

and turn this quiet into shouting Sunday
and make folks forget what she did on Monday.

Oh, Satan sweet-talked her,
and four bullets hushed her.
Lord's lost Him His diva,
His fancy warbler's gone.
Who would have thought,
who would have thought she'd end that way?

Robert B. Jones Sr.

Arnesia's Song

In the year of nineteen and sixteen,
The moneyed world had turned its hands to war.
But deep within the State of Alabama,
Arnesia of Evergreen was born.

> No movies were ever done about her.   (Chorus)
> No history books will ever hold her name.
> But I know her story like I know my own hand,
> And I will sing her story just the same.

In '28 when all the folks were laughin',
Thinking 'bout the money that they'd made,
At twelve years old, in dresses made of patches
Arnesia picked the cotton while she played.
> And she helped her mother raise two orphaned cousins
> 'Cause that's the way they did it in those days.
> Not much older than the children that she cared for,
> That is how Arnesia learned a mother's ways.

In '34 when all the folks were crying,
Over all the money that they'd lost,
Arnesia was all alone and trying,
To understand what love, too young, could cost.
> 'Cause she'd had two children for him out of wedlock
> Back when bastards were a mark of shame.
> And though she didn't wear it in her own life
> She raised her children with their father's name.

Chorus

In '49 Arnesia left for Detroit,
To find the poor man's fabled promise land.
Sold whiskey, in the Bottoms, to the workers,
And she left her problems all in Jesus' hands.

 Detroit was not the same as Alabama,
 And she had to learn to face the cold grey morn,
 And that rags around your feet can keep you walking,
 And that newsprint 'round your legs can keep you warm.

In '56 when Civil Rights was marching,
Her daughter had a baby of her own.
She found out what Arnesia had long known,
That it's hard to raise a baby on your own.

 But these women worked to raise the boy together.
 And they tried their best to give him everything.
 When I think about the way those women raised me,
 I am sure that I was born to be a king.

By the '60s Arnesia's son had married,
And had found success in the mechanic's trade.
Eight children helped to bring his mother pleasure,
While 'round her feet all nine grandchildren played.

 And we all grew in the joy that was around her,
 And somehow we cut out the "middle moms."
 And a neighborhood of children called her "Mother,"
 And she wiped away our tears with calloused palms.

Chorus

But in the '80s while the world was busy spending,
Arnesia did the best that she could do.
Her only son was killed at 37,
And her only daughter died at 52.

And the turns of life had taken all her children
And nearly all the joy that had remained
But, in my son's eyes she met four generations,
And, she knew her life had not been lived in vain.

In '90 in the month that she was born in,
Arnesia of Evergreen went home.
But in '91 my wife came in to bless me,
With another little Arnesia of my own.
    And sometimes when I hear my 'Necie laughing,
    I can hear the other 'Necie in the sound.
    And then I bow my head and pray to heaven,
    That Arnesia's life is better this time 'round.

Robert B. Jones Sr.

The Poor Man's Promised Land

I'm forty mile from Detroit, and the cold is coming down.
I'm headed north on a Greyhound, but it feels like heaven bound.
I'll be staying with my cousin, sending money when I can.
I'm headed for the poor man's promised land.

Seven dollars in my pocket with a suitcase in my hand,
I'm headed for the poor man's promised land.

Some make the cars; some fix them, while others cut the deals.
We're all flocking to a city built on oil, and rust, and steel.
And I got a job at the stamping plant; I'm doing the best I can.
I've made it to the poor man's promised land.

Seven dollars in my pocket with a suitcase in my hand,
I made it to the poor man's promised land.

Sometimes it can be brutal, sometimes it can be mean,
But there ain't no other city where a man can build a dream.
When you don't have much education and you want it o' so bad,
If you work you'll give your family the life they never had.

It's a city on the river that's been calling us so long,
There are folks from every nation; it's the dream that makes us strong.

It seems like I've been here forever, and I'm always on the run.
I met Maxine in '67, Mama died in '81.
And I never traveled south again when they laid her in the ground
I just jumped into my Lincoln and I headed for Motown.

Seven dollars in my pocket with a suitcase in my hand,
My home is in the poor man's promised land.

They paid me for my thirty years, our life's been pretty sweet.
We put three kids through college, but we lost one to the streets.
And our kids don't live around here; they've all got other plans,
Cause when they build the dreams now, they build them in Japan.

Seven dollars in my pocket with a suitcase in my hand,
I'm staying in the poor man's promised land.

Our city fell on hard times; we almost lost the game.
Since the riots in '67, things ain't never been the same.
But I came to love the Tigers, and I became a Pistons fan.
And I still love the poor man's promised land.

Yes, I thank God for the poor man's promised land!

Ken Meisel

John Lee Hooker's Boogie Chillun

I.

Beneath the Dequindre Cut, full of greased weeds & graffiti,
you can see the exact spot where roaming dogs shit,

and lovers, because they're expressions of musical notes & lust,
kiss like lovers kiss, one after another in the front seat

of an old Pontiac, here in the pinguid filth of the Eastern Market
where the slaughter houses and the lamb skin factories

stinking of dead animal carcasses and salt, combine on Orleans
and Monroe Street, so that John Lee can arrive, with a bruised guitar

in a box, the Devil skulking behind him, sometime in '43.
And he can squat in a shack, gone now, long gone in the years

that act like razor blades cutting every shack to bits.
Except for Sam, the guy I talk to, who tells me in busted apart

English because he's from the deep south and he's 73 years old
and his back teeth—the ones that can grab hard on tobacco

and on hard-to-say-words, are old chunks of dead weight.
He can tell me that he still lives in a dusty wooden shack,

just off of St. Aubin, where there's a view of the slaughterhouse
and John Lee's place, even though it's long gone now.

And even though the woman he slept with, in the old '47 Pontiac,
is nothing now except the particulate of dandelions & black ink.

II.

Where it is written that the boogie chillun swing on Hastings Street
John Lee, dark as coal burning in an oven, can sing it,

and you can feel it as heat rising up a fence line, weeds crowding it,
and you can see it as flame bursting out of a rigid chimney stack.

And all the young, festooned girls, portable young things
ready to submit to the anything that guides them like rolling black stars

skipping across the sidewalks of Russell Street & Beaubien,
and then on to Henry's Swing Club, on Orleans, you can see them

now as the gnarled trees & weeds under the Dequindre Cut.
And some graffiti artist down there, a quick moving pulsar of light,

is spray painting the future, because it was always hungry to get here,
and you can go down there, amidst the blown tires & the mattresses

and the old car chassis, and find the boogie chillun, their throats
parched and thirsty from the hot weight of the night, their roots sucking oil.

III.

Ladies & Gentleman of the cornucopias of littered trash, of forgotten
auto hulks never mentioned, of slaughtered animals glazed in blood,

of the wantonness of soiled floors where knife blades divide ribs,
I want to tell you of the boogie chillun, John Lee's kin, yours & mine,

because they are the ones born in music and the ones lost in light,
and they are the ones whose voices go on singing in the low wind

that's wandering like a melody under the Alfred Street Bridge, where Sam's
walking this morning, his mouth full of chewing tobacco and blues,

and I am walking there with him, one of the free ones never a part
of the 1943 riots that slaughtered this town, like a lamb's neck.

And we're getting high on the light that's slanted like a guitar string
through the wreckage of a viaduct, he & I, and we're not alone.

We're never never alone, he shouts out at no one, we're never alone,
our roots and toots live inside the ashes and underneath the weeds,

and he throws his arms up in arrivals & in cataclysmic gestures, and
in soiled lathered sweat; we're never alone, he shouts out to no one, *never alone.*

Ron Milner

From the Porches

(A portrait of a moment with Aretha. A gospel "shout" in her honor.)

Saturday nights? Or, was it, Sunday nights? Hard to place because those at whose feet we—me and my fellas—sat, were not necessarily church-goers. The "Mrs's" of the houses, maybe; or the "Muh-Dears" (the Grands or Great-Grands); or the "Aintees." But these steps, these porches, with we young ones giggling our falsetto ad-libs to each other on the steps, and, the grown folks in the rockers and kitchen chairs, behind us on the porches, chuckling and sighing the " . . . You oughta' be ashamed! . . ." bass, tenor, and contralto, primary notes—were not the steps and porches of the "Sanctified Houses." Not where me and my buddies first heard the music blending with the pulsating dots of cigarette tips, and quick, street-light flashes of gold crowned ivory, gaping wide, framing laughter: All behind us there in the dark with the smell of the beer in mason canning-jars and the echo of the just ended ballgame still glowing from the radio (usually perched on a stool with its wire running through the window to the "front-room").

No, me and my rowdy, jitterbug crew, would hardly be allowed to sit on the "sanctified" steps of the neighborhood's A-Man-Thank-You-Lord stations. Uh-uh, not us. The rhythm-section setting the pace for us was hardly a tambourine chorus: Dresses and skirts pulled up to the taboo point to catch the breeze; switchblades snapped open to clean fingernails and punctuate fables; with the brush-stokes of folded newspapers as fans and fly-swatters. That was our back-up atmosphere. The ones trying to hedge their bets on the hereafter hoping for some angle around the spiritually straight and narrow road through the churches.

So the radio switch from the ballgames to the "church-programs," was the Mrs's and Muh-Dears' efforts to exercise and appease before the naked vulnerability of sleep. You understand: "Grown-folks business." Yeh. And right about then we would begin to feel the constraint of being tied to them there on the porch; feel the pull of the far-off street lights—sign-posts to adventure, to the future. Unable to sit any longer, compelled by an erupting antidote, someone (okay, you know who!) would spring to his feet, performing a carefully edited visual for the steps, with an eye on the gallery. And we would extend and exaggerate our laughter—proclaiming secrets and times of our own. Then would come the command:

"Shhh. Y'all hush! Reverend Franklin's youngest is sangin' . . . What's her name? . . ."

"Yeh, hush boy! . . . Ain't that somethin'?! . . . What is she: 'leven, twelve years old? . . ."

" . . . My Gawd: Listen to that . . ."

"Hush! . . ."

The sound—as young as us and older even than them on the porch—would soar up like a flock of just-released birds, with one straining to get just a little higher, a little further, than the rest. The sound was us and them up on the porch: Them rising to release us—just as Reverend Franklin was revealing and releasing her, his youngest, Aretha—and us, like her, straining to soar a little further, a little higher!

And we would sit, shoulders and knees touching; awed by the fact that we were all being grabbed and bound by an eleven/twelve-year-old. Tingling with wonder. So hushed, we could hear all the other radios up and down the street sending Reverend Franklins' Aretha out to soar with Bessie, Mahalia, and Dinah—taking 'em just a little further, a little higher. Touching and bonding us, making us feel—"sanctified."

John Sims

D-City Blues

Downtown Comeback
ArtTown UpRise
GhostTown DriveThroughs
D-City Blues, Blue City Blues

Economic Rapture, Bailout Capture
Wall Street Views, World Class Muse
D-City Blues, Blue City Blues.
D-City Blues, Blue City Blues.

Home of that Renaissance Phoenix
Of Motown and Blue Labor
Of Movers and Makers
Of Planters and Rakers

Where Cadillacs are plenty
And freeways are many
Where that Belle Isle slide, be Giant
And the working folks be bad ass defiant

Where did the people go, factories slow
What up doe, What up doe?
Broken bricks and corporate tricks
Before Nafta and Afta Nafta

Downtown Comeback
ArtTown UpRise
GhostTown DriveThroughs
D-City Blues, Blue City Blues

Art Scene Rapture, Prime Time Capture
Blue Chip Views, World Class Muse
D-City Blues, Blue City Blues
D-City Blues, Blue City Blues

From the Crevices and Cracks
of Vacancies and Grayness
Rise the colorful Canvasses
for creative minds and constructive hands

Where Art grows on the Buildings
Mindescaping portals to other places
Where Art bes the Buildings
Landscaping a liberty for future worlds

Basquiat is hanging off Grand River
Where Folks and Faces tell stories
Of histories and people that matter
Of places and dreams that matter

Downtown Comeback
ArtTown UpRise
GhostTown DriveThroughs
D-Blue City Blues

Neigborhood Rapture, Subprime Capture
Nightmare Views, World Class Muse
D-City Blues, Blue City Blues
D-City Blues, Blue City Blues

On Sorrento and West Chicago
Spartan's, Sonny's, Dino's and the candy store.
Where community once stayed and the kids once played
On the Street, at the Churchyard and Rosie's House

The Dallases, Maples and the Millers
The Simses, Crawfords and Pearsons
Ms. Best, Ms. Love, Ms. April and Ms. Cotton
Many more, many going, many gone but not forgotten.

In between the space of death and resurrection
Are gutted houses, missing children and silent schools
Copper robbers and uncelebrated westside sunsets
And a rising Phoenix spirit yearning to move beyond

Downtown Comeback
ArtTown UpCome
GhostTown DriveThroughs
D-Blue City Blues

Downtown Comeback
ArtTown UpCome
GhostTown DriveThroughs
D-Blue City Blues

D-City Blues, Blue City Blues,
D-City Blues, Blue City Blues,

Dennis Coffey

Little Willie John

Sir Mack Rice

The Marvelettes

Nathaniel Mayer

Doo Wop

Aretha Franklin

The Temptations

Motown Records

Fortune Records

Marvin Gaye

Funk Brothers

The Falcons

Stevie Wonder

Duke Fakir

Andre Williams

The Supremes

The Contours

Eddie Kendricks

III.

NORTHERN SOUL

Dancing in the Streets

David Blair

DETROIT (while i was away)

Even though I know the air hangs
like a dead dog's ass over River Rouge,
I still miss you.

Your fenced in gardens
filled with sustenance and Saturday
evening blue.

The September stench that creeps
slow as a Woodward bus on Sunday.

Your acoustic guitars and amplified hair.
Your rows of long thin buildings,
arranged on a young man's head.

Last time I saw you,
a woman stood
on a corner conducting traffic.
Her own sunken opera.
A crack pipe baton. Car horns joined
in like a bad man cruising a dream.

She stood on the corner of Cass and Mack
dying to reach Joy Rd.
The moon left its spotlight on a backdrop of burnt out buildings.
Police tape posed like velvet rope.

Do Not Cross.

A picket line of teens careened down Cass
past broken glass that spread
like urban sprawl

Or the Diego Rivera mural
painted across the whole damn DIA wall.

Another time I saw you,
steam barreled out of your manhole covers
like you were about to explode.

A soul imbibed forty ounces of courage
so it could head back to the axle plant
on Lynch Road, or Jefferson Avenue or some other
conveyor belt street that gets everyone moving
in step like a Temptation line dance.

22 ounces of sweat and iron hidden in a bathroom stall.
Away from the plant tours and fat cats,
shop stewards and snitches.

I remember you
old friend.

I'm in another city now.
But, somehow, Martin Luther King Street always looks the same.
It just doesn't intersect with Rosa Parks,
12th Street where '67 fires started,
named for a woman who chose you beyond
a boycott in Montgomery, then rode
the front of that big old dog
straight on home to you.

Detroit, I love you . . .

from your basketball sun, that hangs in the sky
then falls, only to bounce back up again tomorrow.
Down to your alligator shoes.
I'll kiss you on the river.
Meet you in the middle of a suitcase and wonder
do you ever think of me this way . . . ?

Do you even know I've gone?

Say my name, Detroit.

I pray you claim me. A small town boy.
Born in New Jersey, but made in Detroit.

My heart beats like tool and die for you.
Like horsepower and pistons for you,
while mechanized, lumpenized robot
zombies haunt Mack Avenue.

Here they come,
a gang of tank tops and do rags,
marching down to Hastings Street.

Though I never knew you back when
you wore your onyx necklace
like a tire around your neck, I witness
the aftermath.

Dipping your blue black hands
in electric currents of music and art. The circumference
of Outer Drive. Moross and Joy.
Paris of the Midwest they called you.

And every time '67 or Halloween came around,

you lived up to it. The year I was born, you blew up.
I came when I could. I've never left.
I stay, even when I go.

Chosen heart.
Adopted town.
From Belle Isle to Eight Mile.
Chocolate city where the mothership landed.
Late night downtown and the peacocks are out

on Fourth Street,
telling stories to streetlamps that hover over highways.
The moon is a plate full of soul food, Mexican food.
Pierogis and paczkis. Kafka and curry

We mix and separate, mix and separate.

Each Prentis stoop is a garage rock chord
strummed and banged, like a car mechanic's sledge.

A man screams beneath the Ambassador Bridge.
Another drums on plastic tubs for tourists.
"Will work for food" is a piece of poetry
scribbled on an art house wall.

Festival wizards, Saunderson, Atkins and May.
The Big Three. Detroit. De trois, of three.
Black panthers, white panthers and Lions, oh my.
Tight boys in rock pants, the hustlers in Palmer Park.
Lovers, thugs and blues men with axes
sharp enough to chop down another forced overtime shift.

Detroit,

your beautiful hair woven women,
with sundresses flowing like the Detroit River,
Supremely,
Standing next to me on the assembly line,
grabbing tools and teaching me,
what perseverance and being a brother is
all about.

These are the overtime fists clocking.
These are the hands
that braid hair and lock dread, and cook meat that falls
right off the bone into fat, black pots of collards working harder
and harder . . .
and harder
still . . .

. . . so step on, Detroit,

dribble and shoot,
pass and play,
struggle and fight,
darken and light,
riot and quell,
drive and impel,
pick the steel burrs off the cross members at the front of the
Jeep Cherokee.

Look what we have made you.

Steam and steel.

Still . . .

that's how hard I love you.

Heather Bourbeau

Thank You, Berry Gordy

I would act embarrassed,
but even as a young girl,
I could see how she would shine
pure joy
when she danced
(an involuntary reaction
I gratefully inherited),
without care,
to the bass and steady drums,
catchy hooks of carefree sweethearts,
or angst of love gone by.
Motown—Motor City—
Detroit Rock—running through
the maybe sober—
more likely barbiturated veins
of a woman,
my mother,
from small timber town Oregon,
who never realized
this was her calling,
her way to see and love herself,
to feel the strength and beauty
of her body in motion for her—not a man,
her way out of the pain she captured
and swallowed every day
by choice.

Billy Bragg

Levi Stubbs' Tears

With the money from her accident
She bought herself a mobile home
So at least she could get some enjoyment
Out of being alone
No one could say that she was left up on the shelf
It's you and me against the world kid she mumbled to herself

When the world falls apart some things stay in place
Levi Stubbs' tears run down his face

She ran away from home in her mother's best coat
She was married before she was even entitled to vote
And her husband was one of those blokes
The sort that only laughs at his own jokes
The sort a war takes away
And when there wasn't a war he left anyway

Norman Whitfield and Barrett Strong
Are here to make everything right that's wrong
Holland and Holland and Lamont Dozier too
Are here to make it all okay with you

One dark night he came home from the sea
And put a hole in her body where no hole should be
It hurt her more to see him walking out the door
And though they stitched her back together they left her heart in pieces on
    the floor

When the world falls apart some things stay in place
She takes off the Four Tops tape and puts it back in its case
When the world falls apart some things stay in place
Levi Stubbs' tears

Charles W. Brice

Setting Up Soul—1968

Pull the big case that contains the cymbals, snare drum, cymbal stands, and sticks out of the van. Tell the guys in the band to hold on, you're comin.' Haul in the bass drum in its plastic case and the floor tom. Open the bass drum case and pull out your kick beats, the ones that made the bloods smile and caused dancin' in the streets. Unwrap the floor tom and lean it toward the snare drum the way Marvin Gaye inclines his ear to hear the grapevine. Tip the snare drum so it's ready for that rimshot—SMACK—"I feel good ... !" Caress the tom-tom until you slip it onto the bass drum holder, smooth and slow, like Percy Sledge loves a woman. Set the ride cymbal on its stand and coax it down toward the floor tom, lower, a little lower, lower now—I ain't too proud to beg. Please, please, please, place the crash cymbal where you can reach it fast, smash it hard, with force, super bad. Put that sock cymbal stand by me 'till it fits my left foot like a stirrup. I'll ride that mustang, Sally, all night long.

L. Soul Brown

Oh! Mercy Mercy Me! A Family Gathers to Marvin Gaye

"Lord Have Mercy!" rises up
    with the smoke from the grill.
        We gather together under charcoal skies
      our ritual.

"Where did all the blue skies go?"
                      Aunt Helen, are those ribs ready?

    When day's pageants are done, we unfold our tent.
        Mother conducts a spatula
            one hand tucked in a mitt
            her salt-and-pepper fro unkempt
            a grease stained apron hugs her full hips.

    The folks (aunts, cousins, friends, children)
        come strolling in;
        some in Sunday suits
        intoxicated by the day's events.

Our house is where they come to let loose Evening blues.
    Relax coats, ties, stockings, and shoes.
        Watch ball games, play cards, eat as much as you choose.
      Talk . . . Plenty of talk
        Good music on . . .

"Things ain't what they used to be."

We've been thinning for years

Once the plumpest family on the block
  Our faces full of cheeseburgers, potato salad, ham hocks, macaroni
   Aunt Frances put pimento on it.
 collard greens, string beans, rice and peas,
 all washed down with private stocks.
Now the elders have restricted diets, substitutes for salt.

"Oil wasted on the oceans . . ."
       (A saucy pork loin slips into a soggy pulp of paper).
 Seas fish full of
Mercury," the cat prefers to lay low   find a place under the bed or
 next to a window
    hoping the young ones don't get distracted
     start prowling for attention.

One Nephew, one Niece all that's passed on from last generation
  very special place the center of family's future.
   Small and precious heirlooms, we tarnish them
    with silver, dollars, and trust funds.

"Radiation . . . in the sky . . ."

   Jeanie, would you place this casserole in the microwave for me?
 Aunt Elsie coos, figure at 70 like it was at 50 as she was at 31.
  She'll charm you like a locket.
 Cooking is a specialty for her—rare; the dish will probably remain
   in the oven. No one will bother.

"Animals and birds who live nearby are dying."

  The yard is well canopied; an elderly pine holds its center
   ringed by two oaks, lilacs, rhododendrons, and hedges. A pear tree
    where robins would nest has long been bundled away
     left to rot by the side of the fence.

After dark, mosquitos are pests, tickle the ankles.
Citronella torches stand guarded protection.

"Mercy, Mercy, Mercy, Mercy! . . ."

Gloria exhorts swatting the gnats that swarm her plate;
a heaped cholesterol mountain's
juices run down her triple E chest
propped up, *It's amazing!*
She never had kids.

"What about this overcrowded land,
how much more abuse from man can she stand?"

On a patch of land next to the house on a cinder brick
a boom box blares Marvin Gaye's *Sexual Healing.*
Crescent rolls, pork bellies, chicken legs, and seasoned rumps
rub the last sod from the Earth.

Typically stoic Trevor enjoys the pleasure of women
winding themselves 'bout his totem.
Reminiscent of his playa days
ball stolen from his court.   Paternity suits make him less a father
figure more a nigga.

Uncle Richie teases the ladies, consummate bachelor, 76—
adjusts his polished brass buckle,
tilts his Stetson, cocks his leg
slyly to display Durango style.
Gleefully flashes his Fixodent smile.

Sister and her girls they're ripe full of happiness.
They've got homes, jobs, families, and cars
by age 32—Their men hang on the fringes

smacking on succulent barbeque thighs.

"Oh, na na. Help me. Help me."

Kids scurry round each other in a mean spirited game of tag.
    Little T hides behind the gnarled knot of Grandpa
        hoping he'll deter the pursuing gang.
            3-year-old Unique cries at the growing shadows desperately
                wanting to join the fellows.
    Oh, she can't wait.

It's beyond pitch, Mom warns us to move inside
    Grab a dish and a chair; collect the children, stray cans
      It's getting late. Suffocate the dwindling fires as
        Cousins pack up vans and wave goodbye.

"No we can't wait"
    to drape our rum-soaked bodies
      around the kitchen table as youth
        nods off before television stations.

"It's almost too late.
        Oh, mercy mercy me."

NOTE: "Quotations" are interpolations of "Mercy, Mercy Me (The Ecology)" written by Brian Holland/Lamont Dozier/Eddie Holland Jr., as performed by Marvin Gaye and The Sounds of Blackness.

Ecology—The science of the relationships between organisms and their environments and the balances between these relationships.

Come See About Me

"(D)efendant will be required in operating its ships as 'public conveyances' to accept as passengers persons of the negro race."—BOB-LO EXCURSION CO. v. MICHIGAN, Supreme Court of United States, argued December 16–17, 1947; Decided February 2, 1948.

Sarah moves unsteadily through her east side Detroit bungalow, her chestnut skin dusted with age. Her knees are swollen with arthritis, but her 85-year-old spine bends only slightly. Tall as she was in her day, she had never learned to stoop in apology. Not Sarah Elizabeth Ray.

That's what happens when you're raised in an ark of children in the Wauhatchie backwoods. A dozen, plus. No one is ever watching. No one tells you no. You climb higher and run faster than the boys. You shoot possum. You grow up thinking you deserve things. You never learn your place, only that you must fight to hold it.

It was sap rising that set Sarah asea. She eloped from Tennessee to Detroit, barely twenty, on the arm of her country beau. Detroit in the mid-1940s was an anthill of refugees from the Deep South and hillbillies from Appalachia. A place where jump bands and jazz and Black Bottom blues stirred together the races under cover of night. Where women no longer sat at home, but headed to the factories to support the war effort.

This was the promise of Detroit, and Sarah wanted all of it. She enrolled in secretarial school, studied hard, lost her accent and left her husband.

As she thinks about those first years in the city Sarah chuckles: *I was really somethin' in my day.* The sweltering basement parties where she danced to that bluesman fresh from the Delta, John Lee Hooker. The night she fell into the arms of Rafael Haskell at the Flame Show Bar on John R.

Shuffling out of her dingy bedroom, Sarah tries to move to the music of her memory. But her balance is off—like waves are rocking the tongue-and-groove floor. She is hungry, but the kitchen is too far away, so she falls heavily upon the moss green sofa and sits in the half-hearted December sun. From the couch she can see the painting on the bedroom wall of Rafael, her white husband, the second one, his sharp features bleached by the winter light.

A river wind drifts through the lonely house. Rafael's folks used to come by and check on her every once in a while. So did the kids who grew up next door at the Action House. Once, a city councilman even came and took her home with him for Christmas. He had just realized that *the* Sarah Elizabeth Ray lived in his neighborhood. They posed for the newspaper, the councilman standing proudly with "the forgotten Rosa Parks."

Shivering, Sarah pulls a crocheted afghan around her legs and wishes Rafael was there to bring her tea. They hadn't yet met in 1945 when Sarah and her white classmates decided to ferry down the Detroit River on the Bob-lo boat. A cruise to the Boblo Island carnival to celebrate their graduation!

The girls were noisy gulls as they'd queued up. When it was Sarah's turn, the purser plucked the ticket from the white of her palms. His gaze went from her hand to her wiry limbs, to her thin, regal neck, to the grin of accomplishment on her dark face. Before he could say anything, her classmates pushed her onto the gangway so that they could hurry aboard.

"We just graduated!" Dorothy bragged. "This is our party!"

Parties. Oh, my, the parties! thinks Sarah, rubbing her swollen knees to warm them. Knees that used to dance the hucklebuck and rock to the sexy songs of Hank Ballard and the Midnighters. By now the sun is slipping and a pall settles over the room. Her stomach is a hollow of hunger. She shakes her head and thinks about the conversations that stormed all night as her fellow Communists filled the bungalow with smoke, manifestos, the waft of Cuban rum.

Community leaders helped build the Action House next door. Sarah and Rafael had poured everything into that clapboard building where neighborhood children learned to read, write, count and share. Sarah and Rafael were loved by the movement for their buoyant rhetoric, for their endless river of deeds. For years after Rafael died, those who had grown up in the Action House would bring Sarah pies, books, money.

But no more. The children of Detroit have disappeared. So have the Reds; the soulful, street corner doo wop of The Falcons; the contentious block meetings; the union protests; the home schools; the unifying joy of Motown blaring from transistor radios. All gone now, and in their place, a vast tide of abandonment.

The girls from the secretarial school were battening down their dresses and tying their scarves when the steward arrived on the top deck. As soon as Sarah saw him, her nerves prickled. Lording over her, he said, "No coloreds." Returning her eighty-five cent fare, he added, "Let's go."

The summer spirit dampened. Everyone stared. Only two years before, in 1943, a race riot had erupted on Belle Isle when coloreds had tried to cross the bridge to the island park. At twenty-four, before she'd ever met Rafael, before she became a Communist, before she had ever lain down in protest, Sarah knew that another riot would not be her sharpest weapon.

She allowed them to escort her off the boat, and her friends set sail without her. From the dock she headed to the NAACP office and didn't stop paddling upstream until the U.S. Supreme Court upheld her right to ride the Bob-lo boat. It was a victory in principle; she never boarded the boat again.

Sarah realizes that she is quaking. Maybe it's from the cold. Maybe it's from hunger. Maybe it's the surprise of memories erupting from their murky depths. Rising gingerly, she stumbles back to bed. She promises to find something to eat tomorrow. For now, she curls onto her side of the old mattress and thinks about that eighty-five cents sinking coin by coin to the bottom of the river.

iBRAHIM dEATHRAY

Dec 4, 2014 **m e r c y**

i drank with Fleeting Joy yesterday

lukewarm Colts on a specially cold summer night

she said she had to leave

just as things were starting to get warm

splitting

as Marvin Gaye voiced the sum of all my pain

in silent anguish, nailed to the same spot

jungle rot setting in

on

illegally downloaded

heartbreak

Motown soul

mercy mercy

mercy me.

Sean Thomas Dougherty

One Nation Under a Groove

Time to start on a rhythm,
Time to start on a rhyme.

Shim shimmy summer watching my home-girls fly
To a Double-Dutch two step, *feet don't fail me now.*

I remember hearing the cry on my block decades
Ago I wore bell bottoms & carried a radio,

Cool as a Coke can pressed to a sweaty brow, "Everbody,
      FEEL the heat!
Everybody feel the beat pouring over your shoulders."

George Clinton can't see the sun for his shades,

George Clinton can't see the sun for his shades,
And the mothership descending like some bad
Fifties sci-fi set design center-piece.

He's the worst nightmare of the Klu Klux Klan!
He's a sequin caped Christ who gave daddy the finger
And never crawled back up the cross!

He's making all those fat policemen re-dance The Sixties
With a chant straight from his sanctified lips:
Getting down
            Just
for

>   *the funk*
> *of it.*

1979 at Detroit's Cobo Hall
George Clinton passed the big-stick to Booty Collins
Bass-line thumping with Bernie Worrell
Blasting the keys, & the crowd paused:

With as much sway as Martin ever displayed
With a word smooth as the soles of Malcolm's shoes
With the brother's shades signifying
What we knew he did not have to say:

Nothing could stop us now.

George Clinton spread his arms wide that night
Expecting to be given no answers.
Expecting to be given

No answers—except a high-five-hand-slap clap!
And we all understood.

We all understood:

That together . . .
Together . . . *together*

We were all breaking bread
With each nod of our heads.

Rita Dove

Golden Oldie

I made it home early, only to get
Stalled in the driveway. swaying
At the wheel like a blind pianist caught in a tune
Meant for more than two hands playing.

The words were easy, crooned
By a young girl dying to feel alive, to discover
A pain majestic enough
To live by. I turned the air-conditioning off,

leaned back to float on a film of sweat,
And listened to her sentiment:
Baby, where did our love go?—a lament
I greedily took in

Without a clue who my lover
Might be, or where to start looking.

Cornelius Eady

Aretha Franklin's Inauguration Hat

Look at that hat, my mother might have said,
Sitting in that bunker the living room had become,
Her favorite shows interrupted by the sight

Of this woman, who once sang my sister through
One of her major heartbreaks—an I give then
Take-away man

With a truth which rose through the house—I was too young
To know which kind of truth, really, and my sister
Was now learning the words—her belly would swell from it—

Ain't no way, ain't no way, sang the girl who was slightly
Older than my sister, old enough to teach it,
Ain't no way, ain't no way

The needle scratched, and scratched again.
It's not too far-fetched to think of it breaking skin,
A rush of something toxic, tear-raising

Remember when she didn't want to tell us
But told us by playing that damn record all day
Over and over in her bedroom, that's the woman under

That hat I'd tell my mother, if she'd asked.
That church hat.
That black woman's hat.
That testimony hat.

Cornelius Eady

The Supremes

We were born to be gray. We went to school,
Sat in rows, ate white bread,
Looked at the floor a lot. In the back
of our small heads

A long scream. We did what we could,
And all we could do was
Turn on each other. How the fat kids suffered!
Not even being jolly could save them.

And then there were the anal retentive,
The terrified brown-noses, the desperately
Athletic or popular. This, of course,
Was training. At home

Our parents shook their heads and waited.
We learned of the industrial revolution,
The sectioning of the clock into pie slices.
We drank cokes and twiddled our thumbs. In the
Back of our minds

A long scream. We snapped butts in the showers,
Froze out shy girls on the dance floor,
Pinpointed flaws like radar.
Slowly we understood: this was to be the world.

We were born insurance salesmen and secretaries,
Housewives and short order cooks,
Stockroom boys and repairmen,

And it wouldn't be a bad life, they promised,
In a tone of voice that would force some of us
To reach in self-defense for wigs,
Lipstick,

Sequins.

W. D. Ehrhart

Dancing in the Streets

for Martha & the Vandellas

The summer I was fifteen, I discovered
girls, and beer, and cigarettes,
how to dance, and how to lie
and get away with it. That summer,
everyone around the world
was dancing in the streets.
Except in Perkasie, a one-horse town
without so much as a traffic light
where fun was watching Lawrence Welk
or listening to the corn grow.
Christ, my mother didn't get it,
wouldn't even let me go
seven miles to Quakertown to dance.
St. Isadore's, for cryin' in a bucket.
Teen dance at a Catholic Church
chaperoned by priests and nuns.
"There's lots to do in Perkasie," she said.
What did she know? Lawrence Welk.
So I just said I'd be at Larry Rush's house,
hitchhiked up to Quakertown instead,
danced with Andrea Jenkins, had
the best time ever in my life,
concluded what my parents didn't know
wouldn't hurt them. Freedom!
What a heady feeling. All the world
at my disposal; all I had to do was lie.
This was 1964. What did I know?

Selma, Watts, Detroit, Khe Sanh, My Lai,
the cost and consequence of lies
had not yet come collecting what was due.

Thomas Sayers Ellis

Photograph of Dr. Funkenstein

after Christian Witkin

A crazy evil grin, eyelids flipped
Inside out, red hot and pink as pork.
The tongue slipping out the mouth
Suggests fellatio, and a pussy taunting dogs.

He is arrested, in custody,
MOST WANTED, an atomic shaman
With a scratch-and-sniff beard. I'll bet you
He was dreaming of Venus, about to say something nasty
When the photographer bopped him
With a nickel bag of light into a permanent
Type nod, sizzaleenmean, somewhere
Between a mugshot and maximumisness.

Judging from the shirt and tie,
He's well hung and may have been
About to make a house call (reach
Way up and give Sir Nose a splanking
Or photosynthesize, a dandy lion)
When the booty snatchers slapped him
With a warrant, shoving him, handcuffed,
Onto a death row of commodes,

A zone of zero funkativity,
Violating his right to hold
His own thang, his right to pee.

Robert Fanning

Memorial in Open Air

for Blair (September 19, 1967–July 23, 2011)

Skyline blaze, thrown spark, slung guitar, far seer smiling down the avenue, so heart-rare—you sang Detroit red. Your voice a bellow, Motown-loud, proud and queer, *made here,* packing a crackling laugh and roar—you sang Detroit orange. Brazing poem to song, stanza to verse with a welder's glare, hammered lines burned iron black and bright, building a bridge for all to cross—you sang Detroit yellow. Leaving the late-shift line to ignite your words, ear tuned to the city's gear, sky-flung songs shot high as arcing flares—you sang Detroit green. With Urban Folk, and the Boyfriends, rolling neo-troubadour carrying the D everywhere, poet-ambassador—you sang Detroit blue. Performer, teacher, poet, singer, star—on stage, in classrooms, on tour to make your home far and near, you snuffed-breath dear—you sang Detroit indigo. Now Down Cass, Blair—the sky a singed and searing bruise, we sing you violet and never gone, all us patchwork human sore, all us pieces fused by your bright black stitch of flame, for you our put-out star we sing our varied carols one, for you, barrel-chested, operatic, arms thrown wide, your day a harmony of hours weaving into night, for you we lift the poems *you* sang, your hooked-thumb hands turned soaring birds again, in your Detroit and everywhere, we parade beneath your painted air.

Linda Nemec Foster

Dancing with My Sister

for Deborah

We're not talking those crazy Polish weddings
in Cleveland, where we both learned how to dance,
clutching each other's sweaty hands, galloping
to the Beer Barrel Polka, and trying not to bump
into Uncle Johnnie and his whirling Chicago Hop.

This is now, tonight, in a smoky bar in Detroit
where two women dancing together can scandalize
any pimp within range. Where the hot-shot
bartender can mix anything and has the wide eyes
to prove it: bloody mary, wallbanger, a zombie
with a spike of lime that will raise the dead.

Above the crowded dance floor, in the maze
of cat walks, the geek of a lighting man
(who reminds us of every boy in high school
who fast-danced with his hands behind his back)
shines the spotlight right on us. And we glow.

Girl, do we glow. Not for the memory of those
distant high school boys whose faces we can't
remember. Not for the fluid desire ebbing
around us on the floor and beyond where silent
men sit in the dark. We glow for the raw truth
of Aretha's voice spelling out RESPECT;
for the way our hair curls down past our shoulders;
for our legs that can out-dance any young thing;

for the miracle that we survived our childhoods—
mother's obsessive cleaning, father's factory shifts,
the Erwin Street mob of pre-juvenile delinquents.
We glow because we came from the same burnt-out dream
of second-generation immigrants and learned to smile
at the closed mouth of loss and dance, dance, dance.

Stewart Francke

Motor City Serenade

Well the riverside is alive tonight,
a sliver of light keeps the buildings bright.
Cars rumble down Woodward, on to Circus Park
Mitch Ryder on the radio after dark.

Ride from Menjos to the Bluebird to the Minor Key;
Ernie's voice still floats inside the factories.
A hurricane of color waits at Motor's door,
the techno holy trio will fill the floor.

Baby let the night swallow us whole
'cuz we're alive in this city of soul
Hear the music, hear the rock & roll . . .
We've worked so hard, we've paid our dues,
so let's lose ourselves . . . sing a Motor City Serenade.

Drinkin' Stroh's out on the landing of the old canals
Wake up on weekend mornings with Soupy Sales
Through rain & snow & ice we drive to go to work
Then we gather in our neighborhoods and go to church.

Baby let the night swallow us whole
'cuz we're alive in this city of soul
Hear the music, hear the rock & roll . . .
We've worked so hard, we've paid our dues,
so let's lose ourselves . . . sing a Motor City Serenade.

Oh my love, it takes some faith to survive
Sky above, tonight the highway's alive

Well the riverside is alive tonight
A sliver of light keeps the buildings bright
I hear Nolan Strong and Marvin somewhere in the air
Stoney, Wojo, Gordie Howe & John Sinclair.

Baby let the night swallow us whole
'cuz we're alive in this city of soul
Hear the music, hear the rock & roll
We've worked so hard, we've paid our dues,
so let's lose ourselves . . . sing a Motor City Serenade.

Christopher Gilbert

Time with Stevie Wonder in It

Winter, the empty air, outside
cold shaking its rigid tongue
announcing itself like something stone,
spit out, which is still a story
and a voice to be embraced.
Januaried movements but I hear a tune
carries me home to Lansing.

Always waiting for signs of thaw,
dark nomads getting covered by snow,
our parents would group in the long night—
tune frequencies to the Black stations
blasting out of Memphis, Nashville,
still playing what was played down south—
Ray Charles, Charles Brown, Ruth Brown, Muddy and Wolf.

The tribal families driven north
to neighborhoods stacked like boxes—
to work the auto plants was progress,
to pour steel would buy a car
to drive hope further on down the road.
How could you touch, hear
or be alive; how could anybody

wearing our habits, quiet Protestant
heads aimed up to some future?
This was our rule following—
buy at J.C. Penney and Woolworth's,
work at Diamond Reo, Oldsmobile, Fisher Body.
On Fridays drink, dance, and try to forget

the perverse comfort of huddling in

what was done to survive (the buffering,
the forgetting). How could. we not
"turn the head/pretend not to see?"
This is what we saw: hope screwed
to steel flesh, this was machine city
and the wind through it—neutral
to an extent, private, and above all

perfectly European language
in which we could not touch, hear
or be alive. How could anybody
be singing "Fingertips?" Little Stevie
Wonder on my crystal, 1963.
Blind boy comes to go to school,
the air waves politely segregated.

                *   *   *

If this were just a poem
there would be a timelessness—
the punchclock midwest would go on
ticking, the intervals between ticks
metaphor for the gap in our lives
and in that language which would not
carry itself beyond indifferent

consequences. The beauty of the word,
though, is the difference between language
and the telling made through use.
Dance Motown on his lip, he lays
these radio tracks across the synapse
of snow. The crystals show
a future happening with you in it.

Brian Gilmore

living for the city

for stevie wonder

at the lansing school for the blind
the boarded up buildings do the talking.
people here living just enough like a boy
named steveland from saginaw who arrived
here half famous. mouth organ near his fingertips
singing christmas songs way before this became the
frontline. pasttime paradise. ted hull with his
own terrible sight showing the boy how to walk
straight lines he will need badly once he settles down
to sing some songs in the motor city. don't want to
bore you with the morning sun. because lately these
streets aren't happy or lovely. no one is calling to say
they love anything either. this is in need of love today.
the parks. storefront churches with barely any members.
houses welcoming squatters & rats. there is no joy inside
tears. everyone around here would move to saturn if
they could. be there always. this no ordinary pain, no
ordinary pain. knocking many off of their feet in this village
ghetto land that hasn't done nothing in a very long time.

Nikki Giovanni

Poem for Aretha

cause nobody deals with Aretha—a mother with four children—having
    to hit the road
they always say "after she comes
home" but nobody ever says what it's like
to get on a plane for a three week tour
the elation of the first couple of audiences the good
feeling of exchange the running on the high
you get from singing good
and loud and long telling the world
what's on your mind.

then comes the eighth show on the sixth day the beginning
to smell like the plane or bus the if-you-forget-your-toothbrush
in-one-spot-you-can't-brush-until-the-second-show the strangers
pulling at you cause they love you but you having no love
to give back
the singing the same songs night after night day after day
and if you read the gossip columns the rumors that your husband
is only after your fame
the wondering if your children will be glad to see you and maybe
the not caring if they are scheming to get out
of just one show and go just one place where some doe-doe-dupaduke
won't say "just sing one song, please!"

nobody mentions how it feels to become a freak
because you have talent and how
no one gives a damn how you feel
but only cares that aretha franklin is here like maybe that'll
stop:

chickens from frying
eggs from being laid
crackers from hating

and if you say you're lonely or tired how they always just say "oh come off it"
    or "did you see
how they loved you did you see, huh, did you?"
which most likely has nothing to do with you anyway
and I'm not saying Aretha shouldn't have talent and I'm certainly
not saying she should quit
singing but as much as I love her I'd vote "yes" to her
doing four concerts a year and staying home or doing whatever
she wants and making records cause it's a shame
the way we're killing her
we eat up artists like there's going to be a famine at the end
of those three minutes when there are in fact an abundance
of talents just waiting let's put some
of the giants away for a while and deal with them like they have
a life to lead.

Aretha doesn't have to relive billie holiday's life doesn't have
to relive dinah washington's death but who will
stop the pattern

she's more important than her music—if they must be
separated—
and they should be separated when she has to pass out
before
anyone recognizes she needs
a rest and i say i need
aretha's music
she is undoubtedly the one who put everyone on
notice

she revived johnny ace and remembered lil green aretha sings "i say a little
     prayer" and dionne doesn't
want to hear it anymore
aretha sings "money won't change you"
but james can't sing "respect" the advent
of Aretha pulled ray charles from marlboro country
and back into
the blues made nancy wilson
try one more time forced
dionne to make a choice (she opted for the movies)
and diana ross had to get an afro wig pushed every
Black singer into his Blackness and negro entertainers
into negroness you couldn't jive
when she said "you make me / feel" the blazers
had to reply "gotta let a man be / a man"
aretha said "when my soul was in the lost and found / you came along to
     claim it" and joplin said "maybe"
there has been no musician whom her very presence hasn't
affected when humphrey wanted her to campaign for him she said
"woeman's only hueman"
and he pressured james brown
they removed otis cause the combination was too strong
the impressions had to say "lord have mercy / we're moving
on up"
the Black songs started coming from the singers on stage and the dancers
in the streets
aretha was the riot was the leader if she had said "come
let's do it" it would have been done
temptations say why don't we think about it
                         think about it
                         think about it

Jessica Hagedorn

Motown/Smokey Robinson

hey girl, how long you been here?
did you come with yr daddy in 1959 on a second-class boat
cryin' all the while cuz you didn't want to leave the barrio
the girls back there who wore their hair loose
lotsa orange lipstick and movies on sundays
quiapo market in the morning, yr grandma chewin' red tobacco
roast pig? . . . yeah, and it tasted good . . .
hey girl, did you haveta live in stockton with yr daddy
and talk to old farmers who immigrated in 1941?
did yr daddy promise you to a fifty-eight-year-old bachelor
who stank of cigars . . . and did you
run away to san francisco / go to poly high / rat your hair /
hang around woolworth's / chinatown at three in the morning
to go to the cow palace and catch SMOKEY ROBINSON
cry and scream at his gold jacket
Dance every friday night in the mission / go steady with ruben?
(yr daddy can't stand it cuz he's a spik.)
and the sailors you dreamed of in manila with yellow hair
did they take you to the beach to ride the ferris wheel?

Life's never been so fine!
you and carmen harmonize "be my baby" by the ronettes
and 1965 you get laid at a party / carmen's house
and you get pregnant and ruben marries you
and you give up harmonizing . . .
hey girl, you sleep without dreams
and remember the barrios and how it's all the same:
manila / the mission / chinatown / east l.a. / harlem / fillmore st.
and you're getting' kinda fat and smokey robinson's getting' old

so take a good look at my face / you see my smile
looks outta place / if you look closer / it's easy to trace /
the tracks of my tears . . .

but he still looks good!!!

i don't want to / but i need you / seems like i'm always /
thinkin' of you / though you do me wrong now / my love is
strong now / you really gotta hold on me . . .

Peter J. Harris

Some Songs Women Sing

(in homage to "If I Were Your Woman" & "Make Me the Woman (You Come Home To)," by Gladys Knight & The Pips; "My Guy," by Mary Wells; "Don't Mess With Bill," by the Marvelettes; "Jimmy Mack," by Martha and The Vandellas; "I Got Him Back in My Arms Again," by The Supremes; "Natural Woman," by Aretha Franklin; "Alfie" & "Message to Michael," by Dionne Warwick; "Yes I'm Ready," by Barbara Mason; "BABY," by Carla Thomas, & other womansung classics . . .)

some songs by women
so bad even men
sing along without changing words we don't flinch
promising to keep some wayward brother "weak as a lamb,"
we confess "there's not a man today can tear me away from My Guy"
we be warning all the sisters "Don't Mess With Bill" begging Jimmy Mack
"when are you comin' back?" announce with pride
"got him back in my arms again" One Voice sings these songs
no tittering come time
to sing some man back home no stuttering come time
to moan he makes me real feel verse by verse
we holler all the words just as proud to lipsync
Aretha, Gladys, Tammi Terrell just as satisfied
being Diana, Martha, Bernice Reagon
as ripping into a
Mad Lad/Impression/Stylistic type thing anyway
what is a Vandella

a Vandella as in Martha and the . . . what *is* a Vandella anyway
but a call to Imagination
            to rework our minds

to remember the Each Other in each other
to believe in the Vandella
in all of *us*
a Vandella
like one of them
Blackcity names
sisters create to sound French
Fashwan LeJean
Que Sera Que Sera names like Sweet names like no other names
for all to call
with wonderful wonder whatever will be
    will be
    will be sung together whether woman or man sings
long as it touches
the Deep Human so when Aretha say
        "I didnt know
        just what was wrong with me
        till your kiss
        helped me name it"
I don't even *want*
to be a Natural Man
& I wouldn't never be alone
if I could beg a brother
like Jennifer Holliday
onstage/spotlit/sweatswept

sometimes
one of these womensung classics
rise out radios tearing down walls of gender
from under bricks & cinder
our voices float on time/on tune
to the charming neon leadlady singers
who make us understand
just what it mean
to be a memorable Main Squeeze

just what it mean
to be a Marvelous Marvelette
just what it mean
to believe whatever we'll be
          we'll be

Lolita Hernandez

Silver Anniversary

> *You broke my heart*
> *'Cause I couldn't dance*
> *You didn't even want me around*
> *—The Contours, Motown 1963*

That December evening the boys on vinyl blasted their Motown music smack at the people crowded in the tiny house, their faces shiny from kitchen heat and their souls full of anticipation. It was the silver anniversary in the States of a marriage that began back home. You have to celebrate making it here and lasting through the Detroit shit, with the economics of being poor, the cold winters and summers without sea salt.

Notes were all in the atmosphere. Little miss DJ moved her bottom bumpity bump, knees bent and head swaying, hands poised over her small cardboard record player to refresh the 45 RPM soon as the needle hit end.

After many needle endings across the 45 with her hands reaching up, no one, not one single soul was paying attention. No one offered to join. Only she feeling the fun off in the corner in the front room with souce and turkey seasoned their way competing, as well as the usual schtew chicken, pelau, cucumber, curry. In short almost everything you could imagine transporting itself from over there to then. Even guava find its way in the fete. Of course, nips of rum and scotch.

Getting back to bumpity bump in the corner of the front room, some aunt or the other entered the scene, full of practiced Detroit social skills with blah blah blah and so on. Meaning full of she self, thinking she well off. Then she realized that some young someone was off in the corner bumping to something not quite in the fumes of curry and souce and schtew and all that. Bam, just like that she fix up she face like some imperious lady of rule and next thing you know she telling Miss Bumpity Bump: Take that off. Put on Calypso. Like she in she own house.

What to do, but take off the boys and put on a set of donkey wanting watah? All in a sudden the whole house shifting from side to side with the old people dancing, showing their contours. One hip going that way, another going that way. Him, one half of the silver celebrants, got lips pursed like he can sneak some kind of kiss from whoever lady. Miss DJ slipped way back into the corner to see what the other half was doing. That one, like every last manjack, was working the southern regions of the body. She never see anything so in she short life.

What to do? You think you in this city and you trying to get in with the people. All you listening to up to then is music like Mac Beth, the Great and he donkey. Then you discover these boys with their wish for love through dance. They ask, do you love me? And she was convinced she did and that they loved her and that they knew what to do. Young Detroit boys. She thought all that until she saw these folk's bottoms swaying this way and that, house moving all kind of way. Everything and everyone steaming, including the silvers. Let all that cold stay outside. Mac Beth donkey moving the crowd in such a way you didn't worry about who loving who, how the kisses land, where the hips bump. It's silver time in this city right now. We here no matter how you think you can dance. Let we show you. Look, move this thing like that. And then you see chook over here, chook over there. Pampalam, pampalam. Oui foute. Yes Lawd. Nothing can stop we now.

By this time she completely forgot about the woman with her pretensions and the vinyl boys. There was no place to be but then and there with all of them dancing their hearts out. Full.

Dennis Hinrichsen

Radio Motown

I go back to Levi Stubbs and the fog when it's spring again
and I lie awake. Me kissing a girl
the whole ride home, thinking if I pulled my lips away
I'd never get it back, whatever
was happening. Her *yes* in the dark
feeding mine
as Tommy nursed the '98 through the hair-pin turns
of autumn, Ridge Hollow Road,
while the other Tommy held the door ajar
and tambourined the dash, crying
right in time with the bass, or *left, left*
as the tires spit and the car veered, and
we stayed on the road.
Frogs still out in the reeds
because the air was alive. The boys
were alive. And Mary was kissing me
back. Pulse of tail lamp. Four Tops. Fog,
banked road, stench of swamp . . . And then
I was home and dropped at that house by the lake.
Taste of her lips on my lips, the boys' voices swept
to mist in my head—
they would be dead in the spring, I would crawl
unhurt over their beyond-hurt bodies—
I sat alone in the kitchen in the same
radio dark
and guided by the singing,
pitched them all the curved road home.

Edward Hirsch

Let's Get Off the Bus

Let's get off the bus
in 1979
in front of the empty fairgrounds
on Eight-Mile and Woodward
and stop for a few rounds
at the Last Chance Bar.
The moon is tilted
at a rakish angle
and we can toast the unruly
poets of Detroit
and praise our students
who work three jobs
and still show up for class.
Don't get lost
in the sad stories
of the regulars
and make sure to step over
the junkies on the corner
and dodge the cars barreling
past the stoplights
for the suburbs.
Let's surprise my wife
who is napping off her grief
and crank up the stereo
for Stevie Wonder's road trip
through *The Secret Life of Plants.*
Someone has started a garden
on the far side of Palmer Park—

or is it Woodlawn Cemetery?—
where we can throw a party
for our friends
who are still alive.

Lynda Hull

Chiffon

Fever, down-right dirty sweat
      of a heat-wave in May turning everyone
            pure body. Back of knee, cleavage, each hidden

crease, nape of neck turning steam. Deep
      in last night's vast factory, the. secret
            wheels that crank the blue machinery

of weather bestowed this sudden cool,
      the lake misting my morning walk, this
            vacant lot lavish with iris—saffron,

indigo, bearded and striated, a shock
      of lavender clouds among shattered brick
            like cumulus that sail the tops of high rises

clear evenings. Surprising as the iris garden
      I used to linger in, a girl distant from me
            now as a figure caught in green glass,

an oasis gleamed cool with oval plaques
      naming blooms Antoinette, My Blue Sunset,
            Festival Queen. This morning's iris frill

damp as fabulous gowns after dancing,
      those rummage sale evening gowns church ladies
            gave us another hot spring, 1967.

JoAnn who'd soon leave school, 14, pregnant,

Valerie with her straightened bouffant hair.
   That endless rooftop season before the panic

and sizzle, the torched divided cities,
   they called me cousin on the light side.
     Camphorous, awash in rusty satin rosettes,

in organdy, chiffon, we'd practice
   girl group radio hits—Martha Reeves
     but especially Supremes—JoAnn vamping

Diana, me and Valerie doing Flo and Mary's
   background moans, my blonde hair pinned
     beneath Jo's mother's Sunday wig.

The barest blue essence of Evening in Paris
   scented our arms. We perfected all the gestures,
     JoAnn's liquid hands sculpting air,

her fingers' graceful cupping, wrist turning,
   palm in held flat, "Stop in the Name of Love,"
     pressing against the sky's livid contrails,

a landscape flagged with laundry, tangled
   aerials and billboards, the blackened
     railway bridges and factories ruinous

in their fumes. Small hand held against the flood
   of everything to come, the savage drifting years.
     I'm a lucky bitch. Engulfed in the decade's riotous

swells, that lovely gesture, the dress, plumage
   electrifying the fluid force of that young body.
     She, was gang-raped later that year. The rest,

as they say is history. History.
When I go back I pore the phone book for names
I'll never call. Peach Pavilion, Amethyst

Surprise. *Cousin on the light side.* Bend
to these irises, their piercing ambrosial
essence, the heart surprised, dark and bitter.

David James

Floating

*"How can a girl get serious about dancing when
her man can't even float?"*

—*Overheard conversation*

Turn on the Motown
and he begins to drown,
flailing with both arms and legs,
gasping for air. While others
swim gracefully through the notes,
dipping, turning in unison
like a school of tuna on the dance floor,
he is panicking, taking in water,
eyes bulging to touch
the surface of anything.
Within minutes, he sinks into silence,
his stubborn body held still in clear, watery cement,
a statue on the row of folding chairs
along the wall.

The music of *The Supremes, The Temptations,*
The Four Tops floats high above him, untouchable.
From the bottom, wallowing in muck,
he glances up every now and then
to see lights flashing,
bodies curving and bending,
a pale blue sky
dancing
just to spite him.

Mark Jarman

The Supremes

In Ball's Market after surfing till noon,
we stand in wet trunks, shivering
as icing dissolves off our sweet rolls
inside the heat-blued counter oven,
when they appear on his portable TV,
riding a float of chiffon as frothy
as the peeling curl of a wave.
The parade m. c. talks up their hits
and their new houses outside of Detroit
and old Ball clicks his tongue.
Gloved up to their elbows, their hands raised
toward us palm out, they sing,
"'Stop! In the Name of Love" and don't stop
but slip into the lower foreground.

Every day of a summer can turn,
from one moment, into a single day.
I saw Diana Ross in her first film
play a brief scene by the Pacific—
and that was the summer it brought back.
Mornings we paddled out, the waves
would be little more than embellishments:
lathe work and spun glass,
gray green with cold, but flawless.
When the sun burned through the light fog,
they would warm and swell,
wind-scaled and ragged,
and radios up and down the beach
would burst on with her voice.

She must remember that summer
somewhat differently, and so must the two
who sang with her in long matching gowns,
standing a step back on her left and right,
as the camera tracked them
into our eyes in Ball's Market.
But what could we know, tanned white boys,
wiping sugar and salt from our mouths
and leaning forward to feel their song?
Not much, except to feel it
ravel us up like a wave
in the silk of white water,
simply sweetly repeatedly,
and just as quickly let go.

We didn't stop either, which is how
we vanished, too, parting like spray—
Ball's Market, my friends and I.
Dredgers ruined the waves,
those continuous dawn perfections,
and Ball sold high to the high rises
cresting over them. His flight out of L.A.,
heading for Vegas, would have banked
above the wavering lines of surf.
He may have seen them. I have,
leaving again for points north and east,
glancing down as the plane turns.
From that height they still look frail and frozen,
full of simple sweetness and repetition.

Allison Joseph

Junior High Dance

No one wanted to dance with us
in 8th grade, to glide across
the shiny expanse of gym floor,
choosing us from among
the awkward and shy girls,
the boys loud and pushing instead,
uncouth to everyone but chaperones.
I had on the ugliest pantsuit—
matching orange and blue—
homemade by my mother before
she really learned to sew,
before she dazzled us with
cotton and corduroy.
My best friend had an earache,
but stayed anyway, swaying
to the music, letting it
carry her heavy body
a little forward, away
from the wall, back.

The speakers didn't wail
the way I wanted them to,
their volume respectable,
although you could still hear
Diana Ross singing—*I'm coming out*—
her anthem of disco liberation.
We watched the other kids dance,
lithe Hispanic girls who always
seemed to know when to turn,
how to bow and shimmy, or smile.

Watched the older black girls
who, self-satisfied and worldly wise,
knew all the latest steps,
and the variations on the latest
steps, so when I dared once before
to venture on the dance floor,
they hooted at me, said *that's old,*
with surety they had about nothing
else. April and I hung back,
sassy wallflowers joking about
our teachers—their whiteness,
their lack of street savvy.
They still thought Diana Ross
was a Supreme, that she still sang
You Can't Hurry Love with Flo and Mary,
that Motown was still Hitsville, U.S.A.
No one could convince us
we had something to learn
from them, no one could tell us
they were anything more than old
as they blew up balloons,
made sure the lights stayed on.
And we had our corner,
our tiny bit of that place,
where we listened to that garish
seventies music, not letting
our bodies stray far, staying
right there, no matter how funky
the beat, no matter how delicious.

Allison Joseph

Paradelle for Motown

The back-up singers sway from side to side.
The back-up singers sway from side to side.
In bouffant wigs and pointy heels, they dance.
In bouffant wigs and pointy heels, they dance.
Bouffant wigs, pointy heels. The singers dance;
they sway from side to side, back-up, and in.

Tempts and Tops sing swelling songs of love.
Tempts and Tops sing swelling songs of love.
Backed by tight drums and bass, syncopation.
Backed by tight drums and bass, syncopation.
Swelling syncopation tight, Tempts and Tops sing
songs backed by love of drums and bass.

Flo, Mary, and Diana coo demurely in place.
Flo, Mary, and Diana coo demurely in place.
Three skinny girls who made it past Detroit.
Three skinny girls who made it past Detroit.
Three skinny girls who made it demurely,
Flo, Mary, and Diana coo in place, past Detroit.

Drums and bass. Backed by syncopation,
tight Tempts, Tops, Flo, Mary, and Diana—
they coo and sway, side to side, back-up.
From past Detroit and demurely in pointy heels,
three skinny girls who made it dance in place.
Bouffant wigs swelling, the singers sing of love songs.

Lawrence Joseph

Sentimental Education

So no self-centered anarchism
was of use, too manic was the sense
of economy, employment and inflation
curved. Detroit's achromatic
sky for a son of lower
middle class parents like me
glowed. My baptism by fire
in the ancient manner,
at a father's side in a burning city,
nothing sacramental about it.

Everything was—everything fast!
Strips of a twilight shadow sheened
transparency and cast
a concisely stylized groove
you could count on
around the door to the dance.
War-days conscientiously objected to,
the racial on me all the time,
I knew my place, you might say,
and white-hot ingots

in their molds, same time,
same place blue jays among the marigolds
held their own beside
the most terrible rage, tears wept
for no reason at all except
what might have been
—my mother's tears, for instance.

She doesn't sleep well
in this climate
composite pale tints.

But first, back to Henry Ford.
Of the world-famous Highland Park Plant
Otto Moog, the German engineer,
in 1923 proclaimed (Vladimir
Lenin thought so too): "No symphony
compares to the music hammering
through the colossal workplace"
—proof, so to speak,
that speech propels the purposes
by which it's been shaped.

But back, first, to Marvin Gaye,
during an interview in Brussels.
"Remember the Turbans?" he asks,
laughing at the memory. "Cats
sported silk headdresses, sang up
a storm. Had this one hit tune,
'Please Let Me Show You Around Myself,'
the lyrics comparing enclosed
empty space to an open heart
showed me to appreciate language."

Back to, because you want to,
Grand Boulevard, excessive sky
hot and indigo, poured forth
onto Hendrie. Inside the store,
Grandpa lifts you into his arms,
small as a single summer Sunday,
a kind of memory-trance truly
dark, deep and dark, steel dark,

not as pure, but almost as pure,
as pure unattainable light.

What now? The palette's red.
The beggars wear red in their hair.
Red's contained in the place's currency.
The distance sustained between
subject and object looks red.
History, increasingly ephemeral,
is red. The switches of the music are
red while you mark the beat,
consistent with your education,
without any inner dispute.

Zilka Joseph

To the Man Leaning Forward

Inspired by the factory scene on the north wall of the Diego Rivera
Detroit Industry Frescoes in the DIA, and Motown music

How can I stop thinking of my girl
my baby love I have to leave behind

I have no money but this is not what I want
I push so hard my face hits my fists
clenched on the trolley bar

my muscles moan heart drums loud
my feet move in step with my partner
but this is no dancing in the street

I taste iron rusty like blood in my mouth
a sting no after-lunch smoke will mask
these are the tracks of my tears this is real blood

and from above the foremen shout and the furnace is a dragon roaring
burning sunshine of my life
it breathes fire on us all night long

all night long the music of metal blows in my ears
some days the machine sings the inner city blues
or plays bebop and I stomp in step keep up

grinding hard the horns are demanding today
they say let's get it on
and my legs pump like they are pistons

heat wave after heat wave covers me
what's going on you ask
are we ghosts already I say
I can't feel my legs
I can't even feel this old heart of mine

so tired I can do no more than slow boogie
go on then laugh at us these are the tears of a clown
owned by you master with an iron heart
I have nowhere to run

what will become of us broken-hearted ones
still I ask my partner to dance
our feet dragging the weight of steel uphill

and we just roll down again
and again
no there ain't no mountain high
no mountain higher than this one

M. L. Liebler

Rhythm and Blues Fire

for The Falcons & Sir Mack Rice

Tonight gasoline pours
Creating a fire of rhythm
And blues igniting an engine
Of sweet soul dreams

Warm, dark purple
Late summer night songs
That respect themselves
Hot harmonies on an Eastside Detroit street

Falcons singing in the front
Room and across the street
And a young boy hears
Their call and response.

It's a new church
It's Detroit. It's late 1959
And it's our good fortune to have

New hymns for our northern souls.

Dawn McDuffie

Dear Detroit Earthquake,

You show Reggie from the shelter and
and his sister Suzanne from Lafayette Park
the undeniable facts of life: action, change.
Slow or fast your plates slip and stop. You're
adorable when frustrated, stamping your
invisible earthquake foot like a sexy lady
in a 1950 sitcom. Friction traps you, desire
to shake loose all the conflict building up
in your soul. You love Detroit when it plays
your favorite song. I can almost hear you
hum along with Marvin Gaye, "Brother,
brother, brother, / There's far too many of you
dying . . . Talk to me . . ." It's all pressure, no
release. Trust me, I know how much earth
aches when the margins of one plate slam
into another. You're a geological megastar,
thwarted way too long, and you're here to
shake the city until justice is as common as
winter. Earthquake, I'm balancing on my own
skittery floor, house shaking like a huge dog
scratching behind its ear. I hear your exhale
of pleasure as ground shifts the foundation.
I wonder if Belle Isle is safe. A bronze child
holds water in cupped hands, but it bounces
away like rain falling up. Statues of mothers
are crying in churches and graveyards, and
a new crack streaks through carved stone
where broken Jesus blesses broken children.

Ray McNiece

Pop Songs through the Night

In the middle of night
apartment complex,
empty elevators open
on lavender carpets
and long hallways sterilized
with fluorescent lights,
rock muzak and plastic plants.

Curled on the couch
under her mother's frowzy coat,
she would like to have a cat
to be pretty with and lounge
around yawning and petted.
But no one strokes her tonight.

Her voice wavered thin
through the phone lines
in the call that woke me
after I slipped asleep
out of an empty bottle
into my own red wine pity.

She knew as well as I did
I would be right over, driving
through the traffic light
that keeps making signals
all night, cars or not.

I pass windows that seep

blue light and rooms that stay
set and clean. Maybe a man
sits inside in the dark
sipping coffee or whiskey
or both deciding whether
to move or stay put.

I click on the radio and
a golden oldie fills night,
Pop Songs
"Standing in the Shadow of Love,
waiting for the heartache to come . . ."
and so on as I drive on.

In my teenage room,
I longed into every song,
ear pressed against plastic
transistor radio, antenna
pointed towards CKLW,
the Motown sound, crying
the tears of a clown,
when there's no one around.

I imagined snuggling close
to Denise at Big Boy Burgers,
sticking thigh to thigh
in the naugahyde booth.
I had no idea I'd ever be
released from the nervous,
glandular embrace of adolescence.

As I pass through this city
we have both drifted to,
I see there comes a time

neither of us will call,
having moved too often and
ending in too many other beds.

Some saccharine lyric will
make us want, once more,
to hold forever, because "*Sugar pie
Honey bunch—you know I love you . . .*"
the more cliché love becomes,
the more crucial.

Somewhere in the Midwest,
back in the heart of it all,
you will hear one of our songs
Pop Songs as it drones on and on
in an all-night donut shop
and start to hum along.

A middle-aged waitress
will take your order
snapping gum like you
learned back of the Tastee
Freeze summers ago.
She does not hum along.

She only wants to go home
to her double-wide trailer
have someone rub her feet
and call her, *honey,*
so long as it doesn't sound
through the rooms like *lonely.*

Wardell Montgomery Jr.

Michael Was Unique

Dionne Warwick, take a Message to Michael
And tell him to rest in peace
Some say Michael was guilty as sin
The jury said in a loud voice, "not guilty"
This was not a jury of his peers; he had no peers
No one else quite like him; "world's greatest entertainer"
Unique

That was not a jury selected by Michael
He knew that would not be fair
This jury was not selected by his friends
Some of his friends would not want a bad guy to go free
This jury was not selected by his family
They believed him and spoke passionately on his behalf
This was not a jury of his fans who could not get enough of him
This was not a jury of his enemies who would love to destroy him
This was not a jury of main stream media to the surprise of many
This was not a jury of Jay "I'm Bad" Leno who told some bad funny
Jackson jokes on TV but told the jury the truth of what a great man
Michael was
This was not a kangaroo court; they loved Michael too and were offended

How often are poor people who look strange and weird doing time based
only of their looks?
In pursuit of happiness, did Michael fail at success and could not face the
Man in the Mirror?
Prescription drugs, religion and entertainment can be your best friend or
your worst enemy

Children now full grown who slept and played games in Michael's big bed room, had
Milk and cookies, testified under oath that Michael had not molested them or other children
The accusing family has been found guilty of extortion. Michael was their perfect victim.
There was no smoking gun, no soiled bed sheets with DNA, no pictures, no audio or video tapes
This time I think Lady Justice was a real lady and kept her eyes closed and heart open
Los Angeles' Dragnet Detective Joe Friday was famous for saying on that TV show,
"The Facts Please, Just The Facts!"   I would like to add:

not your opinions	not your superstitions	not your stereotypes
not your cynicism	not your homophobia	not your negativity
not your racism	not your nightmares	Just The Facts

It's not against the law to be horny, celibate, asexual, bisexual, or homosexual.
It's not against the law to be weird, a consenting adult;
Unique

K. Michelle Moran

Help Wanted

Everybody wants to be Belinda Carlisle
or maybe Jane Wiedlin—
not Gina Schock—
but somebody has to keep the beat.
The Supremes with just Diana Ross?
Destiny's Child with only Beyoncé?
That's called a solo act,
and it teaches you nothing
about sharing.

Someone needs
to find your size in black
in the Macy's shoe department stockroom.
Someone has to
weigh your package
after you've stood in line an hour at the post office.
Someone must
feed the chickens,
sweep the streets,
be Inspector No. 9.

The trains don't run on time
if no one makes the schedule.
The president can't pilot
Air Force One.
Pancakes burn in the griddle
if no one flips them.
The "CEO's" corporate restructuring memos
don't write themselves.

So look smart
behind that cubicle wall.
Answer your phone like Ed McMahon just told you
you won the Publisher's Clearinghouse Sweepstakes.
And when you ask the next person in line
if he'd like fries with that,
do so knowing
he'll probably say yes
because of you.

Cindy Hunter Morgan

Incident on Grand River, 1967

Detroit was rancid, separating
like a can of paint—thin skin
of the already congealed,
distended lump of what had clotted.
Stir it and nothing mixed, stir it
and riots exploded—mobs, snipers,
army men, guardsmen, looters, paratroopers,
Willie Horton standing on a car
in his baseball uniform,
John Lee Hooker singing
"The Motor City is Burning."

My grandmother lined the shop
windows with geraniums
but learned to keep most of her jewelry
beneath an empty paint can, its bottom
cut out, placed on a shelf
with a hundred other cans.
She'd been robbed before.

That day, two men bound her wrists
with paint rags, took the money
she'd been counting—paint money,
varnish money, ox-hair brush money.
My grandmother, stiff-backed in her chair,
sucked on her wedding band,
which she had tucked beneath her tongue
like a cough drop, silver coating her throat,

the office clock ticking, a shop
full of wallpaper books in cubby holes,
patterns of cowboys on quarter horses—
useless cavalry.

Scott Morgan

Detroit

John Lee Hooker down on Hastings street
Jamerson Benjamin the Motown beat
The Contours singing "Do You Love Me?"

Hey, Hey, Detroit

Barrett Strong "Money, That's What I Want"
Nolan Strong and the Diablos
Shorty Long singing "Function at the Junction"

Hey, Hey, Detroit
Rockin' Rhythm & Blues

Wilson Pickett (Bob Seger)
Jackie Wilson (Mitch Ryder)
Aretha Franklin (Edwin Star)
Deon Jackson (Nathaniel Mayer)
Smokey Robinson (Lavern Baker)
Little Willie John (The Spinners)
Velvelettes (The Four Tops)
Marvelettes (Jack Scott)
The Primes (Paul Williams)
The Primettes (Kim Wilson)
Funk Brothers (Kim Weston)
Grand Funk (Del Shannon)
Funkadelic (Jimmy Ruffin)
And The Stooges

Hey, Hey, Detroit

Rockin' Rhythm & Blues
Hey, Hey, Detroit
Talkin' 'bout, talkin' 'bout you

Florence Ballard
Hank Ballard
Tony Clarke
And Question Mark
Jeep Holland
Holland Dozier Holland
Ohhhhh yeah

The Vandellas, dancing through the street
Mary Wells "Bye Bye Baby"
Tammi Terrell saying "Come On And See Me"

Hey, Hey, Detroit
Rockin' Rhythm & Blues
Hey, Hey, Detroit
Talkin' 'bout, talkin' 'bout you
Hey, Hey, Detroit
Hey, Hey, Detroit
Hey, Hey, Detroit
Hey, Hey, Detroit

Marvin Gaye (Freda Payne)
The Hurricanes (Punch and James)
Stevie Gaines (Gladys Knight)
Tommy James (Della Reese)
Glenn Frey (Dorothy Ashby)
Eddie Floyd (Yusef Lateef)
Al Green (Bob Hodge)
Grant Green (Son House)
MC5 (Elvin Jones)

Bill Hodgeson (Thad Jones)
Johnny Angelos (Alice Cooper)
Junior Walker (Alice Coltrane)
Stevie Wonder (Sippie Wallace)
Gina Washington (Barbara Lewis)
Brownsville Station (Doctor Ross)
Marshall Crenshaw (Bossmen)
The Originals (The Romantics)
The Capitols (Johnny Thunders)
Kenny Burrell (Coachmen)
Patti Smith (Eddie Kirkland)
Norman Whitfield (Detroit Emeralds)
Eddie Burns (Detroit Count)
Amboy Dukes (And Madonna)
Brimstone (Detroit!)
Jake the Shake (Detroit!)
Calvin Frazier (Detroit!)
Baby Boy (Detroit!)
Sonny Boy (Detroit!)
Brother Will (Detroit!)
Maceo (Detroit!)
Bobo (Detroit!)
Washboard (Detroit!)
Whoaaa Yeahhh (Detroit!) (Detroit!)
Whoaaa Yeahhhh (Detroit!) (Detroit!)
(Detroit!)
(Detroit!)
(Detroit!)
(Detroit!)

Thylias Moss

Vashti's First Plane Ride to Manhattan from Detroit Metro Airport

Ryan is sitting in my row. Seat E, I am in
Seat C.

Boarding is such a slow process, I was in
A wheelchair so got to board first,

And in this way, I observe people filling
the plane.

Ryan was nice enough to lend me his pen, a
Tumi pen, "too me" saying I do not have to return
It, so

I don't, and he gets special mention
in my blog . . . unexpected

Kindness. A total stranger just as I was to
my own mother when

I was born, kicking
my way

out of her
(not that I didn't like
where

I was;

and not that I wasn't
already

Thinking about Thomas! Though
I travel to his town, I doubt

I'll be seeing him; I have to get

Used to such

Narrowing of Horizon

So reduced
Nearly to a nothingness that
Horizon should

Never be!

Endlessness!

SUPREME Sounds echo Diana, primed
for Diana, soprano sound shark. horizon of

hearing something possibly otherwordly,
contrail of high C,
high seas

from the lowest delta into which these high
C's plummet past:
Horizon

I think, I demand

That imaginary line

So easy to draw

Separation of sky and ground
Horizon

Only implication road
Into
Out of

pots of gold
-en

Illusion,

Paved jeweled paths
Of unlimited access
—horizons of
Best Possible Lives:

Heavy gray jackets
right across the other other
Horizon

Where laughs begin
And end, wavy ebbs
And flows,

Pyrocastic flows
Debris.

Already learned about

Dahveed Nelson

into the streets

Black children

                        Thousands of

Black children

          Movin   Movin   Movin

In time with magical

                              Black street sounds

Magical Motown sounds

                                   Movin   Movin   Movin

Magical Movin sounds

Like

    The Temptations   *"Ah know you wanna leave me but ah*

                                   refuse ta le you go"

       The Supremes   *"ma world is empty without you babe"*

         The Impressions   *and we're a winner cuz "we're movin on up"*

                                Until

Some lifeless merchant

                    Turns off   The sounds . . .

Richard Peabody

Marvin's Voice

No Cell Phone Use When We Play Marvin Gaye
—sign, CD Cellar, Falls Church, VA

Don't be

messing

with

a chocolate

avalanche

of kisses

that make

your lover

bite

her tongue

hard

and

push

your

head

down.

Lisa Jane Recker

I Wanna Testify

I wanna testify about the city
That taught me how to fly.
A city of workers, of immigrants,
Of strength, fearless with hustle.
Standing up, never backing down,
Pure heart, true grit, metal muscle.

Car tires rattle along the bricks
Of Michigan Avenue. We're racing Downtown.
We're swinging from the rafters of the old Grande Ballroom
We're resting on the shoulders of giants: Yusef Lateef
Walter Reuther, Viola Liuzzo, Coleman Young,
Ms. Rosa Parks, Berry's Motown revolution—the future is ours!

Feet flying high with the FaFaFa kicks
Of the MC5 guitar line jam. The symbolic
Iron fist of Joe Louis in all his glory,
And a young Kirk Gibson rounding the bases.
"He don't wanna walk you!"
Sparky yelling from the dugout

Now, I wanna testify with all
My words, all my music, all my sweet soul
Sweat and determination. We have always
Shaped our own future. The glory of beautiful
Detroit City. A never ending creation
Of love, work and struggle.

Robbie Robertson

Somewhere Down the Crazy River

Yeah, I can see it now
The distant red neon shivered in the heat
I was feeling like a stranger in a strange land
You know where people play games with the night
God, it was too hot to sleep
I followed the sound of a jukebox coming from up the levee
All of a sudden I could hear somebody whistling
From right behind me
I turned around and she said
"Why do you always end up down at Nick's Cafe?"
I said "I don't know, the wind just kind of pushed me this way."
She said "Hang the rich."

Catch the blue train
To places never been before
Look for me
Somewhere down the crazy river
Somewhere down the crazy river
Catch the blue train
All the way to Kokomo
You can find me
Somewhere down the crazy river
Somewhere down the crazy river

Take a picture of this
The fields are empty, abandoned '59 Chevy
Laying in the back seat listening to Little Willie John
Yea, that's when time stood still
You know, I think I'm gonna go down to Madam X

And let her read my mind
She said "That Voodoo stuff don't do nothing for me."

I'm a man with a clear destination
I'm a man with a broad imagination
You fog the mind, you stir the soul
I can't find, . . . no control

Catch the blue train
To places never been before
Look for me
Somewhere down the crazy river
Somewhere down the crazy river
Catch the blue train
All the way to Kokomo
You can find me
Somewhere down the crazy river
Somewhere down the crazy river

Wait, did you hear that
Oh this is sure stirring up some ghosts for me
She said "There's one thing you've got to learn
Is not to be afraid of it."
I said "No, I like it, I like it, it's good."
She said "You like it now
But you'll learn to love it later."

I been spellbound—falling in trances
I been spellbound—falling in trances
You give me shivers—chills and fever
I been spellbound—somewhere down the crazy river

Judith Roche

Detroit Music

Long before Motown,
before Joni Mitchell, not famous yet
in small coffeehouses, Plum Street and the MC5,
before Little Stevie Wonder, Aretha,
Bob Seger and Kid Rock
but after Ma Rainey, Bessie Smith, Ethel Waters
and my mother's memories
of dancing at The Greystone Ballroom,
was my mother's clear but quivery voice singing
"there once was a Union Maid
who never was afraid . . ."
was our nightly lullabies of
"Just like a tree a standing by the water
we shall not be moved . . ."
was "When the union's inspiration
through the worker's blood shall run . . ."
Song was my inspiration, running
through my blood. And her stories
of dropping a stink bomb in a striking
Woolworth store, and the UAW sit down strike
where she smuggled food in the factory
for the dug-in striking workers
who stayed for days.
Others smuggled mattresses in,
which wasn't easy—with Company Goons
guarding the entrance and bloodying
anyone they caught.

History is the water we drink

that gathers in the shallow footsteps of memory.
She was not afraid.

Maybe they were.
Maybe she was.
But they didn't act that way.
Solidarity was solid then.

John G. Rodwan Jr.

More than Motown

Pilgrims to the house Berry built
on West Grand Boulevard
testify to Smokey's Miracles,
marvel at the Wonder of Stevie,
affirm the Undisputed Truth,
succumb to the Temptations.

As they would.
As they should.

Not that many blocks away
over on Second Avenue
Bird led his original five,
Hooker raised boogie chillen,
The MC5 was lookin' at you,
Clinton convened Parliament.

Hardly anyone knows.
No one goes.

Lisa Rutledge

New School Year

At our school (named after the state poet of our state*)
we lived in a bubble
Kindergarteners through 7th graders
Service Squad and Safety Boys
moving grade to grade without much change.

1970 or 1971.
5th or 6th grade.
The bubble didn't break but it stretched.
Every morning the DSR busses brought the new kids to school . . .

We were too well behaved
and afraid of the principal to be mean.
Friendly enough to talk and smile at each other,
but our friends were the boys and girls
from Camp Fire Girls and Boy Scouts
and catechism and the block.

The playground was the equalizer.
Everyone had a transistor radio,
sometimes tuned to the Tiger game on the
voice of the Great Lakes,
but usually to music.

They listened to Martha Jean the Queen,
we preferred Brother Bill and Ted the Bear
coming to us from across the border.

Hitsville was represented in all corners

of the sharp rock covered exercise yard.
Timidly we boogied the line a little closer together
with Smokey, Gladys, Diana,
Stevie, Michael, Marvin,
Tammi and Martha leading the way.

Standing along the fence like call numbers on the AM dial,
we nodded our heads to the same beats
and danced our version of moves we saw on TV
Saturday afternoons on Dick and Don's shows
that came on before Big Time Wrestling.

At 3, the busses came back
and the new kids went home
to their Camp Fire Girl and Boy Scout meetings or
Bible study, and to the kids on their block.
Like they'd never been there.
Leaving no evidence but the Motown Sound.

---

*Will Carleton, whose most famous poem is "Over the Hill to the Poorhouse" and thought to be the first person to use the term "hillbilly."

James Scully

Motown

The rock star
rising
the hard way,
from an auto workers'
neighborhood in Detroit,
playing the beer halls
the grass and acid alleys
of the Great Lakes,
the Ohio Valley
singing
the grungy
neighborhood of Detroit

got a smash hit

a gold record

turned this
disc
into a Corvette,
a river cruiser,
a platinum record,
invested this
in shares
of GM,
cashing in
again
on the lst 2nd 3rd shift
the office drudges

kitchens and kids
of that
neighborhood in Detroit

where his fame
persists,
clings to the street
like confetti
after a wedding,
after the wedding
party has driven off.

Larry Smith

Bo Diddley Died Today—Hey, Bo Diddley

(June 2, 2008)

The man who put the Bomp, da-bomp,
da-bomp, bomp, bomp into rock-n-roll
has left us. Ellis McDaniel his off-stage name,
but for us 1950s rockers, he was none other
than Bo Diddley—Hey, Bo Diddley—
rocking his way over bad R&B radio:
sending those bad rockers
to us white kids in steel towns:
Little Richard, Chuck Berry,
Ronnie Hawkins, Jerry Lee Lewis.
But king of them all was bad Bo Diddley
pounding the electric axe of his square guitar
like a drum, like a violin, like a rocket—
giving us what we lacked and didn't know:
an answer, a response: "Before you Accuse me/
Take a Look at Your-self!" an anthem,
a folk, a pulse, a reason to rock.
"Say, Man" . . ."Tell me, Who do you love?"

In 1959 he filled the CIO hall in Steubenville.
In 1960 Detroit we were turned away from his show
as two too-young white boys,
but they couldn't turn off his music
as we wore it into our heads on
our radios and stereos.
It got into our walk, our talk,
our grin and bear it looks—

"I'm a Man. M-A-N"
We would feel it in our legs, our pelvis,
shaking our ass out on the dance floor—
"Bring it on home. Bring it to Jerome."
Come on now, everybody,
"Hey, You pretty thing." . . . Tell me
Bomp da-bomp, da-bomp-bomp-bomp
"Who do you love?"
Hey, Bo Diddley—Go, Bo Diddley, Go!

Patricia Smith

Motown Crown

The Temps, all swerve and pivot, conjured schemes
that had us skipping school, made us forget
how mamas schooled us hard against the threat
of five-part harmony and sharkskin seams.
We spent our schooldays balanced on the beams
of moon we wished upon, the needled jetblack
45s that spun and hadn't yet
become the dizzy spinning of our dreams.
Sugar Pie, Honey Bun, oh you
loved our nappy hair and rusty knees.
Marvin Gaye slowed down while we gave chase
and then he was our smokin' fine taboo.
We hungered for the anguished screech of *Please*
inside our chests—relentless, booming bass.

*   *   *

Inside our chests, relentless booming bass
softened to the turn of Smokey's key.
His languid, liquid, luscious, aching plea
for bodies we didn't have yet made a case
for lying to ourselves. He could erase
our bowlegs, raging pimples, we could see
his croon inside our clothes, his pedigree
of milky flawless skin. Oh, we'd replace
our daddies with his fine and lanky frame,
I did you wrong, my heart went out to play
he serenaded, filling up the space
that separated Smoke from certain flame.
We couldn't see the drug of him—OK,
silk where his throat should be. He growled such grace.

                    *   *   *

Silk where his throat should be, and growling grace,
Little Stevie made us wonder why
we even *needed* sight. His rhythm eye
could see us click our hips and swerve in place
whenever *he* cut loose. Ooh, we'd unlace
our Converse All-Stars. Yeah, we wondered why
we couldn't get down *without* our shoes, we'd try
and dance and keep up with his funky pace
of hiss and howl and hum, and then he'd slow
to twist our hearts until he heard them crack,
ignoring what was leaking from the seams.
The rockin' blind boy couldn't help but show
us light. We bellowed every soulful track
from open window, 'neath the door—pipe dreams.

                    *   *   *

From open windows, 'neath the doors, pipe dreams
taught us bone, bouffant and nicotine
and served up Lady D, the boisterous queen
of overdone, her body built from beams
of awkward light. Her bug-eyed brash extremes
dizzied normal girls. The evergreen
machine, so clean and mean, dabbed kerosene
behind our ears and said *Now burn.* Our screams
meant only that our hips would now be thin,
that we'd hear symphonies, wouldn't hurry love,
as Diana said, *Make sure it gleams
no matter what it is.* Her different spin,
a voice like sugar air, no inkling of
a soul beneath the vinyl. The Supremes.

                    *   *   *

That soul beneath the vinyl, the Supremes
knew nothing of it. They were breathy sighs
and fluid hips, soul music's booby prize.
But Mary Wells, so drained of self-esteem,
was a pudgy, barstool-ridin' buck-toothed dream
who none of us would dare to idolize
out loud. She had our mamas' grunt and thighs
and we preferred to just avoid THAT theme—
as well as war and God and gov'ment cheese
and bullets in the street and ghetto blight.
While Mary's "My Guy" blared, we didn't think race,
'cause there was all that romance, and the keys
that Motown held. Unlocked, we'd soon ignite.
We stockpiled extra sequins, just in case.

*   *   *

We stockpiled extra sequins, just in case
the Marvelettes decided that our grit
was way beyond Diana's, that we fit
inside their swirl, a much more naughty place.
Those girls came from the brick, we had to brace
ourselves against their heat, much too legit
to dress up as some other thing. We split
our blue jeans trying to match their pace.
And soon our breasts commenced to pop, we spoke
in deeper tones, and Berry Gordy looked
and licked his lips. Our only saving grace?
The luscious, liquid languid tone of Smoke,
the soundtrack while our A-cup bras unhooked.
Our sudden Negro hips required more space.

*   *   *

Our sudden Negro hips required more space,
but we pretended not to feel that spill

that changed the way we walked. And yes, we still
couldn't help but feel so strangely out of place
while Motown filled our eager hearts with lace
and Valentines. Romance was all uphill,
no push, no prod, no shiny magic pill
could lift us to that light. No breathing space
in all that time. We grew like vines to sun,
and then we burned. As mamas shook their heads
and mourned our Delta names, we didn't deem
to care. Religion—there was only one.
We took transistor preachers to our beds
and Smokey sang a lyric dripping cream.

*   *   *

While Smokey sang a lyric dripping cream,
Levi tried to woo us with his growl:
Can't help myself. Admitted with a scowl,
his bit of weakness was a soulful scheme—
and we kept screaming, front row, under gleam
of lights, beside the speakers' blasting vowels,
we rocked and screamed. Levi, on the prowl,
glowed black, a savior in the stagelight's beam.
But then the stagelight dimmed, and there we were
in bodies primed—for what we didn't know.
We sang off-key while skipping home alone.
Deceptions that you sing do tend to blur
and disappear in dance, why is that so?
Ask any colored girl and she will moan.

*   *   *

Ask any colored girl and she will moan
an answer with a downbeat and a sleek
five-part croon. She's dazzled, and she'll shriek
what she's been taught: She won't long be alone,

213

or crazed with wanting more. One day she'll own
that quiet heart that Motown taught to speak,
she'll know that being the same makes her unique.
She'll rest her butt on music's paper throne
until the bassline booms, until some old
Temptation leers and says *I'll take you home
and heal you in the way the music vowed.*
She's trapped within his clutch, his perfumed hold,
dancing to his conjured, crafted poem,
remembering how. Love had lied so loud.

*   *   *

Remembering how love had lied so loud,
we tangled in the rhythms that we chose.
Seduced by thump and sequins, heaven knows
we tried to live our looming lives unbowed,
but bending led to break. We were so proud
to mirror every lyric. Radios
spit beg and mend, and precious stereos
told us what we were and weren't allowed.
Our daddies sweat in factories while we
found other daddies under limelight's glow.
And then we begged those daddies to create
us. Like Stevie, help us blindly see
the rhythms, but instead, the crippling blow.
We whimpered while the downbeat dangled bait.

*   *   *

We whimpered while the downbeat dangled bait,
we leapt and swallowed all the music said
while Smokey laughed and Marvin idly read
our minds and slapped us hard and slapped us straight,
and even then, we listened for the great
announcement of the drum, for tune to spread,

a Marvelette to pick up on the thread.
But as we know by now, it's much too late
to reconsider love, or claw our way
through all the glow they tossed to slow our roll.
What we know now we should have always known.
When Smokey winked at us and then said *They
don't love you like I do,* he snagged our soul.
We wound up doing the slow drag, all alone.

   *   *   *

They made us do the slow drag, all alone.
They made us kiss our mirrors, deal with heat,
our bodies sudden bumps. They danced deceit
and we did too, addicted to the drone
of revelation, all the notes they'd thrown
our way: *Oh, love will change your life. The sweet
sweet fairy tale we spin will certainly beat
the real thing any day. Oh, yes we own
you now. We sang you pliable and clueless,
waiting, waiting, oh the dream you'll hug
one day, the boy who craves you right out loud
in front of everyone. But we told you,
we know we did, we preached it with a shrug—
less than perfect love was not allowed.*

   *   *   *

Less than perfect love was not allowed.
Temptations begged as if their every sway
depended on you coming home to stay.
Diana whispered air, aloof and proud
to be the perfect girl beneath a shroud
of glitter and a fright she held at bay.
And Michael Jackson, flailing in the fray
of daddy love, succumbed to every crowd.

What would we have done if not for them,
wooing us with roses carved of sound
and hiding muck we're born to navigate?
Little did we know that they'd condemn
us to live so tethered to the ground.
While every song they sang told us to wait.

*　　*　　*

Every song they sang told us to wait
and wait we did, our gangly heartbeats stunned
and holding place. Already so outgunned
we little girls obeyed. And now it's late,
and CDs spinning only help deflate
us. The songs all say, *Just look what you've done,*
you've wished through your whole life. And one by one
your stupid sisters boogie to their fate.
So now, at fifty plus, I turn around
and see the glitter drifting in my wake
and mingling with the dirt. My dingy dreams
are shoved high on the shelf. They're wrapped and bound
so I can't see and contemplate the ache.
The Temps, all swirl and pivot, conjured schemes.

*　　*　　*

The Temps, all swirl and pivot, conjured schemes
inside our chests, relentless booming bass
then silk where throats should be. Much growling grace
from open window, 'neath the door, pipe dreams—
that soul beneath the vinyl. The Supremes
used to stockpile extra sequins just in case
Diana's Negro hips required more space,
while Smokey penned a lyric dripping cream.
Ask any colored girl, and she will moan,
remembering how love had lied so loud.

I whimpered while the downbeat dangled bait
and taught myself to slow drag, all alone.
Less than perfect love was not allowed
and every song they sang told me to wait.

Patricia Smith

A Colored Girl Will Slice You
If You Talk Wrong About Motown

The men and women who coupled, causing us, first
arrived confounded. Surrounded by teetering towers
of *no, not now,* and *you shoulda known better,* they
cowered and built little boxes of northern home,
crammed themselves inside, feasted on the familiar
of fat skin and the unskimmed, made gods of doors.
When we came—the same insistent bloody and question
we would have been South—they clutched us,
plumped us on government cereal drenched in Carnation,
slathered our hair, faces, our fat wiggling arms and legs
with Vaseline. We shined like the new things we were.
The city squared its teeth, smiled oil, smelled the sour
each hour left at the corner of our mouths. Our parents
threw darts at the day. They romanced shut factories,
waged hot battle with skittering roaches and vermin,
lumbered after hunches. Their newborn children grew
like streetlights. We grew like insurance payments.
We grew like resentment. And since no tall sweet gum
thrived to offer its shouldered shade, no front porch
lesson spun wide to craft our wrong or righteous,

our parents loosed us, into the crumble, into the glass,
into the hips of a new city. They trusted exploded
summer hydrants, scarlet licorice whips, and crumbling
rocks of government cheese to conjure a sort of joy,
trusted joy to school us in the woeful limits of jukeboxes
and moonwash. Freshly dunked in church water, slapped
away from double negatives and country ways, we were

orphans of the North Star, dutifully sacrificed, our young
bodies arranged on sharp slabs of boulevard. We learned
what we needed, not from our parents and their rumored
South, but from the gospel seeping through the sad gap
in Mary Well's grin. Smokey slow-sketched pictures
of our husbands, their future skins flooded with white light,
their voices all remorse and atmospheric coo. Little Stevie
squeezed his eyes shut on the soul notes, replacing his
dark with ours. Diana was the bone our mamas coveted,
the flow of slip silver they knew was buried deep beneath
their rollicking heft. Every lyric, growled or sweet from
perfect brown throats, was instruction: *Sit pert, pout, and
seamed silk. Then watch him beg.* Every spun line was
consolation: *You're such a good girl. If he has not arrived,
he will.* Every wall of horn, every slick choreographed
swivel, threaded us with the rhythm of the mildly wild.
We slept with transistor radios, worked the two silver knobs,
one tiny earbud blocking out the roar of our parents' tardy
attempts to retrieve us. Instead, we snuggled with the Temps,
lined up five pretty men across. And damned if they didn't
begin every one of their songs with the same word: *Girl.*

Kevin Stein

Upon Finding a Black Woman's Door Sprayed with Swastikas, I Tell Her This Story of Hands

How to say hate was in rancorous bloom,
spiking my town's tepid April breath
with florets of white sheets & raised,
gloved fists. How to say we seethed
around our school, white & black splayed

on either side of Lincoln Street, its broken
promise. Tick, tick, tick, & I was late
for chemistry, prelude to explosion
as flushed & spontaneous as any combustion
you'd swear won't happen, fists & chains

catalyzing our frothy breath. I screamed
"Be cool, man!" beneath a pitiful catalpa,
beneath its blossoms the Creek called *kutuhlpa,*
"head with wings," though some of us
had surely lost our heads & any chance

of flight. I screamed, "Peace!"
& took a punch in my white face.
After the sirens & nightsticks, after
snarling dogs & the mid-morning spritz
of Mace, after the curses & bloody lips,

we felt exotic, lured to some fine madness
we'd never recover from. What I had
in mind involved my girlfriend, not Clayton

thumbing a ride, huge defensive end
who'd trashed halfbacks as he lilted

"Going to a Go-Go" & I piled on. His black
hand swallowed mine, his knuckles bruised,
bleeding. We didn't say "brother." We didn't
sing of slain Jack & Bobby & Martin.
We didn't swear we loved this life, either—

the woof & warp of hour upon hour tottering
like a palace of the lost, beguiled,
befuddled. It wasn't exactly cruising,
though we drove windows down, AM 1470
spooning out Smokey Robinson & the Miracles,

their honeyed voices as smooth as
my parents' powder blue Bel-Air.
How to say I felt spring waft its redolent
insistence across the cracked dash
as I harmonized with Bill "Smokey" Robinson.

How to say Clayton's hand daubed
my split lip with iodine, all the while
a bloody sunset reeled in the night:
fish of dark, fish of peace, speckled fish
of forgiveness he knew more of than I.

Rodney Torreson

Since You Always Threw Yourself
Out There, David Ruffin

in that drizzle called life, such as onto the stage
for that impromptu audition with the Temptations,
maybe in the end it was easy for NBC
in the mini-series to throw the facts about.

Framed by your trademark black glasses,
while the other Temps danced a labyrinth behind you,
you would whirl around, throwing the microphone up
with one hand, snatching it with the other,

then hitting the floor with a leg split so crisp
that before you'd rise, the other Temps saw
the fortune of the moon and stars breaking your way,
your extended hand offering it to the crowd.

In the sun's turn-around time, you'd lunged
into stardom. Or maybe after the opening riff,
with its climbing guitar notes that scaled the heart,
you flung yourself into "My Girl"—

which Smokey Robinson wrote just for you—your baritone,
that gritty scuffle, going sweet as water over stones,
so that 700 miles away, in Terril, Iowa, cold wind
at our ribs, the song would strike up a blue sky:

"I've got sunshine on a cloudy day / and when it's cold outside, /
I've got the month of May," my brother Dean,

while the wind was reduced to a few breezy spumes, rigging
speakers in our upstairs window, so we could broadcast

"My Girl," all over the block—teaching it to the trees,
the flowers, even the crusty, world-weary sidewalks—
as if their cracks could take on your other trademark,
that break in your voice, so that even Beryl Coleman,
the old no-nonsense justice of the peace, who lived next door,
would take store of your song, and her drapes would sway,
though back in Motown, you were leaping into arrogance,
traveling solo in your mink-lined limo, while the rest of the band
hit the turnpike in a station wagon, you going so far
as to have your glasses painted on your limo,
as you hurled yourself into everything but rehearsals,
which you'd miss along with, later on, the concerts,

in your drug-induced exile, all of this leading to a hiss
in your skillet that broke the crying stillness,
and frost on the furniture, and you trying
to sign away your lady friend's Lincoln Continental

for $20 of cocaine, the Temptations soon voting you out
of the group. It was *then,* ironically, you'd show up
at gigs, flinging yourself onto the stage—for the shiny ache
you cosseted—while, for the Temptations

the stage lights stung, the audience weighing in with applause
when you'd pry the mike from the new front man's hands,
for "My Girl" or maybe "Ain't Too Proud to Beg"
or "Beauty's Only Skin Deep" or "I Wish It Would Rain."

And, my God, did it rain! The boiling truth of it is
you died in a Philadelphia crack house,

the limo driver then escorting you to a hospital.
Instead NBC tossed you out with the trash,

so that beneath the strain of streetlights, fans saw
your body being flung from a car into the ashen traffic,
as if it were only what you deserved,
and a funeral parlor pillow was what you were after.

David Trinidad

Meet The Supremes

When Petula Clark sang "Downtown," I wished I
could go there with her. I wanted to be free
to have fun and fall in love, but from suburbia
the city appeared more distant and dangerous
than it actually was. I withdrew and stayed
in my room, listened to Jackie DeShannon sing
"What the World Needs Now Is Love." I agreed,
but being somewhat morose considered the song
a hopeless plea. I listened to Skeeter Davis'
"The End of the World" and decided that was
what it would be when I broke up with my first
boyfriend. My head spun as fast as the singles
I saved pennies to buy: "It's My Party," "Give
Him a Great Big Kiss," "(I Want To Be) Bobby's
Girl," "My Guy"—the list goes on. At the age
of ten, I rushed to the record store to get
"Little" Peggy March's smash hit, "I Will Follow
Him." An extreme example of lovesick devotion,
it held down the top spot on the charts for
several weeks in the spring of 1963. "Chapel
of Love" came out the following year and was
my favorite song for a long time. The girls
who recorded it, The Dixie Cups, originally
called themselves Little Miss & The Muffets.
They cut three hits in quick succession, then
disappeared. I remember almost the exact moment
I heard "Johnny Angel" for the first time: it
came on the car radio while we were driving
down to Laguna Beach to visit some friends of

the family. In the back seat, I set the book I'd
been reading beside me and listened, completely
mesmerized by Shelley Fabares' dreamy, teenage
desire. Her sentimental lyrics continue to move
me (although not as intensely) to this day.
Throughout adolescence, no other song affected
        me quite like that one.
On my transistor, I listened to the Top Twenty
countdown as, week after week, more girl singers
        and groups
came and went than I could keep track of:

        Darlene Love,
        Brenda Lee,
        Dee Dee Sharp,
        Martha Reeves
        & The Vandellas,
        The Chantels,
        The Shirelles,
        The Marvelettes,
        The Ronettes,
        The Girlfriends,
        The Rag Dolls,
        The Cinderellas,
        Alice Wonderland,
        Annette, The
        Beach-Nuts, Nancy
        Sinatra, Little
        Eva, Veronica,
        The Pandoras,
        Bonnie & The
        Treasures,
        The Murmaids,
        Evie Sands,

The Pussycats,
The Patty Cakes,
The Tran-Sisters,
The Pixies Three,
The Toys, The
Juliettes and
The Pirouettes,
The Charmettes,
The Powder Puffs,
Patti Lace &
The Petticoats,
The Rev-Lons,
The Ribbons,
The Fashions,
The Petites,
The Pin-Ups,
Cupcakes,
Chic-Lets,
Jelly Beans,
Cookies, Goodies,
Sherrys, Crystals,
Butterflys,
Bouquets,
Blue-Belles,
Honey Bees,
Dusty Springfield,
The Raindrops,
The Blossoms,
The Petals,
The Angels,
The Halos,
The Hearts,
The Flamettes,
The Goodnight

Kisses, The
Strangeloves,
and The Bitter
Sweets.

I was ecstatic when "He's So Fine" hit the #1 spot.
I couldn't get the lyrics out of my mind and continued
to hum "Doo-lang Doo-lang Doo-lang" long after
puberty ended, a kind of secret anthem. Although
The Chiffons tried to repeat their early success
with numerous singles, none did as well as their
first release. "Sweet Talkin' Guy" came close,
sweeping them back into the Top Ten for a short
time, but after that there were no more hits.
Lulu made her mark in the mid-sixties with "To Sir
          with Love,"
which I would put on in order to daydream about
my junior high algebra instructor. By then I was
a genuine introvert. I'd come home from school,
having been made fun of for carrying my textbooks
like a girl, and listen to song after song from
my ever-expanding record collection. In those
days, no one sounded sadder than The Shangri-Las.
Two pairs of sisters from Queens, they became famous
for their classic "death disc shocker," "Leader of
          the Pack,"
and for their mod look. They were imitated (but
          never equaled)
by such groups as The Nu-Luvs and The Whyte Boots.
The Shangri-Las stayed on top for a couple of
years, then lost their foothold and split up.
Much later, they appeared in rock 'n' roll revival
shows, an even sadder act since Marge, the fourth
member of the band, had died of an accidental

drug overdose. I started smoking cigarettes around
this time, but wouldn't discover pills, marijuana
or alcohol until my final year of high school.
I loved Lesley Gore because she was always crying
and listened to "As Tears Go By" till the single had
so many scratches I couldn't play it anymore.
I preferred Marianne Faithfull to The Beatles and
The Rolling Stones, was fascinated by the stories
about her heroin addiction and suicide attempt.
She's still around. So is Diana Ross. She made
it to superstardom alone, maintaining the success
she'd previously achieved as the lead singer of
The Supremes, one of the most popular girl groups
of all time. Their debut album was the first LP
I owned. Most of the songs on it were hits—
one would reach the top of the charts as another
hit the bottom. Little did I know, as I listened
to "Nothing but Heartaches" and "Where Did Our Love
Go," that nearly twenty years later I would hit
bottom in an unfurnished Hollywood single, drunk
and stoned and fed up, still spinning those same
old tunes. The friction that already existed
within The Supremes escalated in 1967 as Diana
Ross made plans for her solo career. The impending
split hit Florence the hardest. Rebelliously,
she gained weight and missed several performances,
and was finally told to leave the group. The pain
she experienced in the years that followed was
a far cry from the kind of anguish expressed
in The Supremes' greatest hits. Florence lost
the lawsuit she filed against Motown, failed at
a solo career of her own, went through a bitter
divorce, and ended up on welfare. In this classic
photograph of the group, however, Florence is

smiling. Against a black backdrop, she and Mary
look up at and frame Diana, who stands in profile
and raises her right hand, as if toward the future.
The girls' sequined and tasseled gowns sparkle
as they strike dramatic poses among some Grecian
columns. Thus, The Supremes are captured forever
like this, in an unreal, silvery light. That
moment, they're in heaven. Then, at least for Flo,
begins the long and painful process of letting go.

George Tysh

Vintage Soul

It once seemed that love

was an exchange of pleasantries

that sometimes attained elysian fields of joy

a way for "me" to take "you" higher

as the old song goes.

But now it's clear that women

take men for a herd of oafs

grazing at their pleasure

and lead them around by the

nose or other protuberance

An endless procession of drooling studs

the proverbial chain of fools

Crystal Williams

Parable of Divas: Aretha Franklin & Diana Ross

Back in the day, Ree Ree & Miss D were sweet meat, ours
to pick over like vultures. We were Detroiters; after all,
it was duty to learn from our lost.

Ree Ree's house had an untended yard.
D was in flat-out denial: Detroit had given her nothing
&, be damned, she'd return the favor.

We sucked our teeth, harrumphed:
*They're trifling, look, see, fortune has knocked
& the hussies have gained amnesia.*

We were too young to know survival, song, is enough;
combined they are testimony in a city so Black. We thought,
no. Tend yard, offer back. Savor the sweet stuff of our city.

& yet we too moved, forgot the chance gardeners
& thankless hussies of youth, became them
in varying degrees, in spite of ourselves. Unavoidable, this.

There is always some pigeon nipping at the shoelace
because it is there & speaks to stature. Aretha & Diana's
contradictions should have readied me:

from respectable people, damning affronts.
From damnable people, beauty. I cannot be fully convinced
of any good thing. There is no such thing

as a measure for loss. There is only Ree Ree & Miss D trilling:
Silly girl, nothing is so sweet
as not to be sour, somehow, some way.

Crystal Williams

Homecoming

                                                    & when
by some fluke you return, dragging your blue black behind you,
nothing is as it was. The city is stasis,
not dance. Bereavement, not dance. The music has darkened
& stopped its sway, the boulevards are empty theatre.
& who should love this? Who recognizes this? Broken curbs
& potholes & shoes hanging from power lines
& snatches of weave hair blowing like sagebrush. Statues
& statuses. Someone once said that crows are old, wise folks
& today they follow you again, hopping wire to wire, squawk
& squawk until you look up, call: Hey, hey, girl, ain't no other
place knows you, loves you like this, knows that when you shine
out in the big wide, this here is what's sparking your shimmer,
this is the pop, pop, pop lighting your eyes, filling your mouth with stars.
& you nod because the bones of you know
& there was really no escaping
this dance city, this holy morning empty street city,
this dialysis clinic on every other corner city, this be a smart girl city,
this play the harp on Tuesdays & Thursdays city,
this girl-you-look-good-&-we're-called-to-praise-&-lift-you-up city,
this ice-skate city/jazz-dance city, this tote as many talents as you can carry city,
this be-whatever-you-want city, this daddy's sweet pea city,
this drive like you want because we're free city, this quiet & quake city,
this we used to build Lumina/Caddy/Explorer city,
this family reunion on Belle Isle/BBQ hot/thump music city,
this momma dressed as a scarecrow on Halloween city,
this Little Alabama City city, this Smokey/Aretha/Florence city,
this FaygoRedPop/VernorsGingerAle city,

this long memory city, this big wheel chipped tooth city,
this johnjohn & veevee & fernando/robyn/karriem city,
this how could you have stayed away for so long city. This
This city, this downbeat to the secret, irrational life of your heart.

Baron Wormser

Soul Music

The Baltimore evening I saw
Otis and Aretha I knew
Kings and queens still existed:
Poised but get-down, a danceable valor,
The uncharted cry and sigh
Strive and jive
From the shook-up ground of
Plead-it-on-your-knees love.

The founded nation no longer
Was diagrammatic;
Unsevered feeling fit
Into any shade of skin.
Unchurched sound was the test
Of civil progress.

Outside that night
Plate glass fractured like
A sobbing final tone,
A plea that brought white overseers
To the city on a Sunday
While the condemned frolicked
At everyone's expense.

Whole blocks burned gladly,
The tinder of democratic
Promise redeemed in anger,
The grandeur of performance

Burlesqued by riot,
The insurrection of running free.

I too protested:
Hadn't I been good?
Hadn't I endorsed
Both sympathy and force?
Didn't I love the music
As much as I could?

On the televised streets
I watched people dance,
Souls on fire with a passion
That sang of days
No ticket could touch.

The Mutants
Fred "Sonic" Smith
The Grande
Ted Lucas
Lili's Bar
Scott Morgan
The Rationals
White Mud
The Früt
Gordon Lightfoot
Wayne Kramer
Kick Out the Jams
Mitch Ryder
Alice Cooper
Rob Tyner
Patti Smith
The Eastown
Madonna
The Frost
The Stooges
Iggy Pop
MC5
Teagarden & Van Winkle
Dick Wagner
The Sights
Third Power
The Dirt Bombs
Frigid Pink
Crow's Nest East
The Gories
The White Stripes
Cinderella Balloom
The Amboy Dukes
Jack White
Bob Seger
Grand Funk Railroad
Wilson Mower Pursuit
Blacktop
SRC
Suzi Quatro
Scott Richard Case

IV.
DETROIT ROCKS
Kick Out the Jams

Jan Beatty

Love Poem w/Strat

for The MC5's Wayne Kramer & The Stooges' Ron Ashton: Strats Supreme

My baby's got a solid-body
guitar, rocks it hard like dinosaurs
eating cars, plays it dirty like worlds
exploding, like Stevie Ray's battered strat,
Badlands sticker on the back, he's got a fever
for the steamroller, like Hendrix on Voodoo Child,
like Jeff Beck avalanching notes into air/
my baby's a gunslinger, plays
his guitar rock-hard—
he likes it old-style, he likes it Muddy,
likes it Elmore James, bends it crazy
on his '62 reissue arctic white strat
& his head rolls back/
to that precise pain, that one note screaming,
his mouth twisted open & the light crossing
his face like a freight train passing—
my baby's a gunslinger, plays
his guitar rock-hard—
he likes it Freddie King/whole body vibrato/
likes it Howlin Wolf, my baby plays it
strings-against-the-mic-stand dirty/twists
the body to the Hubert Sumlin script/screams
through his Fender vibro-king—he's
got a hard-on for traditional, fuck
special effects, fuck overplay/he's got love
for his whammy bar, got love

for his double cutaway fins, jams
his headstock into the air, rips a hole
in the sky with his song

Jan Beatty

Love Poem w/Strat #2

for Grand Funk Railroad's Mark Farner

it's a cross/

        between/

    a greek lyre and

      a peach

         cadillac

         /it

             /rings/

    like a bell when/

        you play it right—

    my baby

plays the/

    lightweight/

        spring=tension

      tremolo bar at the bridge/

           we hit

      the sweet

         notes

        all

        night

Ben Blackwell (The Dirt Bombs)

The Nain Rouge

I'm holed up in the Yondotega
Just wait 'til somebody dies
Enjoy free food at Fischer's mansion
While you hear those Krishnas cry

Why don't you ski down Mt. Elliott?
Or take a swim in Grand River?
Good luck on finding a newspaper
That will even deliver

For every national news source
Claiming our city is spent
Diggers go and sell our soul to England
Just trying to cover the rent

I'm not a well-respected man
I don't fit in your master plan
I put your parents in Eloise
And elected a mayor from the Klan

Yeah I was burnin' with Bubba Helms
I cut down all those Dutch Elms
I'm the one that made it Bloody Run
I was Sweet's suicide gun

I sunk the Edmund Fitzgerald
I'm the money behind White Boy Rick
I was at the Red Fox with Hoffa
I'm the courage of Eddie Slovik

I got you your People Mover
I pushed Wallendas off their rope
I'm the one who killed the Edsel
I specialize in ending hope

I beat up Nancy Kerrigan
Malice Green and Vincent Chin
I threw that brick out on 12th Street
I filled up Cobo with Flynn's

I clipped the wing of Flight 255
I didn't mean to leave that girl alive
I'm the truth at Algiers Motel
I work so we don't survive

But who would've thought
When the beaver came back
He would choose the name
Antoine Cadillac?

Chief Pontiac?

Ben Blackwell

Bury My Body at Elmwood

Last night in Detroit
I lay awake in bed
I couldn't stop thinking
Of Detroiters who are dead
Suffered from diseases, long since found the cure
Take a walk off Lafayette to see Elmwood endure

On Barent's ribbon farm
Dalzell crept up with guns
Pontiac was a patient man
And made it Bloody Run

The ugliest for pres
Was Lewis Cass they say
He had boils on his face
Now he's hanging here all day

MFIC
Read the nameplate on his desk
Coleman Young never backed down
Now he's catching up on rest

Sonic Smith left us
With his contribution to song
Now Irish ship lane markers
Show us where he's gone

Where Joe Louis would jog
The fighter so adroit

It's the last place left
The landscape of Detroit

Then there's sweet Jim Shaw
The steward of the scene
A kinder man you've never met
A finer you've never seen

I don't ask for much
You can give my shit away
When i die in eighty years
This is where i want to stay

Bury my body
Bury my body
Bury my body
Bury my body

Bury my body at Elmwood

Who knew dying could be so good?

Hayan Charara

Bob Seger's "Night Moves" on the Radio in Winter

Leaving Henry Ford Hospital

The nurse did what she could to ease
her into her death.
The dying was effortless
but not watching it happen.
When it happened, I remembered
her twenty years before
walking through snow at night
to buy milk.

Andrei Codrescu

String City

to my friends, dead and alive, universes all

Detroit you're no string theory
   you're all strings
   I got wrapped into the first string in 1967
when a bush opened her yellow flowers
   in a parking lot at McDonald's

then a string of light and young man's coming out of himself
   wrapped itself around the string of a woman's coming out of herself
     and there was a universe just glowing there on a beautiful sidewalk
       trod by the insane and the hilarious

and there was the string-world of the Lost & Found world
and the smoky dark strings of the Writers & Artists Workshop
   spiraling into Os of wonder
and the string of a world inside a young woman-spider
   who lived a million miles from the known world
projecting purple-hued substrings of feeling
     I followed a black-light string of violence
twisted tautly by an angry lover wrapped around a gun
      in the glove-compartments of an infinity of cars

I saw a violet man busy cutting strings of light into powdered heroin
   on the soon-no-longer-to-exist 12th street
     while red-yellow flames shut their own visions of worlds
      into the same place as all others: into my heart

there were tangled strings of law & anarchy & relief

mauve fake strings in every color on Plum Street
   a plum-colored street
looking for its commercial apps in the next millennium

but repairing and raising the spirit
   there were the always working hands holding brushes and guitars
hiding stigmata in their palms of beauty
   new strings of light inside longer strings of light
     all the way into the 21st century
      when the golden string of Michelle
       spun me around the waist
        she was another universe yet
         twirling decades of the same moment

a sweater of light was knit by my dear ones
   from you Detroit
     from your dizzying history of booms & busts
     of memories in fat flakes of snow

strings cacophonous and beautiful of poets dying
   even as your gas stations
     wrapped themselves in strings of machine-gun fire

I recall all your string universes, gritty town,
     the luminous threads of time defying space
some of them thick like the future
   some spider-thin like a hand-made tsimbal
or thick-steel of guitars exploding electric street battles

Detroit, your strings draw me back I am your puppet
   because when I was new in America your strings vibrated
     in a newness new even to the new world
      a world that must be courage itself or die

Jim Daniels

"School's Out," Alice Cooper, 1972

*The original album cover had the sleeve opening in the manner
of an old school desk. The vinyl record inside was wrapped in a pair
of girl's panties. This original issue was recalled because the panties
were not flame-retardant.*

Fifteen. Alice knew what I wanted:
black vinyl sheathed in sky-blue panties
I hid in my dresser. My mother found them—
threw them out without a word. Panties!

In my tiny room on the edge of Detroit, black-light
glowed on the frayed posters of my minor gods.
I counted the girls I'd kissed, then multiplied
with lust. I fingered the cheap elastic band
and erupted in my sleep.

Alice's desk: marbles, slingshot, jackknife.
Scratched initials, Stuck gum.
Mine: plastic sheet soured with lunch milk,
three gnawed pencils, one hard pink eraser.

A guy named Alice with the face
of cartoon death. Surly mascara barked
from the coffins of my speakers.
The song blew up school. School as prison—
a metaphor made quaint by factories
in our future that offered no graduation.

Lifer, I'd call myself, as my father did.
Afternoon shift. Black vinyl circling midnights.
In headphones: *School's out forever.*
I drifted to the sounds of simulated
damage and counted my hours of overtime
then multiplied myself to sleep.

Flame retardant.
Collector's items now, those panties.

Jim Daniels

Patti Smith at the Punch and Judy Theater

She's one freaky kinda
scarecrow scarin all
the birds away no crop
to protect just scarin
on principle cause ever-
body needs a good scare
get the blood flowin
thinkin bout dyin
or just bein bored.

Us? we're stoned
as always so when
she spits on us
it just feels
like rain.

Jim Daniels

Detroit Hymns, Christmas Eve

Kenny and I down a few beers
circling church in my old Falcon
thinking about Midnight Mass.

White Castle is the closest we get,
sitting at the shiny metal counter
mumbling our little prayers.
Shoulda got a pint of something,
Kenny says.

Shoulda woulda coulda mouda.
It's the guy wearing three hats,
the high priest. He winks at us,
falls asleep.

Let's not argue about drinking.
A young couple slip off their stools,
bump heads going out the door.

Ratburger, I say, chomping down
on one of the four I ordered.
Ratboogers, Kenny says.

Rats ain't got no boogers.
It's the plump woman behind the counter,
safe in her hair net.

Kenny punches the jukebox:
Mitch Ryder's "Little Latin Lupe Lu,"
and a couple old Motown.

Let's dance, Sugar, Kenny says.
The counter woman shakes her hips a little
but she clearly don't got the spirit:
What's that mean, Latin Loop De Lou?

It's a Christmas song, Kenny says.
The grill man with bad skin
laughs at that—his spit sizzles.

Finding Culture Saturday Night

I sit and watch Frank Pahl
fiddling with his instrument creations
homemade gizmos for sound
an organ played by blocks on a rotisserie spit
and I know this is what I should be doing
it's what everybody expects me to do
finding modern bohemia in Detroit warehouses
trying to test the limits of white sound
singing a waltz like a gypsy drone
breaking all conventional wisdom for success
the crowd is totally engaged
and increasing as the time goes on
talking in the corners and sitting on the floor
developing solutions to world problems
in the middle of this white Motown
I find the eclectic experimental avant edge

at the Detroit Art Space
it's an avant-garde extravaganza
young men plink and pluck
the bartender is the sound man
writing poems at events and music events
with a group called terror at the opera
—it's actually 2 young punkish lookers
with an accordion playing blonde woman
and a sweet faced brunette on guitar
sometimes playing steel guitar with a bow
the electric and the accordion fill the room
somehow silly yet seductive
the music is a supplement to the scene
while social interplay is the mode
the sound sets the scene in motion
bringing in an inherent understanding of cool

Don Duprie

what am I supposed to do

I hired on here back in 89
February 28
They put me on that old midnight shift
It became the job that I love to hate
But I found a girl and we set our vows
We tried for a kid but we ended up with two
And now it seems like they're shutting this town down
So tell me what am I supposed to do

What am I supposed to do
Lord tell me what am I supposed to do
Because this is all that I have ever known
So tell me what am I supposed to do

Now we reside on the northeast side
That's where my family came way back in 33
We sold a car just to keep the house
It's getting hard to hold on to anything
And the union boys
Yeah they made some noise
But in the end they
Had to feed their families too
Union dues they can't help me now
So what am I supposed to do

What am I supposed to do
Lord tell me what am I supposed to do
This is all that I have ever known
So tell me what am I supposed to do

Now I sit by as this city slowly dies
And I wonder about my fate
The government checks
Gonna stop coming soon
No more help from the state
Now I'm 45 and I got no place to hide
And I got nothing left to lose
This is what I get after all that I gave
So tell me what am I supposed to do

Elizabeth Ellen

Target

I went to Target to buy the new Kid Rock CD.
The woman who rang me up was young and black.
She said, "Oh, he's still putting out albums?"

She was smiling in a genuine way. I felt like we liked each other even though
she was teasing me about Kid Rock.

I said, "Yeah, this is his new one, it just came out."
"Didn't he have some sort of . . . *trouble* . . . with Beyoncé?" she said.
"Did he?" I said. My mind was blank.
"Yeah," she said. "You can't mess with Beyoncé or Rihanna, their people will
get you on Twitter."

She was still smiling. I still felt good about us.
"Right," I said. I was smiling too.

I seemed to remember something about Kid Rock and Beyoncé but then I
forgot it again.

She handed me my receipt and I started to walk away when I remembered
something.

"Hey," I said. "I just remembered I'm wearing my Beyoncé shirt." I started
unzipping my jacket to show her. She walked toward me to look. The shirt
was red and long sleeved and said "all I'm really asking for is you" and under
that it said "Beyoncé."

"Oh, yeah," she said. We were still smiling even though we had nothing more
to say.

Linda Nemec Foster

History of Sweat

Look for it in the Midwest where sweat was really invented and patented.
You'll find it alive, thriving in Mitch Ryder, the one person who can sweat
more than anyone. Even without the back-up of the Detroit Wheels. Even
when he lip-syncs. Like a dinosaur in heat, Mitch lumbers on the stage.
Sings the same song, the only song he will ever be remembered for. Sweat
of the fossil glides down his neck. Back in 1966, we were sweating, too. If
not on the dance floor with Mitch's grunts blaring from the speakers, then
in the back seat of some guy's Ford. Devil with the blue dress on . . . or off.
But, no boy—furtively holding me in a slow dance embrace or in a parked
car where the air became the moisture escaping our bodies—no boy ever
sweated like Mitch sweated. And for all I know, Ryder was more real, more
alive, more wet than any guy who unbuttoned my blouse or parted my legs.
The car radio playing that one song. The same, calculated Ryder-sweat:
steaming into translucent drops that formed on the windows of the gold '63
Thunderbird; steaming into the sweat of whoever it was that tried to make
me that night.

Cal Freeman

Visiting the Inside Outlaws in River Rouge, MI

And you say I don't stand and deliver,

but you don't know if you don't live here,

in Blood River.

　　　　　　　　　—Don Duprie

I listen to Doop and the Inside Outlaws' record, *The Corridor,*
while making the trek over the pocked and potholed
asphalt of Schaefer Road, past Ford's Rouge Plant
and The Marathon Oil Refinery, into River Rouge
where the road name becomes Coolidge and the air
quality regularly ranks among the worst for municipalities
in Michigan, to grab drinks at Mr. K's Bar and pick
Don Duprie's brain about songwriting. Going here
to hang with Don Duprie and Alison Lewis
seems a bit mythical, perhaps the Michigan equivalent
of visiting Guy and Susanna Clark in Nashville, circa 1970.
The razor wire fence surrounding Great Lakes Steel
takes on a dull glint in the gas light, and the cirrus clouds
with the chemicals at night get tinted a sallow-green,
cirrhotic hue. Doop, Alison, and I shoot pool and play
the jukebox at Mr. K's Bar for an hour or so before
cashing out. The plan is to head back to Doop's
place to drink beer and have him help me with a song
that has been giving me trouble, but first he wants
to show us something. It is winter, a snowless night,
the air dry and frigid. He drives his Ford transit van
down a dark street labeled, "No outlet." He points
toward the Marathon refinery and the glowing ore mills

on Zug Island with his tattooed fingers and says, "See,
lots of folks look at nature and swim in lakes and climb mountains
and shit and say it's beautiful. I consider this stuff beautiful, man.
This is my idea of beauty." I look out and have to admit
I don't quite see it. An outmoded factory, an oil refinery
that is surely depositing ungodly amounts of mercury
into the Trenton Channel, which rushes into Lake Erie,
a fragile ecosystem subject to toxic algal blooms
and resultant no-swim advisories up and down its coast.
But what a place like Rouge can teach you
is that death descends daily on fumes from Severstal Steel
and the Marathon Oil refinery, that the west wind secretes it
one sallow cloud-dollop at a time, that what is here today,
be it a job or a life, might not be tomorrow.
It makes it more difficult to other others' hardships;
it makes it that much more imperative to listen
to the peoples' stories before they themselves are gone.
One of Doop's favorite things to say about empathy
in his writing is, "I'm just a reporter, man.
You gotta listen to the stories people tell you
and write them down. That's all a song is. It's easy."
In recent years philosophers like Timothy Morton
and Slavoj Žižek have suggested that at the end of history
the goal of the radical ecologist must be to admire

the aesthetics of the damage and find the beauty there.
As this irredeemable century trudges on
that ought to be the goal of the great songwriter as well:
to look at what's left over and recognize its precarious worth.

Tino Gross

'I Almost Played with The Stooges'

telephone started ringin' about 2 PM
my friend Jimmy Recca was on the other end
'Hey . . . the Stooges got a show at the Eastown tonite
and our singer, Iggy Pop is getting real uptight . . . '

you see the drummer went and crashed the van
bashed his head, and he broke his hand . . .
rock n roll can be tough, and so full of abuses
I almost played with the Stooges
I almost played with the Stooges

I went into the Eastown Theatre, to the back room . . .
they said 'hey boy can you learn these songs?
. . . we got to play real soon'
now here's a big favorite—it's called '1969'
I said hey Mr. Asheton, that jam is so damn fine!

rock n roll can get you high, so full of abuses
I almost played with the Stooges
I almost played with the Stooges

now this cat showed up with glitter and baby oil in a sack
soon he was applying it, on Mr. Pop's back
now Iggy looked at me and said,
'Man, I know this is a bummer . . .
but tonite, we're gonna let our saxophone player,
be our drummer . . . '

rock n roll can get you high, so full of abuses

I almost played with the Stooges
I almost played with the Stooges
everybody got real high, with all these abuses
but, I . . . almost played with the Stooges

Jim Gustafson

Tales of the MC5

Somewhere between Mainstreet USA
and The Lost Horizon
the bare-breasted Maoist
crashed into band practice
and told everyone
their dialects were do-do.

Jim Gustafson

Jukebox

I would eat a jukebox if it made me fall in love
with my work again. These days I feel
like an obsolete Univac oddly replete
with a functional sciatic nerve and a massive erection
left out on the sun porch during the ice storm of the century.
There are memories and then there are mirrors.
Then there are mirrors shattered by concussion grenades,
concussion grenades that are launched
like rocket-propelled glockenspiels
through walls of salmon paté. They hit the expensive floors
and erupt with "Dancing in the Streets."
Don't forget the Motor City. No chance.
It's a choral rapture, glossolalia for broke dick dogs,
weird howling by the guard shack,
a requiem for a complicated obsession
buried to its chin in succubi excreta.
I VOWED that I would eat a jukebox if it made me fall in love
with my work again. But I'm not going to rip out my heart,
trade it in for quarters, and entertain cheap strangers
no more no more no more no more. The vultures
are eating frozen quiche and the ospreys
are out of town on confidential business.
The law whores have turned everyone else into omnivores.
The passage of time has become an abhorrence to its ownself.
And listen, blubberbreath, I have a boot full
of ball bearings and a trunk full of dynamite,
and to be perfectly honest, I'm fresh out of mercy,
cheap of otherwise. The stupid tyrant
put me in charge of collecting the grog tax,

but I just collected the grog itself,
and now say spew on you, Stooge Rex.
I'm giving it all back to the peasants,
who have *earned* the right to stay drunk forever.
Yeah, yeah, vitriol is a terrific fat-buster.
And raw remorse will release the shredded angels
who have clogged your arteries.
And you too
will figure out
the joy
of variation
assuming you
live long enough
to get real.

Jim Gustafson

Final Wish

When I die I just want
a jukebox for a tombstone
and to leave all my friends
rolls of quarters.

Joe Henry

Written

for Melanie

The first time I lay on top of you I didn't weigh 120 pounds.
I must have felt like a small, broken tent:
a damp skin and spindle frame
moving with barely discernible purpose,
as if to a sudden gust of wind.

It was winter, and all around us black trees cracked when they moved,
without the leaves that only weeks before had them
rushing to impart something sweetly confidential,
before shuddering to a stop all at once
as if someone unexpected had entered the yard.

I had taken the bus from Ann Arbor
and had been crowded into a back seat by prison wives with small children
who all disembarked at Jackson
leaving the aisles stale, wet and silent;
the rest of the ride to Lansing a lurch without ballast.

I found the house on Linden St. you described,
and your room left warm and ticking:
the antique heater glowing orange,
its coils abuzz and dangerous behind a bent cage;
a bowl of water beside it giving up small wisps of steam to the air.

A lamp leaned from a stand of books,
a shirt draped over the torn shade and raw bulb.

I dropped my bag in a corner,
brought coffee from another room, undressed, climbed into your bed,
pulled rough covers up and around me.

I set a tiny and old black typewriter on my lap and waited,
still and quiet,
for something to come to me.

Brooke Horvath

I Thought We'd Never Get Over That First Album

Got live on the Zenta New Year, Detroit's Grande Ballroom, out on vinyl in
    January '69.
Less "sha na na na" than "no one here gets out alive."
High school almost done with me, believer
in the strobe-lit dream
(*it takes five seconds to realize it's time to move, to choose, to testify*),
in rock-n-revolution, Yippie sages, candle magic, Blake.
Ready to trip out with John Sinclair's
evangelical, alchemical, *almost unimaginable*
Trans-Love Energies White Panther *rama lama fa fa fa* freak-out.
Ready to *kick out the jams* with the bare-chested boys,
    brother Wayne & brother Fred, brothers Mike & Dennis & Rob
("music," sd. Sinclair, "*is* revolution").

Far left was far out,
& Johnny Rotten's bad-ass uncles—
    less ramblin' roses
    more handful of thorns, strung out
    & dangerous
    (*black to comm,* motherfuckers)—
Potawatomi voices from the whirlwind out of Lincoln Park
prophesying starship rides (hang on, *we're leaving the solar system*) &
    burning cities,
snipers on the rooftops, revolution for the sheer white noise of it,
pot, free love, & the end of waiting (*god it's so close now*).

    Don't take my word for it—the boys were "the counterculture at its
    most volatile and threatening" (Stephen Erlewine), "a catastrophic
    force of nature" (Robert Bixby).

Wayne & Sonic wannabes, we listened loud, *born hell-raisers*
& were transmogrified, glorified,
wanting to be both problem & solution
        (*This is the high society,* men for girls who *can't stand it*
        when you're doin' it right)
high on booze disgruntlement, on acid possibilities—
the future almost now, scary & exuberant & inexhaustible
        (the brothers played eight hours anything but straight
        at the Festival of Life in Chicago, August '68,
        the pigs in the street freaking out)—
punk seventeen-year-olds learning what we needed
from *The Big Us,* the *Fifth Estate, Crawdaddy! Rolling Stone,*
protesting the draft in front of the wrong building,
desperately sweet-talking every sweet young thing
(*I want ya right now* not the best come-on),
stupidly scoring oregano more often than not,
learning songs from the boys & Mitch Ryder, Terry Knight & the Pack
with a rhythm guitarist who knew maybe ten chords
& shirtless an unsavory sight to see.
But anyway & what the hell, our hair was right,
the blotter for real & potent, a few girls willing.

Come together, come together, yes yes yes yes yes

. . . . .

Today, the vinyl's scratched and obsolete,
Detroit in its dotage (*let it all burn*).
The dream, heaven knows, is over. Don't
look up the brothers in their decline, two dead
of heart attacks, one of liver failure.

Yesterday, standing on the corner
with no girls going by, waiting for

the light to change, I watched a car pull up,
music blasting from its open windows.

My first thought: "why's an old bald guy drumming
the wheel & singing along to the MC5?"

John Jeffire

sonnit: i luv you suzi quatro—

the one true suzi q could ever do
first time i seen her i grew and i grew
i canned every can just be suzi man
vinil undercuver creemy ham jam
jus one tuch suzi black lether butt
lick this sick hunger from out my gut
fret my neck up to devil gate drive
teenage man handle throtled alive
detroit dinamo tenshin releiver
rolling stone cover plesure seaker diva
mi motor city missy thumpin her bass
trust mama gonna love sweet suzi face
so we all come a stumblin to a 48 crash
jus mash me back suzi slick licrish ass

George Kalamaras

Fifteen Hundred Miles (Through the Eye of a Beatle)

for Dick Wagner

You were an old man, Dick, even when you
were young. Twenty-seven when *Frost Music*
appeared. So few remember The Frost.
Like a July day when we can't understand why
we vowed to escape the winter. Why we made
our way to Phoenix or Nogales and the cactus thorns
of the heart. Fewer still recall your next band, Ursa Major.
"Stage Door Queen." "In My Darkest Hour." Yes,
you wore black leather. The kind of dark
that might drive a Chevy with dice. The kind of dark
from the inside scar of a star. I'm glad you later played
with Alice and Lou, but the early stuff threw me
by chance to the galaxies. As if scorpions in Morocco
bit my wrist so hard I had to leave my body
starved on a rock. *Frost Music. Rock and Roll Music.*
And *Through the Eyes of Love.* What does it mean to move
"Fifteen Hundred Miles (Through the Eye of a Beatle)"?
And why did you misspell the insect, blurring
arthropod with the angst of teenage screams? I'm here, now,
among the bug husks of Indiana. Threading
the needle through the eye of a camel. It hurts
our animal selves to slip so slim. To moisten
and measure and see if we can *see.* You were old, even
when you were old, Dick. The heart. The stroke.
As if you had left it all on stage at Detroit's
Grande Ballroom, or in Meadow Brook
in Rochester Hills with Gordy and Bob

and Don. Whatever became of the toenail
clippings you kept secreted in a box to remind you
to keep both feet. On the ground,
before us, we find, perhaps, a dead possum.
If we open the pouch there might finally be a way
to sustain our eternal young, peeking out their marsupial heads
and clinging to us even when we leave. Raccoons disguise
their night in marvelous masks. Polecats protect themselves
with the distinctive stripe. You never hid
behind your guitar but let it shriek like nocturnal
trains. What if it had only been thirteen or fourteen
hundred miles through the beetle's eye? What if it
hadn't been a round number but grasped the cliff-
edge of fourteen hundred ninety-nine? Was it real
distance or the gap in the universe you felt
when the music wore off? There is so much empty space
in our lives. Like last night when I woke
with night-sweats. My friend's sick cat. My dream
already grieving my sleep. And the loss
of a guitar god, like you, which left
the world unforgivably unknown. Yes, I mean it
both ways—with the world equally incomprehensible
without you. Sure, you played with Cooper
and Reed. People always remember them

first. As if you somehow painted the palm fronds
behind the golf course where Alice retired. But you, Dick,
drove the guillotine and its steel. Charmed the boa—
with your heaving harmonic scales—to never strangle out a song
around the madman's neck. It was the chops
you honed with The Bossmen, with The Frost.
With what it felt like to constrict yourself through
the very eye of what was looking at you—
whether a beetle or the bones of the bereft. What looks
at us—what looks *into* us—also often looks,

barnacled, from within. Was the beetle
in your brain? In your heart? How might it fit inside
all you ever desired? What if the beetle itself
had traveled sixteen or seventeen hundred amoeba
miles through the curving canals of your intestinal
tract? Please don't wince. Smaller things
have lapsed. Like the great unknown—you
journeying all those years to simply one day die?
You are not dead, Dick. You died with a guitar
in your hands, even when you were alive. You are reborn,
now, in the beetle's eye, in *our* eye. To moisten
and measure and see if we can *see*.
And in seeing, *hear*. Fifteen hundred miles
forward and backward at once.

Christina Kallery

On the List

Tonight, my friend is sad because
we couldn't get into The Magic Stick
to see some band. She wasn't on the list.
But I'm not thinking, "Get a real problem."
Nor will I remind her of the dying and the destitute.
I feel it like a grade school snub.

O List, I, too, have longed to be on you.
And for a few hours immune to life's
disparate assaults against my mattering
at all: form rejection letters, texts
that never return, backless medical gowns,
the clerk who eyes me like I'm fixing to filch some pens.

Inside the music thumps a smug refrain
as the bouncer's hairy forearm waves
on the cool, the black leathered,
the crusty guy who knew the MC5.
Our names are nowhere
for a girl with charcoal eyes to cross
off, so we could enter, feeling a little chosen.
We wouldn't even need a balcony seat or to make
out with the bassist on a disgusting couch.
We'd be content to stand before the stage
with our little plastic cups, belonging.

There's the list of the seventh grade lunchroom
to the nerd with his trembling tray;
or, to my aggrieved aunt, the clique lording

the list over the front pew of her Pentecostal church.
On the office list, the chisel-jawed glide
like yachts on an indigo sea, past frumpy rowboats
to their island of promotions.

As twilight drapes its purple cape across the sky,
we stand, dust off our skirts and settle for the neon
of an all-night diner in Hamtramck.

The way all our lists resolve in time,
to an ever-smaller, brighter orbit;
where *plus one* means there's someone to watch a movie with,
a flick that's not that great but has its moments.
Someone to call when the dark fog of aloneness looms,
or to sit with on the front porch and watch the lunar eclipse—
its halo scripted on the broad black night
that goes on without us forever.

Christina Kallery

Burnouts

Downriver Detroit, 1987

There's enough burnouts out there to go hands across America.
—*Heavy Metal Parking Lot*

I went to a party last Saturday night. I didn't get laid, I got in a fight.
—*Lita Ford*

You'd see them rolling joints in class, textbook propped
to hide the task, feathered hair fringing their eyes,
a starter mustache shadowing their upper lips. Always
a few hanging out on empty bleachers, trading swigs
from something bottom shelf in a paper bag.

And always the jagged lettered logos of their concert tees,
their suede boots like the ones worn by the guy in 7th hour
fine arts. He pulled them on every day, in snowbound December
and blazing June, laced to the knee over jeans tight
as snake's skin, belt buckle shaped like a woman's
clutching hand forever poised just short of third base,
a heavy metal send-up of the poet's Grecian urn.

I never knew his name, but I recall his cloud-grey,
half-mast eyes, his Bic-penned scrawls
of fiery skulls and undead guitarists,
his public makeouts with some girl by the acrylic paints.
He'd float through hallways, an apathetic ghost

gliding onward to its dead-end job, jail term
or other bad turn. But it would be sweet
justice if he dodged the old clichés and got by ok.

It would be a flipped bird from the window of a black
Camaro they said would never make it off the blocks—
watch it peel onto the entrance ramp, rebuilt engine roaring,
to catch the last gleam of sunlight fading fast behind the trees.

Wayne Kramer

Back to Detroit

It's a hard wind blows through the buildings and empty lots
As the corner of michigan and 31st waits in ruin
And the echoes of happy shoppers faded long, long, long ago
Back when chrysler, gm and ford went mad with greed

Oh, how we hoped it would turn out right
Going back to detroit

Kid could ride his bike through any neighborhood in town
No fear of getting jacked for his sneakers
Drive-bys only happened to the purple gang
Back before the rebellion of '67

Still we dreamed it could turn out right
Movin back to detroit
Drove down from st. claire, took all night
Going back to detroit

From east grand boulevard to michigan and 31st
Over to livernois and warren
And then the upper duplex of elmer and mcgraw street
And then the big move to our own whole house in lincoln park
Which shattered into a rental in taylor
And the endless search for the great good place
Was redeemed by the power of loud electric guitars

Up the river it's all forests and secret trails
And forts and swamps and dogs and boats

And the day held a million adventures for a boy of seven
But that was before the time of later ghosts

Lost paradise left behind
Huck finn hits the steets and the neon light
Hope against hope it'll turn out right
Going back to detroit.
Drove down from algonac, took all night
Going back to detroit

Jan Krist

State of Sin

I know this guy who's from the south
Sings about how he was raised
Singing songs of Jesus' love
Living in a state of grace
But me I come here from the north
From Detroit, Michigan
And I've struggled all my life
Living in a state of sin

Once we came here to Detroit,
Nothing ever was the same
We were never quite that sure
If we were happy that we came
But I found my first guitar,
Found my voice and a few friends
Found that Jesus came to save me
From the pain that I'd been in

       And my mom taught me to be kind, and to always try my best
       Life may not bring what you want, make good choices with what's left

And I was raised to go to church
Wash my hands and say the grace
Do the dishes fold the clothes
Hold the planets in their place
Raised to know that talk is cheap
And that love demands action
And to know we're not alone in the landscape of our sin
Life is thinner than we know
May we all find grace within. . . .

Gerry LaFemina

The American Ruse

My first guitar was a Japanese Les Paul wannabe
with a warped neck I'm certain was manufactured
in Staten Island, in Paul Majewski's basement,

circa 1982. We knew the best ones were built in the States
Gibsons & Fenders we couldn't afford.
The best amps British HiWatts or Marshalls

hand wired, tubes glowing like party lights, those parties
we never attended. We were poor children of poor parents.
Our heroes made do, made music from distortion—

Wayne Kramer, James Williamson, Ron Asheton
names so ordinary they might have been written
under a class photograph. In school the sisters

assured us we could do anything, just not rock n roll,
or art; not anything sexy, anything glamorous or fun.
What we were ravenous for we never received:

that guitar refused to stay in tune & turned
my left hand into a claw. Don't ask
what happened to Majewski—maybe jail,

a jealous husband. More likely he just drove off
into an adulthood of average jobs,
an above average mortgage: that slow drizzle that never

becomes a full blown torrent. He lived with his mother, &

we'd escape, nights, into punk dives or else
into cassette tapes delivered by boombox, the first song

always the same, Robin Tyner insisting
we kick out the jams, motherfuckers. We wanted
to kick out the doors & windows, too. Kick out the night.

*   *   *

There was that small brick ranch in Royal Oak
with its flower gardens & sadnesses
of in-laws with their secret hurts. My wife & I

would visit on summer holidays until the barbecue grill
became just another smoldering. So many hot coals
in the suburbs, in that marriage, in the country

so that I'd just take off some afternoons
stop at the stores on Woodward Avenue where out-of-luck
axe-men pawned old Gibsons & Vox amps, & where

I could play for awhile, first a Mosrite
followed by a Rik then a Gretsch or whatever else
hung on the walls. Nickel strings stinging again

into my fingertips. I'd move from shop to shop:
Music Castle, Motor City Instrument Exchange,
Woodward Guitars, take a pick from the glass jars,

plug in. I wanted what the guitars had to say,
the inflection of sustain & overdrive, a feedback
barrage Fred Smith & Wayne Kramer understood,

a revolution in fuzz tones. It was the third of July.
Already those streets of pastoral names reeked

of sulfur & lilac, maybe a lead lick of honeysuckle.

We could be anything, we once believed, but even
then, all I recognized were the frowns of my wife,
the gospel of bills & bank statements to which we tithed,

so I knew I couldn't afford that American Flag
Fender Coronet with the single humbucker
just like Kramer used to play

on *Back in the USA* (it could have been his, he was
made in Detroit, after all). From the tuning pegs,
a price tag dangling like dog tags. I knew

in a way I hadn't known I'd been taught, I was
finally getting hip to the American Ruse.
I couldn't afford the revolution. But still, it came.

John D. Lamb

The Day's Last Cigarette: A Tobacco Memoir Poem

Dad is pensive when he smokes. One eye squints. He is singing "Nel blu dipinto di blu." It means, "In the sky, painted blue." Most people know the song as Volare (to fly). He's from Italy but we live in Michigan. He works at Ford's. When he takes a drag, he looks faraway. Smoke emanates from his mouth and nose. He could have been a singer.

We listen to albums by Modugno, Gianni Morandi and Peppino Di Capri. Claudio Villa has the best voice. Villa's photos show him smoking a pipe or wielding a long cigarette holder. Dad used to smoke Viceroys. He switched to Tareyton. At school they tell us that smoking is bad for you. I have asthma and he should quit smoking.

Our house is in Redford Township, a western suburb of Detroit. Ted Nugent was born near here. Ted is ten years older than me. He and Steve Farmer have a band called The Amboy Dukes. They wrote a song called Journey to the Center of the Mind. A lot of my neighbors go hunting. Dad grows tomatoes.

My first cigarette is a Kool. Kenny, the older boy next door, hid a pack in his Beatle boots. The taste of smoke makes me want to spit. His mom let him join a mail order record club. He says Mick Jagger uses a bad word in the song Honky Tonk Women. I don't know which word he means. Kenny's sister loves Grand Funk Railroad. On one album cover they don't wear shirts. Grand Funk is from Flint, an hour from here. When Mark Farner sings I'm Your Captain (Closer to my Home) I sing along on the chorus. Kenny's favorite is Footstompin' Music. Guys in my neighborhood smoke menthol cigarettes.

Dad has a thick Italian accent. He works on the assembly line with a lot of black guys. He says, "Hey baby" when he sees a guy he knows but can't remember his name. That's a soul thing. Derek St. Holmes sings Hey Baby on a Ted Nugent record. He sings it to a girl who's hanging around while he's "too busy messin' in this town."

At the Wixom plant they make Lincolns and Marks. Dad is a quality control inspector. When he gets home from his shift we eat pasta. After dinner he changes his clothes and goes to a second job as a tailor. That's what he apprenticed to do while growing up. I am learning how to play the guitar. Guys my age like to play House of the Rising Sun. Frijid Pink does a good version. Dad does alterations on men's suits in the back room of Harry Thomas Fine Clothiers. He has an ashtray full of butts next to his sewing machine.

At the Pierson Junior High canteen I saw a band called Tanglefoot. They do mostly Jethro Tull covers while the lead singer dances barefoot. I meet the drummer in the band. He goes to Redford Union High School and he smokes Salem. He says it's easy to be a guitar player. You just learn how to play chords and change them fast.

Bob Seger has a couple of songs on the radio. I hear he plays high school dances. Bob grew up mostly in Ann Arbor. His dad works at Ford's, too. Even though Bob is white, he can sound black when he sings. But he does this one slow song called Turn the Page. I think he wrote it because it sounds like he's talking about himself. In the song he says, "You smoke the day's last cigarette, remembering what she said." I think about my dad.

I'm scared to see Alice Cooper. He uses a guillotine on stage. Kenny has the Love it to Death and Killer albums. We crank out Under My Wheels and Be My Lover. Alice's band tried LA but they didn't get him. I hear he lives somewhere in Oakland County. In Detroit we get the MC5. And we get The Stooges with this guy who grew up in an Ypsilanti trailer park. Alice and Iggy have weird names. They sound like smart-asses from my neighborhood. Not sure what they smoke.

After school I make pizzas at Mama Mia's on Beech Daly near Grand River Ave. The guys I work with, their favorite band is The J. Geils Band. We listen to their live albums. One was recorded at the Cinderella Ballroom in Detroit. Another one is called Blow Your Face Out. They're from Boston but they call Detroit their second home. We like to rap along to the intro of Must Have Got Lost. We toss the pizza dough with our hands and do the Detroit Breakdown. On break, I bum a Newport from the dishwasher. It gives me a rush and makes me a little dizzy.

The Smokin' O.P.s album cover has a pack of Lucky Strikes. It's Bob Seger singing other people's songs. He smokes them instead of writing his own. I'm learning how to sing other people's songs. My Ford Torino has an 8-track player (and an ash tray). Turned up loud is Bob's new album Beautiful Loser. He wrote all of the songs except for Nutbush City Limits. Katmandu smokes. On Jody Girl he sings soft and low while strumming an acoustic guitar. Alone in the car I listen to the words. They make me think.

Freshman year at Central Michigan University is the year of the live album. Big on the radio is Kiss Alive and Frampton Comes Alive. Here in Mt. Pleasant and all across Michigan, we're into "Live" Bullet. Bob Seger and the Silver Bullet Band is at Rose Arena. It's just walking distance from my dormitory. Bob makes his voice go way up firm and high. How does he smoke and not lose his voice? I have a band with some guys down the hall. Every time we do a show I get hoarse. I switch to a non-menthol brand.

My band is playing at Legs Inn, a roadhouse in Cross Village, 23 miles south of Mackinaw City. Bob Seger is hanging out (he has a cabin nearby). People are dancing to our covers. Bob yells out, "Play some originals." He says it with a kind smile; not like a smart-ass. We do a couple of my songs. After the set I step outside to get some air, see the moon and stars over Lake Michigan. There's a group of others doing the same. I ask if anyone has a cigarette I can bum. Bob emerges and gives me a Marlboro Light.

Dad tried to quit but never really did. He ate a plate of pasta. Before going to bed he stepped out to the garage. There he lit up a Marlboro 100, an extra-long. He smoked half and butted it. He was saving the other half for tomorrow.

Gordon Lightfoot

Black Day in July

Black day in July
Motor city madness has touched the countryside
And through the smoke and cinders
You can hear it far and wide
The doors are quickly bolted
And the children locked inside

Black day in July
Black day in July
And the soul of Motor City is bared across the land
As the book of law and order is taken in the hands
Of the sons of the fathers who were carried to this land

Black day in July
Black day in July
In the streets of Motor City is a deadly silent sound
And the body of a dead youth lies stretched upon the ground
Upon the filthy pavement
No reason can be found

Black day in July
Black day in July
Motor City madness has touched the countryside
And the people rise in anger
And the streets begin to fill
And there's gunfire from the rooftops
And the blood begins to spill

Black day in July

In the mansion of the governor
There's nothing that is known for sure
The telephone is ringing
And the pendulum is swinging
And they wonder how it happened
And they really know the reason
And it wasn't just the temperature
And it wasn't just the season

Black day in July
Black day in July
Motor City's burning and the flames are running wild
They reflect upon the waters of the river and the lake
And everyone is listening
And everyone's awake

Black day in July
Black day in July
The printing press is turning
And the news is quickly flashed
And you read your morning paper
And you sip your cup of tea
And you wonder just in passing
Is it him or is it me

Black day in July

In the office of the President
The deed is done the troops are sent
There's really not much choice you see
It looks to us like anarchy
And then the tanks go rolling in
To patch things up as best they can
There is no time to hesitate

The speech is made the dues can wait

Black day in July
Black day in July
The streets of Motor City now are quiet and serene
But the shapes of gutted buildings
Strike terror to the heart
And you say how did it happen
And you say how did it start
Why can't we all be brothers
Why can't we live in peace
But the hands of the have-nots
Keep falling out of reach

Black day in July
Black day in July
Motor city madness has touched the countryside
And through the smoke and cinders
You can hear it far and wide
The doors are quickly bolted
And the children locked inside

Rachel Loden

Tumbling Dice

I thought all your walled cities
would fall
to rock & roll,
I thought no suffering was safe
when Smokey sang.
If Otis
could not teach you tenderness—
Aretha sweet love—
then I was wrong.

Do roses push
up through the streets
of Spanish Harlem,
is "Ooo Baby Baby"
still the melting point of ice?
Will we always find
some rooftop we can drift on
to the roll of the tumbling dice,
sweet darling
the roll of the tumbling dice . . .

Art Lyzak

SO AMERICAN

CHICKS
CARS
SO AMERICAN

DRUGS
BARS
SO AMERICAN

IM NOT GONNA TRY
TO TELL YOU WHY
I FEEL THIS WAY

BUT IM SO GLAD
IM AN AMERICAN
IM AN AMERICAN GUY

ROCK
TV
SO AMERICAN

YOU
AND ME
NUTCASE AMERICANS

KEEP ME IN NEW YORK
OR IN LA
ILL BE OKAY

CAUSE IM SO GLAD

IM AN AMERICAN
COOL AMERICAN GUY

UPS
AND DOWNS ARE
SO AMERICAN

BUDDIES
AND CLOWNS
SO AMERICAN

THE OTHER COUNTRIES BORE ME
LETS DRINK TO THE USA

IM SO GLAD
IM AN AMERICAN
IM AN AMERICAN GUY

GIVE STEVE MILLER A CHEESEBURGER
IM A COOL AMERICAN GUY
LETS GO SEE THE MUTANTS TONIGHT
CAUSE IM A COOL AMERICAN GUY

Art Lyzak

AFRAID OF DETROIT

WE WILL RISE FROM THE ASHES
IT SAYS IT ON MY CITY FLAG
BLACK AND
WHITE AND
LEFT AND
RIGHT AND
WE WILL HAVE
A REAL COLD BEER
TONIGHT

I THOUGHT ABOUT YOU TODAY
EVEN THOUGH IM IN LA

COME ON, BABY
DONT BE
AFRAID OF DETROIT
DONT BE AFRAID OF DETROIT

ITS IN YOUR FACE
MY FAVORITE PLACE
DONT BE AFRAID OF DETROIT

WE HOPE FOR BETTER THINGS
IT SAYS SO ON MY CITY FLAG
I MISS THE LOVE
AND HATE
AND HAPPINESS
IN THIS PARIS OF THE WEST

YOULL NEVER FADE AWAY
EVEN THOUGH IM IN LA

COME ON, BABY
DONT BE
AFRAID OF DETROIT
DONT BE AFRAID OF DETROIT

313
WITH NO APOLOGY
DONT BE AFRAID OF DETROIT

I THOUGHT ABOUT YOU TODAY
YOULL NEVER FADE AWAY

COME ON, BABY
DONT BE AFRAID OF DETROIT

BACK FROM THE DEAD
WITH A BRAND NEW HEAD

TOUGH AND LOUD AND
TOO FUCKING PROUD

DONT BE AFRAID OF DETROIT

Peter Markus

On Turning Fifty-Two

Up early on the morning of my fifty-second birthday.
To read poetry in the dim yellow lamplight of pre-dawn.
My son, about to turn twenty, asleep on the couch.
My wife in our bed sleeping too. Hopefully dreaming.
Of us making a love made strange through its maneuvers.
That it lasts with something resembling fortitude.
The dog licks her own paws to get at something there.
The quiet that hums between my ears. The guitar
across the room with its missing strings wishing I knew
how to play. Accepting that I don't. At least not much.
Still I pick it up. My fingers make the shape of the familiar.
A silver sound jangles out. I have heard it all before.
Give me instead the muted or even the out of tune.
The not knowing what to name the chord. Dissonance.
Discord. The feedback I remember when I was sixteen.
Negative Approach. The Necros. Misfits. Minor Threat.
Standing too close to the amp. Facing it. Not turning my back.
How the impulse would be to reach up and touch our ears.
But I never did. Which explains why I often hear myself
saying the words "Say again." I want you to know I care.
That I'm wanting to listen. Even when the past gets in the way.
We carry our mistakes with us into the present forever.
You can go home again but the house is now abandoned,
or torn down, or painted yellow, and the people inside
don't know your name and are indifferent to your story.
The birds go on singing regardless. The new day and year
fill with either snow or light or sometimes if we're lucky both.

Adrian Matejka

From the Edge of the World

A whole new world
is opening up
—"Intro," Blacktop

This city is a fulcrum of bent intentions
while late-model cars spin in unpredictable
potholes & rust puddles. Who cares if
we ever get back? The penitents in black
neck ties going door to door? The sleeping
man using a box for a house? Block after
block of wet brick arches & slim windows
cut sideways from here to the Mississippi—
what ifs in river waves, as if being shot
in the back is the fault of the man who
got shot in the back. The assemblages
keep moving in belted circles: rock-broken
windows & cracked factory bits everywhere.
Who cares about guitar histrionics inside all
of this rust & flaking blacktop crust?
Here's to the free-falling brick & skin
of the city. Here's to the sculptured husks
of industry opening up to a less-abandoned
world full of sweet-sounding surprises right
next to the dirty river. The city goes & goes
while the litany of have & have not makes it
difficult to talk about anything. We end up
sitting on folding chairs in somebody's
basement, knuckles propped on either
side of our faces as the music fumes

all around us. We end up in the cleft
of gentrification & scented candles, lights
puttering against our chins. All that teeth
grinding & ingenuity cornered between
the working street lights & brocaded river.
The city's feedback is right outside
when the air conditioner stops working.

Ken Mikolowski

At the Grande Ballroom 1968

John Sinclair, poet
and manager of the MC5,
asks other poets
to read at the Grande
between sets.
The night I get to be
the intermission
the Stooges are the opening act.

Iggy cuts himself up and bleeds
all over the audience.
They love it and
go nuts and
can't calm down.

Brother J. C. Crawford calls out
"And now a poet will read some poems."
Most everyone boos and
retreats to the parking lot
to smoke some dope.

That leaves me
to read a couple poems
about life, love and revolution.
One of the few remaining members
of the crowd yells,
"Fuck the revolution. Bring on the MC5."

Someone drops a drum on stage
and on that note my reading is over.

Scott Morgan

16 With a Bullet

Billy grew up down south
His family has some cash
A modern day plantation
I wouldn't call 'em trash
They sent him up to the prep school
To be a doctor man
Forty miles from Detroit
Up in Michigan

16 with a bullet
They were glory bound
16 with a bullet
Now they're goin' down

Johnny came from up north
He was city born
Didn't have much money
He wasn't on the dole
His folks owned a grocery
Detroit, Michigan
He worked behind the counter
Cashin' bottles in

16 with a bullet
They were glory bound
16 with a bullet
Now they're goin' down
One night Billy walked in
He was packin' heat

Got a taste for drugs
And he can't be beat
Johnny opened up the till
Just like the man said
Came up with a pistol
And now they both lay death

16 with a bullet
They were glory bound
16 with a bullet
Now they're goin' down
Well its just don't matter
Who was wrong or right
And it sure don't matter
Who was the black or white
But 16 with a bullet
In the cold hard ground
It's not the way they planned it
But now they're glory bound

Nancy J. Rodwan

Night Moves

She claims to have lost her virginity to Bob Seger. Sipping Jim Beam and Pepsi listening to Live Bullet my mother tells me once again that her best friend in high school was Pep Perrine, the original drummer in The Silver Bullet Band. That Pep often took her to band practice. The way she tells it you are left to believe that "Night Moves" was written about her. My father was convinced my mother was a virgin when they met. The first time they had sex, she tells me, she made sure it was when she was having her period to help keep the illusion alive. The story is brought up while she is mildly intoxicated and it ends with her deep in a quietly morbid drunk. She chose my dad over a successful pop star and I am supposed to feel sorry for her.

In 1996 I had a chance to see Bob Seger in concert. Never having been a big fan, mainly because of my mother, I wasn't overly enthusiastic but my boyfriend thought it would be fun so we went. It surprised me to find myself dancing and singing along. In the middle of the show he performed "Night Moves" and it struck me. It was not true. Her story was nothing more than that, a story. Not the entire story. She did know Pep Perrine. There are old photographs of the two of them together and a later one that included my dad. The bourbon-induced renditions of the story always made me uneasy but it never occurred to me that mother would lie to me about it.

My parents met the day she graduated from high school. They married a month later. I came along a respectable nine months after. Four days before their ninth wedding anniversary my father shot himself in the head while sitting at the breakfast table. My mother was making oatmeal. I was brushing my teeth.

I was twelve the first time I heard the tale and was shocked by her smugness at deceiving my dad. It seemed important to her to make it clear to me that she had other options. Listening to her recounting her secret affair made me determined to live a life free from regret. To be always clear in my choices. To not be her.

At the concert it became clear that she tried to make her sad life seem fuller. Instead she just made it sadder. I never knew why my father killed himself. When he did he made a choice that made all of my mother's choices irrelevant. She chose him but he chose death. To console herself she invents a love affair that would have broken my father's heart. She never seemed to realize that her lie didn't work. My dad could never hear the story.

Nancy J. Rodwan

Waiting on the Revolution

He sat in my section in the rear
The manager begged me
To let him take the table
I just looked at him

But that is
Mitch Ryder!
He claimed ignorantly

Oh my god!
It's Bob Seger
Said the woman who let the bear
Out at the Belle Isle Zoo

No, motherfuckers, just no
You're obviously not
Part of the solution

I am here
Brothers and sisters
To tell you
That is not Mitch Ryder

I am here to testify
Are you with me?
That is not Bob Seger

I am here
To kick it out to you

My brothers and sisters
Sitting at my table is Rob Tyner

He takes his eggs
With hot sauce
His coffee black

Corie Rosen

Madonna for the Damned—a 1980s Heroine

You stretched out your hungry voice
And grabbed Music Television
With fingerless black lace back-beats
And shocking pink lyrics.
From nowhere-nobody-nothing
New York
—sweaty streets full of Italian girls just like you—
You claimed your fame.
The teenybopper soul of the nation,
Your hollow trophy,
Moved to the music of big blonde hair
Moved by the bitter flavor,
The thin white lines
Of jagged, sweet cocaine.
Excommunicated matriarch of underage millions,
A sexual, bisexual, polyamorous parent of two,
America's own Eva Peron
In a black vinyl bodysuit,
You shoved the world into open-sided boxes
As you saw fit
And wouldn't take "no" for an answer.
The holy mother of pop,
You televised, musicalized, revolutionized,
For the very first time,
The spike-heeled sexual longing of fresh young girls.
Aching midnight dancers
Free at last
To wear big cheap earrings.

Raquel Salaysay

Mutants and Monsters, Pillows and Truncheons: A Garage Punk Reunion

We were wild creatures, out to show the world how fierce we were
We kept our claws sharp, our leather black
Ripped clothing, mad symbols inked in our skin
Mutants and Monsters, Pillows and Truncheons

Now look at us
Claws manicured, soccer mom haircuts
Animosities erased like the once graffitied walls of Alvin's dressing room
Vintaged and serene

Our 20's more legend now than reality
We joke and tell stories like soldiers from a forgotten war
I sip my Bushmills out of a plastic cup and take it all in.
I feel the heat that comes with August nights
Soaking into my skin
Electric and hot like that moment in the set
When you're three songs in and ready to release the hounds
At Paycheck's, at Lili's and now PJ's

I lean on a chair and close my eyes
I listen to the raucous intent of random conversation
Mixed inflections evolving into one single wave of sound
Rolling smoothly into my ears like fine whiskey down my throat
We have nothing to prove now
Perhaps this gives us peace of mind
In the wizened golden of here and now

"This is heaven," I hear someone say.

If heaven could be like tonight for eternity, then who among us would be afraid to die?

Ed Sanders

Going to a Meeting on Bank Street

I had written a tune, "Ten Years for Two Joints,"
which I intended to perform with my autoharp at Crisler.

Then I ran into Phil Ochs, who had just spoken with
John Lennon over the phone, and learned that John
had written a song for Sinclair.

Phil sang a snatch of what Lennon sang o'er the phone:
"It ain't fair John Sinclair, ten for two for smoking air"!

Oh no! I thought, what about my own tune, with the chorus,
"Ten Years for Two Joints," that I was going to sing at the
Sinclair concert, so I deferred to Lennon and didn't

perform my song, which would have brought the house down,
as it did when I sang it shortly later at a benefit
for Sinclair at the St. Mark's Church.

So, instead I read a section from "The Entrapment of John Sinclair."

I regret today not performing my own tune.
Here it is, published for the first time:

Ed Sanders

Ten Years for Two Joints

for John Sinclair

10 years for 2 joints
10 years for 2 joints
burn and burn and burn and burn
burn the prison down

in godless walls of stone & steel
the poet lies alone alone alone

hold down the tide
stop the rain from falling
bend away the bars
& set him free

the blubberous judge with pain & puke
and the long haired hippie cop
shall feel the wrath of the angry mob
as we tear the prison down

10 years for 2 joints
10 years for 2 joints
burn and burn and burn and burn
burn the prison down

locked up away from his lady's love
locked up away from the hemp of Ra
locked up away from the streets & the crowds

John Sinclair Poet-Warrior
John Sinclair Poet-Warrior
John Sinclair Poet-Warrior

10 years for 2 joints
10 years for 2 joints
burn and tear and burn and tear and
burn the prison down

Patty Seyburn

Wild One

Dimitri threw his arm into the crowd
I'd fallen under, bodies bowed against
each other, bouncing back like rubber bands
as though we were elastic. We were not.
I was Eurydice, my brief descent
into the underworld aborted by
my friend, who watched me, standing on the fringe
at Iggy Pop, playing in West Chelsea
before that part of town was spic' n' span.
Or wait—was I Persephone, abducted by
the mosh pit's joyful violence? Once out
I found a beer. I couldn't think—which girl
had eaten pomegranate seeds and had
to stay in Hades half the year? I licked
a little blood off my teeth. A guy flicked
ashes on my shoes. This was before tattoos.
The bodies slammed. I'd had enough damage.

Paul Simon

Papa Hobo

It's carbon and monoxide
The ol' Detroit perfume
And it hangs on the highways
In the morning
And it lays you down by noon
Oh, Papa Hobo
You can see that I'm dressed like a schoolboy
But I feel like a clown
It's a natural reaction I learned
In this basketball town

Sweep up
I been sweeping up the tips I've made
I been living on Gatorade
Planning my getaway
Detroit, Detroit
Got a hell of a hockey team
Got a left-handed way
Of making a man sign up on that
Automotive dream, oh yeah, oh yeah
Oh, Papa Papa Hobo
Could you slip me a ride?
Well, it's just after breakfast
I'm in the road
And the weatherman lied

Fred "Sonic" Smith

Sister Anne

Sister Anne don't give a damn about evolution
She's a liberated woman, she's got her solution
Like a dinosaur, she's going off the wall
She's gonna make it her own crusade

She's got a heart of gold
Gonna save a bitch's soul
From goin' down
Satan's hot way

She can, I know she can
I know she can, she's my Sister Anne

Such truth, such beauty, such purity
She wears a halo around her head
She's got the Ten Commandments tattooed on her arm
If she died she'd rise up from the dead

She's every man savior and
Mama too
If you do it she said
She'll save hell from you

She can, I know she can
I know she can, she's my Sister Anne

Sister, won't you tell me where I went so wrong
I used to say my prayers baby, all night long

I'd listen to the Gospel ringing in my ears
Come on Sister Anne, save me from my fears

If you can, I know you can
I know you can, you're my Sister Anne

Sister, won't you tell me where I went so wrong
I used to say my prayers baby, all night long
I'd listen to the Gospel ringing in my ears
Come on Sister Anne, save me from my fears

If you can, I know you can
I know you can, you're my Sister Anne

After Sunday school Mass she goes to see her man
She always does the best that she can
She never tries to tease, she always aims to please
She's gonna squeeze you tight and make you feel alright

'Cause she can, I know she can
I know she can, she's my Sister Anne
I know she can, she's my Sister Anne
I know she can, she's my Sister Anne

She's my Sister Anne
She's my Sister Anne
She's my Sister Anne

Fred "Sonic" Smith

City Slang

Some dirt in my hand
A part of the land
Slip and slide communication
Downtown on the street
They measure the beat
To understand the situation
A taste on the tongue
And no place to run
With all the chances to be taken
The stranger he buys
The angel she flies
My heart is cold just like the nation
Like a dog they kick at night
Gypsy laughin' but that's alright
Momma's cryin' sister thinkin'
Well you know it's just city slang

We rode in the car
Slept in the car
All the way to the citadel
Slept on the floor
Surfed on the floor
All the way to the Coronet
Rock was pissed in Paris
Mad in Madrid
Took the sonic European way
Gary and Rock
Sonic and Scott
Meet again up in Ishpeming

When you hear that hammer fallin'
Ain't no reason to feel left out
Ain't no reason to call any names
Well you know it's just city slang

With Funky and Dog
To Minni and Mad
All the way to the Aragon
Cleveland and Chi
Ann Arbor, Detroit
All the way back to the Second Chance
Je suis un son
Un autre son
Qui n'entend qu'une cloche n'entend qu'un son
Je suis le son
Je suis son son
Hey what kind of fool do you think I am
Keep a-talkin' those city dreams
Well you know alright you know what I mean
Detroit, Chicago now New York to L.A.
They all been talkin' bout city slang

Note: There are no definitive lyrics to this song. This is one version of it.

Carolyn Striho

City Music Lights

Got to get going
Detroit rock and roll
under my fingers
with delicate soul

you can't believe it
it hasn't been told
harder and harder
dance passion the goal

this isn't explained in words
just by action
expression extension
of my own ascension

to take all inside
and let it come out
from the streets, from the city
never a doubt

from the Lodge to 7 Mile
and near Van Dyke
Belle Isle music
we played every night
Rosedale Park over to Cass Avenue
back near The Southfield
the clubs with a view
to Plymouth Road and under
by the tracks southwest

Mexican Village to the backstage mess
we went in those old cars
we walked on the barge
down to Masonic Temple
where we were living large

Marshall amps downtown
in places all the rage now
Midtown was Cass Corridor
home of the hip now

loving the vision of the wild road
loving the incision of the poetic load
we traveled everywhere in the streets so cold
wasn't called the after party 'cause it was just bold

we're out in the streets
we're out on the stage
things haven't changed
ambassadors made

in the motor city,
it was never a deal
because writing and performing is what makes us real

Russell Thorburn

Woodward Avenue on the Bus Downtown the Bus Driver Turns around to Say

They killed Marvin Gaye. What's going on
nobody listens to good music, and the wipers
clear ice from the windshield

but not much of Woodward visible
and the ice-battered bus from a hundred years
of passengers delivered downtown

slides across the frozen skin of road,
bumping against at least three smaller
vehicles with drivers cursing.

Marcellus, the black bus driver,
younger than me, manages to shout
around his lowered shoulder

at the visible presence of a white man,
older than yesterday now, yellowed teeth,
hair like growing plants out of my nose.

My defense drifts past his head-boned
driving, both hands on the large circle of a wheel
that turns us around the Chevrolet

dead on the road, and he's singing,
must be singing, "I'll Be Doggone"
his tenor voice deeper than a drum

but able to ride a flat tire over the bad
notes of "And I'll be doggone
if you ain't warm as a breath of spring."

A black woman with fiery white hair
of an oracle, her pillbox hat from another
generation hangs onto the rope

that buzzes for the next stop, but Marcellus
ignores that hanging which would become
a noose growing louder

when the white-haired fire of a woman
mumbles, "Why ain't you stopping?"
And a bus on Woodward like the whole

Motown era adrift in time can't stop
on the surface boned down to an ice
with new snow falling every minute

his grin that does not hide the stubbornness
as if he knew the brakes won't work
shown to everyone in his refusal to listen

and brakes or not, they all go skidding
sideways through an intersection,
and he won't stop singing Marvin Gaye.

Thomas Trimble

Muscle Car

performed by American Mars

white boy, black city
and history won't let it bend around me
show me, no liberal pity
losers hate to see a winner gloat
but it's so easy
in the wake
it's such breezy
real estate

power and position fade
when you try to get behind the cathode face
dance hall, empty floor
the People Mover is moving around the core
but it's so sleepy
when it gets late
it's so breezy
like the batcave

take me for a ride in your muscle car
show me all the places that you know
tell me, where the people are
where did all of Henry's money go?
man confess

take me for a ride in your muscle car
show me where the Tigers used to play
tell me, is the river far?

was Black Bottom all the things they used to say?
man confess

take me for a ride in your muscle car
show me all the places that you know
open up your petals
dust off your medals
in the city
in your muscle car

Rob Tyner

Grande Days

If I had a time machine
I'd take you back with me
To the heyday of the Grande, and
All the wonders there to see.
The walls ablaze with colors
Smell the incense in the air
Hear the music's sound and fury
When the English bands were there.
In the psychedelic ballroom
As the light show whirled about, and
All the people freaking freely
While the jams were kicking out.
Grande days, Grande days
I had some wild nights
Back in my Grande days.
You were there at the Grande,
I remember you
You had hair down past your shoulders, and
You wore rainbow-colored shoes.
You were there with a chick in a miniskirt,
They called her "Sister Mystery," and
One of us was blasted, and
It wasn't her or me.
Cause you spoke to me in Day-glo words, and
You swore it was true
That you could hear the colors, and
You could see the music too.
Alone at night in the Ballroom,
I heard a mournful, eerie call,

As though a tortured soul was sobbing
Deep inside the walls.
Of my memories of the Grande,
This one disturbs me most,
I didn't believe the place was haunted
'Till I heard the Grande ghost.
Now the Ballroom stands empty
Nobody ever comes to play.
They took out the PA system, and
Put the light show away.
But, if the Grande could talk
What stories she would tell,
Of when the music rolled and thundered
Like fireworks from Hell,
Of the violence in the parking lot, and
The craziness backstage
When the Detroit scene exploded, and
The Grande was the latest rage.
Grande days, Grande days,
I had some wild nights
Back in my Grande days.

Andrew Vinstra

Detroit Rock & Roll 2 am Séance for Jesus

Sunday July 27, 1984

I heard a muted rumor once of one of the greatest
Detroit concerts nobody ever saw.
In an almost hushed whisper, one night
in a college dorm, somebody told me
of the Detroit concert for Jesus
where a bunch of calloused road-worn
Detroit rock warriors tried to break
the devil's extortionary hold.

The roll call of this infamous yet strangely
hopeful gathering included such bastions
of Detroit rock as Bob Seger, Drew Abbott,
Alto Reed, Jim McCarty, Mitch Ryder,
Johnny B, Dave Gilbert, (and rumors swirl
and abound) even Ron Ashton, Iggy Pop,
Glen Buxton and Alice Cooper! Some people say
Brownsville Station was there. Some people
even say Question Mark and the Mysterians,
but the exact names and numbers will always
be a mystery.

It was really just supposed to be one more
rock & roll Saturday night drunk fest
which first mushroomed, then strangely
mutated as legends of Detroit musical rebellion
tried to levitate salvation from the stupor
of a drunken haze.

Just goofing around on the piano, Bob Seger
suddenly began a mournful and heartfelt
rendition of *Just a Closer Walk with Thee.*
Dave Gilbert joined in on harmony, and then,
it was as if this entire little Union Lake house
began to rise.

Remembering their childhoods, their mamas,
their Sunday school teachers, their little old lady
piano teachers, their hard working daddies,
the rockers poured heart and soul into one hymn
after another, mournful and plaintive as the twelve
disciples on the night of Christ's crucifixion. The rockers'
piston engine voices, calloused guitar playing fingers,
tried to grasp the light of the far away midnight stars
and hold it close like a childhood lantern of fireflies in a jar.
They sang and played so fierce and so bright that the ghost
of Elvis Presley appeared, sang *Peace in the Valley,*
only to be followed by a duet of Marvin Gaye
and Jackie Wilson singing *His Eye is on the Sparrow.*

Some saw John Lennon stop in and sing a song or two
in a brief appearance on his sojourn across the universe.
Some even say Hank Williams put in an appearance to sing
I Saw the Light before he faded back into the dark.

After singing themselves hoarse for hours from midnight on,
the gray dawn light of Sunday crept in and each
hard partying rocker found a place to curl up and nap.
Several hours of fitful sleep later they awoke.
After many hugs, slaps on the back, the slightly acrid
smell and taste of coffee, bacon and eggs around a large
table family style, a few hits each of coke or grass,
the rockers slowly drifted out one by one
to walk into the brilliant Sunday afternoon sun alone.

Jack White

Courageous Dream's Concern

I have driven slow,
three miles an hour or so,
through Highland Park, Heidelberg, and the
Cass Corridor.
I've hopped on the Michigan,
and transferred to the Woodward,
and heard the good word blaring from an
a.m. radio.
I love the worn-through tracks of trolley
trains breaking through their
concrete vaults,
As I ride the Fort Street or the Baker,
just making my way home.

I sneak through an iron gate, and fish
rock bass out of the strait,
watching the mail boat with
its tugboat gait,
hauling words I'll never know.
The water letter carrier,
bringing prose to lonely sailors,
treading the big lakes with their trailers,
floats in blue green chopping waters,
above long-lost sunken failures,
awaiting exhumation iron whalers,
holding gold we'll never know.

I've slid on Belle Isle,
and rowed inside of it for miles.

Seeing white deer running alongside
While I glide, in a canoe.
I've walked down Caniff holding a glass
Atlas root beer bottle in my hands
And I've entered closets of coney islands
early in the morning too.
I've taken malt from Stroh's and Sanders,
felt the black powder of abandoned
embers,
And smelled the sawdust from wood cut
to rehabilitate the fallen edifice.
I've walked to the rhythm of mariachis,
down junctions and back alleys,
Breathing fresh-baked fumes of culture
nurtured of the Latin and the
Middle East.
I've fallen down on public ice,
and skated in my own delight,
and slid again on metal crutches
into trafficked avenues.

Three motors moved us forward,
Leaving smaller engines to wither,
the aluminum, and torpedo,
Monuments to unclaimed dreaming.
Foundry's piston tempest captured,
Forward pushing workers raptured,
Frescoed families strife fractured,
Encased by factory's glass ceiling.

Detroit, you hold what one's been seeking,
Holding off the coward-armies weakling,
Always rising from the ashes
not returning to the earth.

I so love your heart that burns
That in your people's body yearns
To perpetuate,
and permeate,
the lonely dream that does encapsulate,
Your spirit, that God insulates,
With courageous dream's concern.

Michael Zadoorian

The Jams

I don't care much for rock music when I first hear it. I find this out in a classroom that fall, when one of the tough kids in my class brings in a record for Show and Tell. Before class, I hear talk between the desks that the record Barry Wegner is going to play has swearing on it. His plan is to trick our teacher Miss Ferlin into playing it in front of the class.

I have certainly heard swearing before from my mother and father, yet I somehow fear that having curse words spoken aloud in the classroom will cause some sort of disturbance, possibly even a riot. (But then I'm always worried about something causing a riot.) If that happens, I naturally assume that Barry Wegner and the other bad kids will take over the classroom, hold our teacher Miss Ferlin hostage, then maybe burn down the school for good measure.

I feel like it's up to me to do something since I'm the only boy in the class who has won a citizenship award. (Me up on stage with dozens of girls, bursting with pride, not knowing that it will make me a target for every mean kid in the school—the tauntings, hat-stealings, book up-endings, and lunch money muggings began shortly after that.) Yet I can't bring myself to tell Miss Ferlin that she's about to play an obscene recording. I don't want to be a tattle-tale, and besides if there is a riot, what will they do to me? I have to keep my mouth shut.

An older, sandy-haired kid from the A/V room rolls in a tank-like gray record player on a cart and plugs it in. The turntable silently starts to rotate.

Miss Ferlin looks out over the class. She has milky smooth skin and a "That Girl" brunette bouffant, offset strangely by a slightly oversize and stationary glass eye. (No one knows how it happened, but it's impossible to not look at it when you talk to her.) "Everyone. Barry Wegner has something for Show and Tell today."

Barry, sloth-eyed and loping, gets up before the class. When he says, "I have a new record that I want to play." Barry holds up the album and I can feel the tension in the classroom.

Miss Ferlin takes a look at it, at the collage of images on the front, at the liquidy red, white and blue letters across the top.

"It looks very—" she searches for a word. "—patriotic," is what she settles on, spotting an American flag on the cover. "Barry pulls the album out of the sleeve and holds it up. The label is black and red with a large E at the top. He leers at the class, making a big show of placing the record on the ashy felt of the turntable.

"And what is this record called, Barry?" asks Miss Ferlin.

I sit at my desk paralyzed, feeling bad about how I am letting Miss Ferlin and her glass eye and the American educational system down by allowing this to happen. Yet I'm also fascinated, wanting desperately to see what's going to happen next.

"It's called Kick Out The Jams, Miss Ferlin."

Miss Ferlin seems not exactly sure what exactly to make of the title, but she smiles pleasantly anyway. "And who's the recording artist?"

"The Motor City Five," says Barry, grinning hard.

"Oh, like the Dave Clark Five," she says approvingly. "All right then, class. Barry is going to play his record called—" She looks to him for confirmation. "Kick out the Jams?"

"Yeah," he says, staring at her glass eye.

Barry places the needle on the record and with a lurid glance toward the class he reaches over and turns up the volume all the way. The whole class somehow knows something big is coming. A sizzle of amplification fills the room. We hear the recorded whistles and hoots of an audience for a few seconds, then finally a man's voice booms out of the speaker, talking like he's being held prisoner in an echo chamber.

"Right now . . . right now . . . right now it's time to . . .

There's a long pause, then the jangle of a guitar before the man screams:

" . . . KICK OUT THE JAMS, MOTHERFUCKERS!"

After that, a series of grunts and ahhs, guitar screeches, and drum beats that sound like gunshots. There is energy crackling in the air from the record, which reminds me for a brief, gleeful moment of the drags.

And I feel pretty good—

Which is when Miss Ferlin, one eye shocked wide open, the other bored and non-committal, rushes over to the record player, where her foot hits the bottom of the tank-cart, sending it rolling across the front of the classroom. The record keeps playing.

and I guess that I could

get crazy now, baby

The music is raucous and angry and thrilling and scary. Even over all the noise, I can hear the sigh of approval from the class. Finally, Miss Ferlin pulls the plug from the wall outlet and the music grinds to a distorted halt. She pulls the needle from the record, grabs the record from the turntable, hands it to Barry Wegner, who is very obviously thrilled with what has happened. Less so when she grabs him by the arm and drags him out of the classroom.

"You are going to the Principal's office right now."

I'm happy when it's over, but there's something about the music, maybe just the volume of it, that haunts me for the rest of the day. I think about it later, when I'm in the basement building the model cars. It crosses my mind that the music I hear on my stations is not at all like what I heard today in class. Just as quickly, the idea evaporates and I continue to sing along to Sugar, Sugar.

Juan Atkins

Black Milk

The Electrifying Mojo

Proof

J. Dilla

Slum Village

Eminem

D12

Awesome Dre

Champtown

Kevin Saunderson

54 Sound

DJ Assault

Carl Craig

Steve King

Big Sean

Esham

Obie Trice

The Belleville Three

V.

HIP HOP INTO TECHNO

Lose Yourself with The Belleville 3

Eminem

Eight Mile

Sometimes I just feel like, quittin' I still might
Why do I put up this fight, why do I still write
Sometimes it's hard enough just dealin' with real life
Sometimes I wanna jump on stage and just kill mics
And show these people what my level of skill's like
But I'm still white, sometimes I just hate life
Somethin' ain't right, hit the brake lights
Case of the stage fright, drawin' a blank like
Da-duh-duh-da-da, it ain't my fault
Great big eyeballs, my insides crawl
And I clam up [wham] I just slam shut
I just can't do it, my whole manhood's
Just been stripped, I have just been vicked
So I must then get off the bus, then split
Man fuck this shit, yo, I'm goin' the fuck home
World on my shoulders as I run back to this 8 Mile Road

I'm a man, I'ma make a new plan
Time for me to just stand up, and travel new land
Time to really just take matters into my own hands
Once I'm over these tracks man I'ma never look back
(8 Mile Road) And I'm gone, I know right where I'm goin'
Sorry momma I'm grown, I must travel alone
Ain't gon' follow the footsteps I'm makin' my own
Only way that I know how to escape from this 8 Mile Road

I'm walkin' these train tracks, tryin' to regain back
The spirit I had 'fore I go back to the same crap
To the same plant, and the same pants

Tryin' to chase rap, gotta move ASAP
And get a new plan, momma's got a new man
Poor little baby sister, she don't understand
Sits in front of the TV, buries her nose in the pad
And just colors until the crayon gets dull in her hand
While she colors her big brother and mother and dad
Ain't no tellin' what really goes on in her little head
Wish I could be the daddy that neither one of us had
But I keep runnin' from somethin' I never wanted so bad
Sometimes I get upset, cause I ain't blew up yet
It's like I grew up, but I ain't grow me two nuts yet
Don't gotta rep my step, don't got enough pep
The pressure's too much man, I'm just tryin' to do what's best
And I try, sit alone and I cry
Yo I won't tell no lie, not a moment goes by
That I don't pray to the sky, please I'm beggin' you, God
Please don't let me be pigeonholed in no regular job
Yo I hope you can hear me homey wherever you are
Yo I'm tellin' you, dawg, I'm bailin' this trailer tomorrow
Tell my mother I love her, kiss baby sister goodbye
Say whenever you need me, baby, I'm never too far
But yo, I gotta get out there, the only way I know
And I'ma be back for you, the second that I blow
On everything I own, I'll make it on my own
Off to work I go, back to this 8 Mile Road

I'm a man, I'ma make a new plan
Time for me to just stand up, and travel new land
Time to really just take matters into my own hands
Once I'm over these tracks man I'ma never look back
(8 Mile Road) And I'm gone, I know right where I'm goin
Sorry momma I'm grown, I must travel alone
Ain't gon' follow the footsteps I'm makin' my own
Only way that I know how to escape from this 8 Mile Road

You gotta live it to feel it, you didn't, you wouldn't get it
Or see what the big deal is, why it was and it still is
To be walkin' this borderline of Detroit city limits
It's different, it's a certain significance, a certificate
Of authenticity, you'd never even see
But it's everything to me, it's my credibility
You never seen heard smelled or met a real MC
Who's incredible upon the same pedestal as me
But yet I'm still unsigned, havin' a rough time
Sit on the porch with all my friends and kick dumb rhymes
Go to work and serve MCs in the lunchline
But when it comes crunch time, where do my punchlines go
Who must I show, to bust my flow
Where must I go, who must I know
Or am I just another crab in the bucket
Cause I ain't havin' no luck with this little Rabbit foot, fuck it
Maybe I need a new outlet, I'm startin' to doubt shit
I'm feelin' a little skeptical who I hang out with
I look like a bum, yo my clothes ain't about shit
At the Salvation Army tryin' to salvage an outfit
And it's cold, tryin' to travel this road
Plus I feel like I'm on stuck in this battlin' mode
My defenses are so up, but one thing I don't want
Is pity from no one, the city is no fun
There is no sun, and it's so dark

Sometimes I feel like I'm just bein' pulled apart
From each one of my limbs, by each one of my friends
It's enough to just make me wanna jump out of my skin
Sometimes I feel like a robot, sometimes I just know not
What I'm doin' I just blow, my head is a stove top
I just explode, the kettle gets so hot
Sometimes my mouth just overloads the ass that I don't got
But I've learned, it's time for me to U-turn
Yo, it only takes one time for me to get burned

Ain't no fallin' no next time I meet a new girl
I can no longer play stupid or be immature
I got every ingredient, all I need is the courage
Like I already got the beat, all I need is the words
Got the urge, suddenly it's a surge
Suddenly a new burst of energy has occurred
Time to show these free world leaders the 3 and a third
I am no longer scared now, I'm free as a bird
Then I turn and cross over the median curb
Hit the 'burbs and all you see is a blur from 8 Mile Road

I'm a man, I'ma make a new plan
Time for me to just stand up, and travel new land
Time to really just take matters into my own hands
Once I'm over these tracks man I'ma never look back
(8 Mile Road) And I'm gone, I know right where I'm goin'
Sorry momma I'm grown, I must travel alone
Ain't gon' follow the footsteps I'm makin' my own
Only way that I know how to escape from this 8 Mile Road

Eminem

Lose Yourself

Look
If you had
One shot
Or one opportunity
To seize everything you ever wanted
In one moment
Would you capture it
Or just let it slip?

Yo
His palms are sweaty, knees weak, arms are heavy
There's vomit on his sweater already, mom's spaghetti
He's nervous, but on the surface he looks calm and ready
To drop bombs, but he keeps on forgettin'
What he wrote down, the whole crowd goes so loud
He opens his mouth, but the words won't come out
He's chokin', how, everybody's jokin' now
The clocks run out, times up, over, blaow!
Snap back to reality, oh there goes gravity
Oh, there goes Rabbit, he choked, he's so mad, but he won't
Give up that easy, no he won't have it, he knows
His whole back's to these ropes, it don't matter, he's dope,
He knows that, but he's broke, he's so stagnant, he knows,
When he goes back to his mobile home, that's when its
Back to the lab again yo, this whole rhapsody
Better go capture this moment and hope it don't pass him

You better lose yourself in the music,
The moment you own it, you better never let it go

You only get one shot, do not miss your chance to blow
This opportunity comes once in a lifetime

You better lose yourself in the music,
The moment you own it, you better never let it go
You only get one shot, do not miss your chance to blow
This opportunity comes once in a lifetime you better

His soul's escaping, through this hole that is gaping
This world is mine for the taking, make me king
As we move toward a new world order
A normal life is borin,' but super stardom's
Close to post mortem, it only grows harder,
Only grows hotter, he blows, it's all over
These hoes is all on him, coast to coast shows
He's known as the globetrotter, lonely roads,
God only knows, he's grown farther from home, he's no father
He goes home and barely knows his own daughter
But hold your nose 'cause here goes the cold water
His hoes don't want him no mo, he's cold product
They moved on to the next schmo who flows,
He nose dove and sold nada, so the soap opera
Is told and unfolds, I suppose it's old, partna,
But the beat goes on: da da dumb da dumb da da

You better lose yourself in the music,
The moment you own it, you better never let it go
You only get one shot, do not miss your chance to blow
This opportunity comes once in a lifetime

You better lose yourself in the music,
The moment you own it, you better never let it go
You only get one shot, do not miss your chance to blow
This opportunity comes once in a lifetime you better

No more games, I'ma change what you call rage
Tear this motherfuckin' roof off like two dogs caged
I was playin' in the beginnin', the mood all changed
I been chewed up and spit out and booed off stage
But I kept rhymin' and stepped right in the next cipher
Best believe somebody's payin' the pied piper
All the pain inside amplified by the
Fact that I can't get by with my nine-to-
Five and I can't provide the right type of life for my family
'Cause man, these God damn food stamps don't buy diapers
And it's no movie, there's no Mekhi Phifer, this is my life
And these times are so hard and it's getting even harder
Tryin' to feed and water my seed, plus teeter-totter
Caught up between bein' a father and a prima donna
Baby mama drama screamin' on and too much for me to wanna
Stay in one spot, another day of monotony's
Gotten me to the point, I'm like a snail I've got
To formulate a plot or end up in jail or shot
Success is my only motherfuckin' option—failure's not
Mom, I love you, but this trailer has got
To go, I cannot grow old in Salem's Lot
So here I go is my shot: feet fail me not
This may be the only opportunity that I got

345

You better lose yourself in the music,
The moment you own it, you better never let it go
You only get one shot, do not miss your chance to blow
This opportunity comes once in a lifetime

You better lose yourself in the music,
The moment you own it, you better never let it go
You only get one shot, do not miss your chance to blow
This opportunity comes once in a lifetime you better

You can do anything you set your mind to, man

Sasha Frere-Jones

Haiku for Eminem

The Slim LP ruled
It came right out of the blue
You were a cipher

Happy music and
self-loathing and all those words
made for good music

The way you sound black
when you are conversating
but white when you rap?

That is the one thing
people have not acknowledged
this jewel in your crown

It's original
and it obviously has
not hurt your sales, no

You don't get credit
for your answer vocals thing,
the second voice trick

Which Slick Rick did first
but you do such a good job
I cannot complain

Now it's all fear, hate

and allegedly shocking
rhymes full of fake blood

You should have won for
the great Slim Shady LP
not peevish Marshall

But like Russell Crowe
you won for Gladiator
not The Insider

Marshall heard just once
is kind of scary and fun
like a rubber mask

But things like sex and
drugs and rock and roll and joy
are fun more than once

Me myself and I
can't imagine playing it
more than once or twice

RZA wrote a song
about his wife—it was raw
and people complained

You did bad Brando
on that embarrassing song
"Kim," and people clapped

There is no excuse
for your treatment of your wife
aesthetic or no

Why is your version
of "real life" so Hollywood?
Nic Cage, please stand up

Who are these people
who allegedly hate you?
Critics wet their pants

And all the young dudes
buy and memorize your work
the day it comes out

In the New York Times—
the Eminem newsletter
perhaps I should say

They talk about you
daily and on the weekend
maybe once or twice

If you are so tough
why go after Everlast?
He's not so badass

If you are so tough
why don't you snap on black folks?
(Leave Bob Herbert out)

And why 'N Sync, huh?
You think they are equals?
Maybe that's it, yes

Insane Clown Posse?
For this you risk a record?
Please, Marshall, sit down

Brian "Champtown" Harmon

Armageddon

Sometime I wanna laugh, sometime I wanna cry
thinking about I have to live my life and then prepare to die.
Why, you ask? Don't ask me ask the maker,
the sky is falling down and pretty soon they'll be a lake of
fire, they say that's how this world's supposed to end
tornado full of fire, blowing with the winds.
The fires getting higher the heat's hot like a dryer,
the man is here to judge us, the angel's in his choir.
So if you down with God sing along with him,
cuz ain't no telling who my man gone bring along with him.
See God is coming back that's a fact, just look at how we act,
the world is based on being white or black.
See black and white are colors I judge people by their souls,
not by how they wear their hair or how they wear their clothes.
Keep em separated, that's what you hear and seeing,
the whites the black the jews and japs, we all are human beings.
So being we human, we are the human race,
the grand finale's coming he speeding up the pace.
The pace is so fast like gonzalez its speedy,
he's shutting down the liars, evil forces, and the greedy,
I can tell the difference in the world especially by the clock,
the minutes are like seconds, prepare for the big shock.
The days go like hours, the church girls are freaks,
the days go by so fast to me, a year seems like a week.

The kkk is ready, but so is farrakhan,
but Clinton got the juice he push a button that's the bomb.
The air stinks, the water from the sinks looks pink,
we better off if we start drinking ink.

The church is packed on Sunday i'm not going, am I wrong?
Why should I have to pay to pray when I can pray at home?
You love that crooked preacher, how he greet cha and treat cha.
Pay me pay me what he teach ya, then he try to beat ya. He
pass that cup around, I oughta knock it out his hand.
He picks it up and still collects and makes over a grand.
When he go to the bank to drop it off i'm waiting on his ass,
to take the money that he stole and slam him on the grass.
You crooked ass preacher cheat my people but not me i'm not dumb
you gets no love from above when revelation comes.

The Electrifying Mojo (Charles Johnson)

The Painting

On the night's sky
    The great canvas of time
        With words, music, and moods—I paint
            Wisdom, beauty, and truth
                Need never to experience restraint.

June Jordan

Owed to Eminem

I'm the Slim Lady the real Slim Lady
the real Slim Lady just a little ole lady
uh-huh
uh-huh
I'm Slim Lady the real Slim Lady
all them other age ladies
just tryin to page me
but I'm Slim Lady the real Slim Lady
and I will
stand up
I will stand up

I assume that you fume while the
     dollar bills bloom
and you magnify scum while the
     critics stay mum
and you anguish and languish runnin
     straight to the bank
and you scheme and you team with

     false balls so you rank
      at the top and you pop like the jury the
        victim
      the judge
      but the ghetto don't trip to the light
        stuff you flip
      on the chain saw you skip
      with
      the rope and the knives and that bunk
        about tying who up like a punk in the

back of the trunk
    or that dope about mothers and wives
        give you worse than a funeral hearse
    fulla
    hickies and hives
    you fudge
    where you come from or whether you
        mean it
    the shit you can't make without
    sycophants see'n it
    but nobody's dumb
    enough to believe that you grieve
        because folks
    can't conceive that you more than a
        moron
    or why would you whore on
    the hole in your soul?

    At this stage of my rage
    I'm a sage so I know how you blow
    to the left then the right and you maim
    every Columbine game about "No!
        Cuz he's white!"

But I am that I am
and I don't give a damn
and you mess with my jam
and I'll kill you
I will!

And if you insist listenin close for a dis
then you missin more than the gist in
    this
because

I gotcha pose by the nose

I hear how you laugh and cut corners
        in half
And I see you wigglin a line that's not
        flat
while you screwin around with more
        than all that

But I am that I am
and I don't give a damn
and you mess with my jam
and I'll kill you
I will!

Don't tell me you pissed or who's
        slashin whose wrists
or pretend about risks
to a blond millionaire
with a bodyguard crew that prey
behind shades and that pay
to get laid—What?
What's that about fair?

I'm not through with you!

I'm the bitch in the bedroom the
        faggot

you chump I'm the nigga for real so get
        ready to deal
I'm tired of wiggas that whine as they
        squeal
about bitches and faggots and little

girls too!
I'm a Arab I'm a Muslim I'm a
    Orthodox Jew!

I'm the bitch come to take you
I'm the faggot to fake you
outta the closet
outta the closet
fulla the slime you deposit
for fun

rhyme and run
you the number one
phony-ass gun

Oh! I am that I am
and I don't give a damn
and you mess with my jam
and I'll kill you
I will!

(Hey, Shady
you know what I'm sayin
I'm just playin!
You know I love you!)

Sincerely,
Slim Lady

Janice A. Lowe

Whazzup Nod 2 Cybotron Cosmic Cars

D-D-D-D-D- D-Troit is a 33-hour drive to LA
9 hours gets you to *NY* 4 hours is Chi-Town
and you can swim to Cleveland
but when you're a **Rhythm Origin**ator
your *Cozzmic Chrome* slices through midnight midwest funk
floats you above overlooked Lake Erie
submerges in *D-D-D-D-D-D-Troit* River deepspace
oily revolutions of 7 infinity inches

Vinyl is gas is acceleration to reverberated electro echo
Moves you to everywhere synthy horns go

Bass bath   vacation supreme
tone over tone over boom over dream
5minutes29seconds of cruise non control   ecstatic modulation
to the percussive rims

Tire writing up in this crazy is the new tagging—*Livernois* fast
combustible fantasy   consou*lllllllllllll* of beats running fat

I rarely reflect but my sound waves do
We rigged a muffler into a thrum machine right before your ears's eyes

This rolling chassis is better than the Schwinn I tricked out
with a steering wheel
badder than a union of raging lawnmowers
is the Roland TR-909 I got
thanks to *on the line* overtime

Pump the *Om-e-ters*
Om-e-ters
       Om-e-ters
Speed far away from all alone

speed far away from all alone

Nandi Comer

Detroit Tells Its Techno Story

Let me be honest.
Back in the day, I had to go to Chicago

to see my music.
We had to go Europe to be validated.

We were preps, holding up our high school clubs.
Back then rec centers turned into after hour gay bars.

Dudes would roll their coffins anywhere they'd let them play—
social clubs, supermarkets. As long as we could drop tracks,

we'd drop them big black boxes and showed the world
our speakers and turntables. And the people would break dance.

That was before NWA.
Techno was Detroit's response to Germany.

We turned Tour de France into a breakbeat.
We took Kraftwerk and mixed it with the breath of the machine.

Canadians tried to come over here and take our style,
but whatever sound they pushed out their studios

just wasn't right. It had no funk. Detroit found a way
to add a break in the breath.

Then computers had all kind of regular kids
thinking they could be creative and now we got

all kind of DJ-Noodle-Finger wannabes
dropping that booty like it's hot with no liner notes,

no album art, no live venues, no radio personality pledging by
your new hook. No way to know where you stole it from.

You can hear us in French Techno, Dubstep
in Nikki Minaj, in K-Pop and AfroBeat.

Kanye say even got his sound from us.
And still folks stumbling around the hood

talking 'bout we got no legacy. I couldn't see myself
until someone from outside told me how I looked.

Until they put my picture in the paper
my mother thought I was selling drugs.

I was always gone, always came home
with new clothes.

My friends thought I was a nobody, but they heard
my shit on the radio. They just didn't know who it was.

I ain't go to computer class. I worked three jobs
and still stole clothes from Eastland mall,

so I flew. Got on the plane a nobody
got off in Japan and I'm a somebody. A superstar.

Came home and my boys still said "Fuck that nigger."
I had a gold record and a beat up Toyota that damn near wouldn't start.

It's hard to be people in Detroit thinking on another level.

No matter how much foreign dirt I kick,

I still got home running through me.
This music passion is one of the few things that make me.

Nothing else works.
Nothing else put me on the other side of the planet.

Not the army,
not some woman,

not some rich man.
Me. My music. My machines.

Nandi Comer

Dear Derrick

Dear Derrick, because at 4am night's
broad canvas pulls tight over Detroit,
because at the end of their workday
suburban businessmen turn downtown
into a ghost town, because freeway asphalt
goes cold from no cars peeling
through city streets, your silent motor reverberates
through Detroit. Your tid-da-da tid-da-da tid-da-da
blares from my stereo. Dear Derrick,
what beat skipped in your head?
How your song stacks samples like pliable crates,
the high tuned trick you turn and build.
Dear Derrick, how many times did you
sit listening to that 1950s album
of the Detroit Symphony Orchestra before
you caught the exact moment, the exact
lull in the strings. Dear Derrick,
before I get too comfortable in your sound
you grab my ears and lead me down
another rhythm road as if to say,
"Don't get too comfortable in my song."

Dear Kevin, decades ago an alarming sound swung
through our neighborhoods. Crack turned the inner city
into an addict. While others bet their bones
in a crystallized narcotic trade you took to tracks,
trading the intergalactic. Made Deep Space as loud
as Radio Raheem's boom box. How you and
your Midwest crew quaked the world with your sound.

Dear Eddie, in every downbeat of Chaka Khan
you saw an octave waiting to be kicked down,
In every funky hook was your basement ear sweating
over a BPM measure, your damp hand, your whetted tongue,
your pull back, your missed scratch, your muted clap,
your ripped symbol. You split a jazz baseline into a 180 tempo.
At a deep sighing seconds break, you are there,
clipping up another round of Chaka's voice, turning up
treble and screwing up her tone to something
ugly enough to draw suburban kids
and garage children to an abandoned tenement.

Dear Juan, you took your Motor City
tripped it and turned it out.
You music maker breaker,
how your melody flails in my ear.
You've gone and churned another dilapidate
tune and rearranged it into this sick ass flow.
I've watched your arms' bow and arc, the space
under your fingers measuring new meters smoother
than the taut muscles in the Joe Louis' fist. Dear Juan,
you bend into yourself, turn notes over in your head,
pound out a newer, shinier, futuristic Detroit.

Dear, DJ Assault
As a girl, I slid it. I worked it. I popped it.
I freaked it. I banged. I sweated. I rump shaked.
I shook what my momma had not given me yet.
And you made me repeat. You were relentless.
You made me think I could rap.
Made me wanna grind up on some boy.
Made me wanna learn how to jit.
You made me wanna,
made me wanna,

made me wanna keep up.
But I never could.

Dear Stacey,
How you sprinkle Black Girl Magic Fairy Dust
in your wax, turn up the bass in your beat, slipped
that funk in your thump. Miss Hotwaxx,
what ghosts haunt your house enough
to make crippled men come up out of their chairs
and wobble a little two step. Miss Halle—Dear Starbooty,
why didn't you keep that name?
A girl in Detroit too young to attend your shows,
never sees your dreads live whipping around
in tune with the spin and turn of turntables
until she stumbles across your SoundCloud
and plays you on repeat. She Youtubes,
googles and Facebooks you.
Watches you bob and gig on the screen,
her quick clicks still rip and rock to your 1995 mix.

Dear Mojo, while Detroit's buildings crumbled,
you gathered the rubble, set it on repeated.
The rivet and drill of our assembly of song
clamped and cinched. You saw how the big three
was abandoning us, so you managed the approaching storm,
saw a hail driven tornado and green sky,
recorded that shit, named it our new soundtrack.
Dear Mojo. Dear futuristic songbird, churning out
the rumble and thunder of tomorrow's tunes.
You double handed man. Disco pioneer.
You had a song tucked in the fringes of your lapels.
Through your wide taste and broken tongue,
some hated you for your strayed song,
while a generation followed you till the last note.

Dear Jeff, we are still listening.
Dear Mother Cyborg, Dear Superdre, Dear Kyle,
Dear DJs, Dear sound artists, Dear Detroit. I am patient.
create your destiny, shape your future.
Do not give up on our ears.

A'leetzia Burns

Between Dexter and Linwood

I vibe out, letting my brain expand,
filling in the blank spaces
that our techno song leaves for the bruisers
and the breakers. Those who embody their graffiti
and jit their tags on its walls because
the silence of an empty space is heavy like
two tons of dried cement and builder's brick.
I think that's why, I am always standing
in the middle of two houses
with my hands extended outward,
my head back.
I'm trying to bridge the gap between present and past.
On the Westside, even the dope dealers sway
and let their arms swag,
getting ready to Crunk battle for territory
among houses that are now fields of tall grass.
The spaces are used for ghetto parking lots,
dump sights, and/or community gardens.
I dance in memory of the hopes that were abandoned here
and the hopes that are stillborn here,
I dance for the dreams with broken windows
where the doors are open, because the doors
were stolen off the hinges,
in broad daylight, yet nobody saw a thing.
The roof has caved in right there on the grass.
I jump up with every du doe du doe du doe
accompanying red and yellow flashing lights
at 7 in the morning. I shake my bones
until they synchronize with the tit tit tit tit tit tih

of the trees that line my neighborhood
as the winds knock the leaves together.
I bang bang bang my head
til I am in sync with the dribbling basketballs
boam boam boam in summer,
until I become the car-window-wobbling-bass.
I feel it rise from my feet to my chest
and reverberate here like Motown voices
in an echo chamber rose and became other-worldly.
My body and soul ignites here,
becomes a squatter's house fire in winter
where the rhythm is so hot it burns
to the bones and the bones keep burning
burning burning the house down
down down down down
until the gaps, the missing houses
resemble a smile with missing teeth.
Makes one want to ask "what happened here?"
one less house each year until there are no more.
Sounds like the breakdown of this—
our techno song
du doe du doe tit tit tit tit bang bang
boam boam   burnin' burnin'
down down down down tit tit bang
burnin' burnin' down down down
burnin' down down burning   down
Between Dexter and Linwood.

A'leetzia Burns, Ashley Rae, Nandi Comer, and Terrell Morrow

My Body as a Spaceship

1.

All systems: loaded
Hair: locking ; cotton picking Thick, and loaded. Packed [in close] with,

rocket fuel, Baby—fire baby,

take off . . .

Let this journey evolve you.

Age Continuum Travel Time

Air . . .
    Born
through layers
Mother Earth

Spins dimensions distant
Sent a distance into heavens

SYSTEMS
;Synthetic Consciousness
Meant to Inhibit Inhuman Inhabitants "SCMIII"

Some foregone pasts future predictions
free like/space travel . . .

Black/large bodies deprived of oxygenated extremities
RealTime

mission?. .to venture
before I get off'd

Take off. .into the unknown

Sending snippets of some blips of information in some pictures of a species

unwitnessed, Unwitnessed. . Un
Wit. . wit. . wit. .witnessed
(g-glitches)

In the system

Information. . . . Information:Civilization
g-(glitches)
Pre-dating

(g-glitches)

Information. .
Buffering . . .
Uploading . . .

Upload; Selfie
U-S-A, N-A-S-A

Internally, some sad poor souls
loved one's back home's gravitational pull

Like . . . somehow belong their

They can wait, it won't be long

Lights: neon,
ETA: eons away

distance:
counts: time
dreams:earth:
Corkscrew en flight pattern upon sun

Jupiter, mercury, Sodium fluoride, Mercury,
                        neurotoxin Entities

-Gas bodies

drip in JetSweat fuel
Going, fucking, nowhere.

all sciences conclude Ship optimal

Melanin suck sun into black titanium automail prosthetic

Deploying; FireArm
Retreat. .

Might get swallowed by any blackness entirely

inter-dimensional, motionless, or shallow
Mutual exclusivity

Inevitable

No matter vote

No matter hope
No matter

No man captain
On this voyage

A boy and a poem interline
Alone,

Yet, life back home depends on how well I can project

I come and peace
packing no weapon

I'm a liability in myself

My body is a spaceship

Our future depends on me.

2.

NASA has documented over 3000 potential planets.
My body is prepared to explore every one.
Your planetary systems don't include me.
My body is a spaceship. My body
has broken sprockets, a dented motor.
My jet propulsion is all rusted.
My body is a spaceship, but it is grounded.
I have not seen the dark freedom
of the galaxy for 200 years. My owner
constructed this tight planet for me,

but my body is a spaceship and this is not a metaphor.
When a record spins and the drum machine is banging

I am already lifting off, chasing my dragon
through the atmosphere. My body
a floating machine and the dance floor,
the lights, the sweaty men, the abandoned building
are all shrinking so small.

When I say my body is a spaceship
you can't wrap your head around the many wires
and systems combusting inside my chest.
In another city I am already tilt headed landing
on my own planet. My body is a spaceship.
A pulse races WARP speed toward the unknown.
Don't you see? I have been trying to escape
this atmosphere. I can't breathe this air.

There have been times my body tried imitating other machines;
attempted reconstructing metal and fuel into some earthly,
accepting image; tried to ignore the fuel running through my veins,
but I was built to run through space,
through mesosphere, through thermosphere—gone.

Earth, just try bringing me back before I start this journey.
The world is itching to wiggle its spindly fingers
through my engine. What scientist has not wondered how far
the body of a black woman can travel and bend through space?

Try to pull the sprockets for my belly. Rearrange my flight pattern.
Try collecting the start dust I've picked up. I am no planet or sea.
I am breaking the solar system with this body. My body is a space ship

3.

My body as a spaceship is smooth, titanium
Sawed in half, And propped open wide
Like some sort of freak show

Now my metal magic is
Rusting away in this dusty ass museum
This body was once home to great astronauts,
And now it is a playground for preschoolers
On field trips
Little boys with sticky hands
Leave fingerprints on my precious interior
I'm way too young of a model to be talking
Bout some back in my day
My day still today
Today I begin to rumble the engine beneath my bellowing belly
Today I rev my engine
Ready to once again
Explore all this blackness, I have been shut out from
But this time with my body as a spaceship.

4.

Self-Innovation
Is the equation I spend most of time solving
Like a 1,000 piece jigsaw puzzle if the pieces are pixels
Scatter across 20 years' worth of Televisions
When blown to supersonic proportions it is clear
That I am a Cybertron

My body is my spaceship
The kind pimped out war bus I explore in
Made of purely organic materials
I produce clean air with my metaphorical oxygen
My conversation zin
Hipped to the hip with words I spit bars that hit
Hard enough to split atoms

My mind large enough to untangle time-warps, forget quadratic equations
I slam shut black holes

Like steel clad doors
Like mouths hanging from the hinges
Negative forces are always talking
Yet have nothing to say but pixy dust and dragons
Fire breathing

When I ask them what they
Are willing to do to solve some of these very realistic problems
"Unproductive" is the type of talk that flips my switch to automated pilot
Signaling close call prayers
To thank god my engine's still running and my pipes aren't clogged with
The type of lung cancer some call global warming

I love long, because life is too short
And lonely
When you eternalize steam
So I, block
Passive aggressive messages sent
By means of purely negative charges
That is what you get for visiting intentionally distant cousins

I refrain from
Laying hands on the minutes
And packing my things
Every time I have to dodge arrows tipped with poison
From the mouths of those who claim they aren't the enemy
Instead, I practice meditation
Release steam. Breathe deeply
Focus
Purpose
I am the mission
In this body, my spaceship

Hajjar Baban, A'leetzia Burns, Ashley Rae, Nandi Comer, and Marrim Akashi

A Meditation on Music

We are swaying and then,

Effortlessly our bodies begin rising
And falling with the music
Curving into a trance like rift

And the chorus grows

It sounds too subtle not to be magic
Can't escape the night

This song becomes running

This song becomes dreaming

Becomes suspended floating
In a tricked out carousel
Where there are no horses

You can't pin this down

Without darkness being wrapped within its skin

The thunder of a pulse beating under Detroit's wrist
Under the Belle Isle Bridge

How I humble my arms and knees
To the repetition, bend to the thwack

Of a drum   Music runs through me
Like a spirit force it mounts me
Turns the ache in my neck into a head nod

Sometimes the quiet hum is enough
To take me back to the first day of my life
Or where future me says it began
In the summer we measure days by sunsets
And those by which songs call us home—to prayer
Or my mama ready to yell at me for mud pie dirty fingers
And even more vulnerabilities.

I listen to Wu Tang with my sisters
I play Mobb Deep for my love
I cry to Kendrick

I scream Jack White lyrics

My dad has an entire wall in our living room dedicated to his records
We've been told all our lives never to touch them
My sister and I make jokes to guess
At the titles of these mysterious albums
That we are banned from

I want us to make love to Frank Ocean
I want Rodrigo Amarante to play at my wedding
I want to play Nas for my kids
I want Biggie playing when they lower my casket

Sounds like pleasure
Sounds like pain
In a theater when the curtains open
And your heart is dancing a weird hustle in your chest

Building up like
Kisses to your lover
In a secret garden

T-Pain blasts at the parties I go to
Kanye plays while I clean
Payroll Giovanni played the first time my heart was broken

My crooked arms wave in praise
Praise each blip, tick and hi hat.
Each 808 or synth.
At every press of the awkward
Black and white keys listen for each
Holy hymn or hallelujah
In this future design
How it enfolds our day the hum
Of human heartbreak

Daddy taught us young,
This music was holy
I don't think we really understood
Until we built shrines of our own
'till we had tracks that we saw
Sacred
2am lying on hardwood floor
Headphones snuggly fit around my curled crown
I'm being baptized by these beats
Damn after a day like this I just need
To hear a really good song

When Kid Cudi bangs I drown in the beat
When Mary J vibrates through the speakers
I set my hands over them and feel her pain
When I rhyme with Missy Elliott I hear my childhood

When Beyoncé sings about the man she loves
I know exactly how she hurts

When I think this is memory enough
The loud beating of her creating some sort of life I never understood
In the kitchen downstairs takes me two years later
The quiet hum is a mud pie in the rear view
I can talk about it but not too much
Not when I think myself more loud beating and metals
Than hum and mellow

If veneration is in each beat
Then let everyone 1–2 1–2 1–2
Rain down on this dance floor.
Let us all bless the space with song.

Franziska Ruprecht

DETROIT

Mama, you still rock me more than Berlin
I wanna be far from my kin—just like my genes.
Wear Motown glitter plus factory jeans.
They raped at gunpoint, drive-by shot, stole wallets
gang stuff too bad for me to know it.
I walked safely in non-pedestrian areas . . .
They gave me everything I care about:
Space. Faith in me. Secret hours.

When winter paints *Eisblumen* in your lungs,
spring: voices are cracking up from the alley,
summer dirt and alcohol soup on liquor store floor
grow hunger for chili cheese fries and rock.
Fall tonight in that thing with me, free tonight
I'm generosity! Stumbling with my *Dioptrin*
imagining under huge yellow sky that over time,
and elsewhere, things would blow up more.

I should have trusted you then, Detroit,
it was the amazing all-you-can-give.
Should have stayed with you stiff,
like an inner city nerd, then
made and kept a promise like a rare man.
But since I was little in a small German city

I've known how to swim.
I remember how he carried your downtown code
with no currency below the slope of his back.
I remember the smell of American detergent plus chrome;

You'll never erode in my mind Detroit even though I bury daily
future pictures under your old railroad station . . .
swagger after this to the bridge slide down slick
I breaststroke away on my deeper straits,
can't be weighed down now by churches and disappointment.

Today. From the other side of a big lake
I take in your light from my Gatsbymansion, Detroit.
I don't even give a "whatever" if it is too dark for some.

I hug the air when no one's lookin.'

Lawrence Joseph

Epilogue. What the World (and Bob Dylan) Learned from Detroit Music

> *and in the end*
>
> *—The Beatles*

"By the 1960s Middle Eastern and Indian rhythms, scales, instruments, and time signatures were making wide inroads in modern jazz, but in 1957 Lateef was clearly a pioneer in this regard," Lars Bjorn and Jim Gallert note in *Before Motown: A History of Jazz in Detroit, 1920–60* (certain to be a classic). Born Bill Evans in 1920, changing his name after he became a follower of the Ahmadiyya Islamic movement, Yusef Lateef first became interested in Middle Eastern music while he was working in a factory. "I realized I had to widen my canvas of expression," Lateef told Jim Gallert in an interview, "Meet the Artist," at the Montreux-Detroit Jazz Festival on September 6, 1999. "I spent many hours in the library on Woodward studying the music of other cultures. At this time I was also working at Chrysler's. I met a man from Syria and he asked me if I knew about the rabat. He made me a rabat and Ernie Farrow played it on the recording. I was looking to widen my expression and made bamboo flutes on my own."

Nat Hentoff, in *Downbeat,* January 9, 1957: Detroit had become "a spawning ground . . . for modern jazz. Their blowing here is primarily of a low flame, conversational kind. They fuse and pulse well together with the rhythm section, a finely knit, flowing texture of full-sounding but not overbearing momentum." The Detroit style, according to Roland Hanna, "tells a story. You hear other pianists running notes and changes. But a musician from Detroit makes an effort to arrive at his own story and tell it in his music."

"Woodward Avenue. Big parades. The library, the museum"—Saeeda Lateef writes on the jacket of Yusef Lateef's *Detroit: Latitude 42° 30'—Longitude*

83°—"the Toddle House—BEST pecan waffles; cheap . . . Paradise Theatre . . . . The old Mirror Ballroom . . . World Stage . . . New Music Society . . . Detroit Symphony . . . Latitude." "Woodward Avenue," one of my favorite tunes on that recording—"Woodward Avenue," and "Belle Isle," and a version of "That Lucky Old Sun"—and oh yes, I almost forgot: "Eastern Market."

When I was ten years-old, I used to go to that Toddle House on Woodward and Palmer. My father and my uncle owned a store on John R., a one-way street that ran downtown, one block east of Woodward. If, from the Toddle House, you walked one block east on Palmer to John R., then one block up, there, on the southeast corner of John R. and Hendrie, was Joseph's Market. "The latter half of the 1940s," note Bjorn and Gallert, "saw the development of the 'Street of Music' in two blocks of John R., between Forest and Canfield" (nine to ten blocks south of Hendie). There's a photograph of the store from that time. Above it, a billboard, "CHEVROLET," with a two-tone-silver-and-white, '57 Chevrolet, "filled with spirit and splendor!" "JOSEPH'S MARKET. MON. WED. THUR. 9 TO 9. FRI. SAT. 9 TO 11." "YOUR NEIGHBORHOOD GROCER SINCE 1935 FREE PARKING AROUND THE CORNER." "5770 JOHN R." "BEER. WINE." "DETROIT PACKAGE LIQUOR DEALER." "BAR B. Q. TO TAKE OUT. RIBS. CHICKEN. PEPSI COLA." I'd walk to the Toddle House for lunch. For less than a dollar you could buy a hamburger, BEST fried potatoes, a Coke.

On the corner of the "Street of Music" and Canfield was a "show bar," the Flame. "Detroit's premier venue in the 1940s for black musical entertainment had been the Paradise Theatre"—Bjorn and Gallert relate—"but with the opening of the Flame in 1949 and the closing of the Paradise in November 1951, the action moved over to the Flame." The Flame was a solid testing ground for black entertainers who wanted to cross over to an adult mass audience. It was similar to the Paradise in presenting top national acts, but it also gave some room for local talent. "Berry Gordy's sister Gwen"—Bjorn and Gallert continue—"had the photo concession at the Flame with camera assistance from her sister Anna and two other brothers in the darkroom." Among the top national acts: Ella Fitzgerald, Count Basie, Billie Holiday, Dinah Washington, Billy Eckstine ("Jelly, Jelly, Star"), Sara Vaughan, Erroll Gamer. Local talent: Della Reese, Jackie Wilson, Little Willie John, Hank Ballard.

Della Reese, quoted in Arnold Shaw's *The Rockin' 50s:* "The Flame was the place to be. In Detroit, in an area of five to six blocks, there wasn't one without spots of live entertainment. Friday and Saturday nights were get-up-and-go nights, get dressed and go out. But every night was nightclub night. The Flame was the hottest spot in town. The Flame was letting your hair down."

"The Flame was a continuous show, right through the night," Johnny Ray told Shaw. Ray was "the only white guy" who appeared there, but, as far as the club was concerned, the scene was black and tan. The Flame's house band, led by Maurice King, backed Ray on his first two records. Ray's next tune, "Cry," was a number-one hit on both the pop and R&B charts. Many listeners, hearing "Cry" on the radio, assumed that Ray was black. During live performances of the song, Ray, in the middle of singing, would break down in sobs. A band member would come to his aid, helping him back onto his feet.

"I always wanted to be a guitar player and a singer," Bob Dylan, born Robert Zimmerman in Duluth in 1941, says in the notes to his *Biograph* collection. "Since I was ten, 11, or 12, it was all that interested me. That was the only thing that I did that meant anything, really." "Henrietta" was the first rock and roll record he remembers hearing. Before that he listened a lot to Hank Williams and, before that, Johnny Ray. "He was the first singer whose voice and style, I guess, I totally fell in love with. There was just something about the way he sang [the opening to 'Cry'] 'When your sweetheart sends a letter' that just knocked me out. I loved his style, and wanted to dress like him, too."

On November 22, 1980, at the Fox Warfield Theater in San Francisco, Dylan told the audience that across the lake from Duluth is a town called Detroit. When he was around twelve, he happened to go to Detroit with a friend of his who had relatives there. Though he couldn't remember how, he found himself in a bingo parlor, where, he said, people came to eat and to dance to a dance band. Where he was from, said Dylan, he'd heard mostly country music—Hank Williams, Hank Snow, "all the Hanks"—but the first time that he was face to face with rhythm and blues was in Detroit. He then broke into a wailing gospel rendition of Little Willie John's "Fever."

Amiri Baraka: "Flame itself has different colors. The old blues, spirituals, quartets, and rhythm and blues, the jazz and bebop plus the multicolored pop, the identifiable American flying object."

My father, I remember, pulled the car over to the curb on Woodward Avenue in Highland Park—in the background Henry Ford's original assembly plant, used already as a warehouse—a July Sunday afternoon, the sky absorbed by a solid red sun, and told me to listen, to listen closely—he played with the radio dial to get the sound as clear as he could—listen to how beautiful the voice was in the song that was playing: Dinah Washington's rendition of "Harbor Lights."

"I've been writing songs since I was six years old," William "Smokey" Robinson told Bill Dahl for a December 10, 1993, article, "Going to a Go-Go with Smokey Robinson and the Miracles," in *Goldmine.* "My mom and my two sisters played a lot of Sarah Vaughan. I heard all kinds of music in my house. Mostly Sarah Vaughan, Billy Eckstine, Ella Fitzgerald, Count Basie, people like that." Sarah Vaughan, Robinson said, was "probably my favorite vocalist out of all of them. She used to cry her songs. She was like an instrument to me. She just did things with her voice that only she and Ella could do." (Robinson's playmates included the Motor City's first family of gospel, the Franklin's—sisters Aretha, Carolyn and Erma among them . . . By the time he was in fifth grade, Robinson was writing songs and singing songs regularly, forming a vocal quartet in junior high school that included Aretha's brother, Cecil Franklin.) When he was eleven or twelve, Robinson became interested more, he said, "in what they termed then as the R&B music and rock and roll kind of sound." He had five idols: Clyde McPhatter, Nolan Strong, Frankie Lymon, Sam Cooke, and Jackie Wilson. (Prime examples of the R&B rock and roll kind of sound at the time were Nolan Strong and the Diablos' local hit "Mind Over Matter" and Hank Ballard and the Midnighters' top-of-the-charts "Work with Me, Annie." Ballard also wrote, and with the Midnighters recorded, "Finger Poppin' Time," and, later, "The Twist," covered by Chubby Checker.) The "greatest idol" he ever had "as far as an entertainer," Robinson told Dahl, was Jackie Wilson. "The other guys could sing, but Jackie could sing *and* dance *and* entertain."

Replacing Clyde McPhatter, who had followed Billy Ward as lead vocalist of the Dominoes, Wilson (who credited gospel singers as the main influences on his style) helped shape the doo-wop vocal group tradition in which McPhatter had been a pioneer. Wilson's first record, "Reet Petite," was written by Berry Gordy, Gordy's sister Gwen, and Tyran Carlo. "Reet Petite" never showed on the R&B charts, but went pop, selling a quarter of a million 45s. In *To Be Loved* (the title of Jackie Wilson's first number-one hit, which Gordy also wrote), Gordy tells how, in 1953, he opened, in the Gordy family's building on Farnsworth and St. Antoine (eight or so blocks from Joseph's Market), the 3-D Record Mart. At first, Gordy said, he sold only jazz recordings, but, as time went on, more and more blues. "I finally had to admit to myself blues was in my soul," he said. This probably stemmed from his early exposure to gospel. "There was an honesty about it. It was just as pure and real as jazz. In fact, jazz had its roots in the blues." Ironically, he said, the simplicity that he'd rejected in the blues was the very thing that people related to. Bjorn and Gallert: "Wilson's recordings of 'Reet Petite' and 'To Be Loved' gave Gordy a name, and singers started coming to him for material. One of them was singer/songwriter Smokey Robinson, who was the seventeen-year-old leader of the Matadors (later the Miracles)."

In his liner notes to *Detroit Blues—The Early 1950s* (which includes John Lee Hooker's "House Rent Boogie"), Paul Oliver defines the Detroit blues style. "Often [the Detroit blues musicians] play with strong piano blues and boogie players who—from the days of Will Ezell and Charlie Spand, through to Big Maceo and Floyd Taylor, to Boogie Woogie Red or Bob Thurman—have been a strong feature in Detroit blues." Drums also feature prominently in Detroit—"socking, hard-hitting, played by a Tom Whitehead, or in primitive imitation by a Washboard Willie." A number of guitarists, like Eddie Kirkland and Eddie Bums, double on harmonica, and can play the organ too, "weaving in with the sax players, who play a bigger part in Detroit blues than in that of Chicago." This complexity of instrumentation, played against steady-beat rhythms, gave birth to "a smoother, more sophisticated music where the instrumental lines were carried by vocal groups against similar rhythm backgrounds, and which borrowed freely from the gospel idioms which also form an important part of the Detroit musical scene."

Bjorn and Gallert: "Gordy decided to form his own record company, and with an eight-hundred-dollar loan from his family, Tamla was born in January 1959." In his November 7, 1959, column in the *Michigan Chronicle,* Bill Lane observed that Gordy was "the first Negro in the city to open a recording studio of any noticeable consequence" when he purchased the former Gene LeVett photo building on West Grand Boulevard. Bjorn and Gallert: "Gordy christened the new headquarters Hitsville USA and his increased control over the production, distribution, and marketing of music led to a steady flow of hits. Motown's first number-one R&B hit was the Miracles' 'Shop Around' in 1960, and the first number-one pop hit was the Marvelettes' 'Please Mr. Postman' in 1961. The Motown organization grew rapidly and eventually became the largest black-owned enterprise in the nation."

Berry Gordy: "The 'feel' was usually the first thing I'd go for. After locking in the drumbeat, I'd hum a line for each musician to start. Once we got going, we'd usually ad lib all over the place until we got the groove I wanted. Many of these guys came from a jazz background. I understood their instincts to turn things around to their liking, but I also knew what I wanted to hear—commercially. So when they went too far, I'd stop them and stress, 'We gotta get back to the funk—stay in that groove.'" Gordy would make it, he said, as plain as possible. "I would extend my arms a certain distance apart, saying, 'I want to stay between here and there. Do whatever you want but stay in that range—in the pocket.' But between 'here and there' they did all kinds of stuff—always pushing me to the limit and beyond."

William James (with whom both W. E. B. Du Bois and Gertrude Stein studied philosophy at Harvard): "When I say 'Soul,' you need not take me in the ontological sense unless you prefer to." Soul? "Only a succession of fields of consciousness: yet there is found in each field a part, or subfield, which figures as focal and contains the excitement, and from which, as from a center, the aim seems to be taken. Talking of this part"—James continues—"we involuntarily apply words of perspective to distinguish it from the rest, words like 'here,' 'this,' 'now,' 'mine' or 'me.'" To the other parts are ascribed "the positions 'there,' 'then,' 'that,' 'her,' 'his,' 'it,' 'not me.'" But, says James, "a 'here' can change to a 'there,' and 'there' become a 'here,' and what was 'mine' and what was 'not mine' change their places." What brings such changes about? The way in which the emotional excitement alters.

There: the funk, the groove. Here: in the pocket.

Are you ready?

"When the beat gets the feel, it's hard to get parted"—"you got yours and I got mine": "Monkey Time," written by Chicago's Curtis Mayfield, sung by Major Lance.

"Mickey's Monkey," written by Eddie Holland, Lamont Dozier, and Brian Holland, sung by the Miracles. "When the people see the dancing they begin to sing—lum di lum di lie." Lum di lum di lie—Detroit's Masonic Auditorium, May 1980. Smokey stops and smiles. "We don't know how to spell it, but we sure know how to say it."

Is everybody ready?

In a small yellow circle on the original purple Gordy label: "It's what's in the grooves that count."

John Lee Hooker, "Boogie Chillen'": "You know it's in 'em and it's just got to come out."

Thursday, December 16, 1965. The Fox Theatre, downtown Detroit. The *Motor Town Review.* Junior Walker and the All Stars, Martha and the Vandellas, Stevie Wonder, the Temptations, Marvin Gaye. In *Smokey: Inside My Life,* Robinson recollects: "Junior was such a big-sound, stomp-down saxist, once at the Fox he was dancing so hard, he tripped and fell into the orchestra pit. The pit was deep, but Junior was a showman, and he kept playing, his wail growing more distant the farther he fell, until he landed on his feet, his 'Shotgun' still firing." That was the night. We arrived early. Sat in the tenth or eleventh row near the aisle, as close to the stage as we could. "Shotgun"—you know—"shoot 'em before they run." Dig potatoes. Pick tomatoes. Stevie Wonder, fifteen years-old, Clarence Paul beside him scatting gospel on Bob Dylan's "Blowin' in the Wind," followed by a long, pure, frenzied expression on the mouth harp. Music. Sweet music. Music everywhere. Swinging, swaying, records playing: "Do you love me / now that I can dance–The Contours"—the epigraph to Al Young's first book of poems, *Dancing.* "The field open / the whole circle of life / is ours for the jumping into, / we ourselves the way we feel / right now": from Young's poem "Dancing in the Street." Eddie Kendrick's falsetto, a Whitfield-and-Holland song, "The Girl's All Right with Me." "Ain't that peculiar—peculiarity": written and produced by Smokey, on the Tamla label, sung by Marvin Gaye. Later, on the radio, Sam Cooke's "Having a Party," so we stopped the car, opened the doors, and danced slowly in the street.

In his unauthorized biography *Van Morrison: Inarticulate Speech of the*

Heart, John Collis reports on Morrison's appearance at the King's Hotel, Newport, South Wales, on October 6, 1993. Morrison began to lecture the audience. "This is not rock, this is not pop," he said. "This is called soul music. So instead of all the motherfucking bastards who say something different, this is what it is." After several attempts to start singing—never getting beyond "I'm a trans-Euro train"—Morrison continued. "I'm talking about soul. I'm a soul singer. I'm more a motherfucking soul singer than some motherfucking motherfucker. I'm a soul singer. I sing soul songs. Blues."

George Clinton, in an interview, "Brother from Another Planet," with Vernon Reid in *Vibe:* "We came from Motown. I always knew that I had been trained as a producer and a writer and there was nothing else like the discipline they had at Motown. Having done that, then we saw Cream and Vanilla Fudge and all of them take the music my mother liked, flip it around and make it loud, and it became cool. We realized that blues was the key to that music. We just speeded blues up and called it 'funk' 'cause we knew it was a bad word to a lot of people."

Van Morrison's *Saint Dominic's Preview,* the first cut: "Jackie Wilson said (I'm in Heaven When You Smile)." The opening lines: "Jackie Wilson said it was reet petite, kind of lovin' she gives knocks me off my feet . . ." On *The Healing Game,* the song "Sometimes We Cry," Morrison sings, "Gonna put me in a jacket and take me away, I'm not gonna fake it like Johnny Ray." On *Enlightenment,* in "In the Days before Rock 'n' Roll": "Come in, come in, come in Ray Charles, come in the high priest." "I'm down on my knees at those wireless knobs." Telefunken. Searching for Budapest. AFM. Fats and Elvis, Sonny, Lightnin', Muddy, John Lee, did not come in, no they did not come in, did not come in without those wireless knobs. Soul. Radio. This is the sound of my wavelength and your wavelength—ya radio. You turn me on when you get me on your wavelength—ya radio, ya radio.

"Pulsars, blue receding / quasars—their vibrant / radio waves. Cosmic Ouija, / what is the / mathematics of your message?": the fourth of five parts of Robert Hayden's poem "Stars."

Released in early 1962, Ray Charles's *Modern Sounds in Country and Western Music* remained on *Billboard's* pop album chart for nearly two years, fourteen weeks in the number-one position. "Not only did it gain him millions of new fans," writes Todd Everett, "the album firmly booted the thirty-one-year-old Charles from the 'R&B' category and let general (let's face it) white audiences know what connoisseurs had taken for granted for several years, that Ray Charles had something to say to virtually everybody and that there's nobody else who can tell it like Brother Ray." The LP's second-to-last cut is "That Lucky Old Sun," according to Everett, "a 1949 smash hit by Frankie Laine, written by the Tin Pan Alley tune smiths Haven Gillespie and Fred Coots."

In a three-day recording session at Blue Rock Studios in New York City in March 1971, Bob Dylan, after recording "When I Paint My Masterpiece," did covers of "That Lucky Old Sun," Ben E. King's "Spanish Harlem," and the gospel classic "Rock of Ages."

There are those who maintain that Aretha Franklin's version of "Spanish Harlem" ("a rose in *black* and Spanish Harlem") is one of her finest tunes. The June 28, 1968, cover of *Time:* "Singer Aretha Franklin. The Sound of Soul." She was around nine, Franklin recalled, when she decided to sing. Her father was the prominent Detroit clergyman, the Reverend C. L. Franklin. "The best, the greatest, gospel singers came through our home in Detroit. Sometimes they stayed with us. James Cleveland lived with us for a time and it was James who taught me how to play piano by ear." Most of what she learned vocally she learned from her father. "He gave me a sense of timing in music and timing is important in everything." The opening to Bob Dylan's 1966 book *Tarantula:* "aretha / jukebox queen of hymn & him diffused in drunk transfusion wound would heed sweet soundwave crippled & cry salute to oh great particular el dorado reel." Say what? Sweet soundwave cry salute hymn diffused great particular C-a-d-i-l-l-a-c El Dorado real. Yes, Aretha told *Newsweek* in August '67, she learned a lot from Sam Cooke. "He did so many things with his voice. So gentle one minute, swinging the next, then electrifying. Always doing something else." When he was still with the Soul Stirrers, Cooke brought his dub recording of "You Send Me" over to the Franklins' house for the family to hear. "The song became a hit, and Sam went pop." When Cooke made the change, Aretha said to herself, "I'd sure like to sing like that, too."

Soulin' Sam Cooke. "Cherie LP 1001." "Two Record Soul Pack." Written in a small box on the front cover: "BONUS 45 RPM RECORD INSIDE! Never-Before-Heard 25-Minute Rap Session by SAM COOKE 'What is

Soul.'" On the back cover: "Dedicated to J. W. Alexander, who knew the true meaning of Gospel Soul Music and became the first to convert it into Rhythm and Blues." Recorded on it, a two-part rendition of Gershwin's "Summertime," each part exactly two minutes, seventeen seconds long.

> The desire of truth bursting from within.
> Rapping and mapping every generation's survival.
> Igniting a brighter and dedicated flame.

The recently released "Deluxe Edition" of Marvin Gaye's *What Going On*. Two discs. On disc One: "Original LP Release (May 21, 1971)"; "Original Detroit Mix (April 5, 1971)" (previously unreleased); "The Foundation" ("'What's Going On' rhythm & strings mix") (previously unreleased). On disc Two: "Live at the Kennedy Center (May 1, 1972)"; "Original Single Versions"; "In the Meantime" ("Head Title aka 'Distant Lover'"). The live performance at the Kennedy Center was Gaye's first in four years. He opened with a medley, the first three songs, "That's the Way Love Is," "You," and "I Heard It Through the Grapevine," originally produced by Norman Whitfield. When he recorded for Whitfield, Gaye told David Ritz, "he had me singing so high and hard the veins in my neck nearly popped." After the medley, songs from *What Going On*. Almost two minutes into "Inner City Blues (Make Me Wanna Holler)," Marvin stops singing and begins conversing, while the band continues to play. "Now Maurice, Maurice King—Maurice King here is my arranger, here, on the piano, and, and, because I want this to be a groovy tune, what I want to do is start all over again from the top, because I want to do it, because we're in the groove now"—the band was still playing—"it's a bit more groovy now, and I want to keep it where it is, from the top, we gonna take it from the *top,* take it from the *top* now . . .

> "One, two, three, four, all right, all right, yeah, I got to have it groovy . . .
> "Dah dah dah, dah dah dah dah dah dah . . .
> "Rockets, moon shots, spend it all on have-nots . . .
> "Money we make it, 'fore we see it, you take it . . .
> "Make you wanna holler, the way they do my life, make you wanna

holler, the way they do my life, this ain't livin', no, no, ain't livin', no, no, no . . ."

Nelson George, in his beautiful elegy "The Power and the Glory," in the *Village Voice,* May 8, 1984: Marvin said he had "three different voices, a falsetto, a gritty gospel shout, and a smooth midrange close to his speaking voice. Depending on the tune's key, tone, and intention, he was able to accommodate it, becoming a creative slave to the music's will."

Marvin's "Trouble Man": "I know some places and I see some faces, got some connections, they dig my directions, what people say, that's okay, they don't bother me—I'm ready to make it, don't care about the weather, don't care about no trouble, I got myself together, I see the protection that's all around me."

Smokey's "A Love She Can Count On": "I know that you know how precious to care is, and you know, my darling, that I know that there is . . ."

Like sunshine. I got sunshine. You are my sunshine. I feel like this is the beginning, though I've loved you for a million years, and if I thought our love was ending, I'd find myself drowning in my own tears. You are the sunshine. You are the sunshine of my life. That's why I'll always be around.

Phil Spector, on the radio commenting on the Four Tops' "Reach Out": "If you *feeeeel* that you can't *goooooo oooonnn* . . . it's black Dylan."

From *The Changing Same (R&B and New Black Music),* Baraka: "But it is interpretation. The Miracles are spiritual. They sing (and sing about) feeling. Their content is about feeling . . . the form is to make feeling, etc . . . 'Walk On By,' 'Where Did Our Love Go?' 'What Becomes of the Brokenhearted?' 'The Tracks of My Tears,' high poetry in the final character of their delivery . . . A blues which bees older than Ray Charles or Lightnin' Hopkins, for that matter. 'I got to laugh to keep from cryin',' which the Miracles make, 'I got to dance to keep from cryin',' is not only a song but the culture itself. It is finally the same cry, the same people. You really got a hold on me. As old as our breath here . . . James Brown's screams, etc., are more 'radical' than most jazz musicians sound, etc. Certainly his sound is 'further out' than Ornette's."

As old as our breath. The ancient streets. The back streets. Back on the street. The street only knew your name. Back on the street again.

George Clinton answering Vernon Reid's question "How did funk come into being?": "Our show was basically R&B and we got happy and we became, you know, like churchy. And once we experienced what you could do to people just jumping around from the soul to the blues parts of our songs, we realized that nobody could even be our competition, and we didn't have to worry about doing it fast—everybody in the band would tell you that I said it's gonna take fifteen years for this to work."

Space? Marvin: "Funky space. Peaceful space. It's every place" ("A Funky Space Incarnation"). "Time for countdown, please. Give me the countdown, Zack. Here we go, here we go—you ready?"

"One, fun. Two, you. Three, me. Four, more. Five, no jive. Six, no tricks. Seven, we in heaven, eight, everything is straight. Nine, fine. Ten, next week we'll do it again."

From the top. All over again. Back on the top again. From the *top*.

Stevie Wonder's second LP—he was thirteen years-old—*Tribute to Uncle Ray*.

John Rockwell's December 26, 1986, review, "Pop: Smokey Robinson in Six-Night Engagement," in the *New York Times:* "But Mr. Robinson has hardly abandoned his falsetto. Instead, he has integrated it ever more seamlessly into his total method of vocal production, so that most of the time, one can't say for sure exactly what the proportion of 'chest tone,' 'head tone,' and falsetto really is. The now-moribund French operatic style of singing that flourished in the nineteenth century called this blending of registers a 'voix mixte,' and Mr. Robinson mixes his registers as well as any singer alive, operatic or otherwise."

Aretha Franklin's first album in seven years, the CD *A Rose Is Still a Rose*. In an interview with Christopher John Farley from "her hometown of Detroit" in *Time,* March 2, 1998: "I'm a very versatile vocalist. That's what I think a singer should be. Whatever it is, I can sing it. I'm not a rock artist. But I've done some rocking. I love the Puffy song ("Never Leave You Again") on my album. It's very jazzy, very cool, very easy."

Van Morrison, "Queen of the Slipstream": "There's a dream where the contents are visible. Where the poetic champions compose. Will you breathe not a word of this secrecy and will you still be my special rose?"

Thought. Feeling. Form. Emotion.

A rose in . . .

A bit more groovy, now, right?

A rose is . . .

Two.

Me. You.

Need a shot of rhythm, need a shot of blues. On the side? A little rock and roll just for good measure. Like, you know, when the chill bumps come up on you. When the hands start to clapping and the fingers start to popping, and your feet want to move around. When the feeling finally gets you . . .

Hey. Hey now. Hey now, go easy now, keep on keep on pushin' easy now, in the easy now, and, if you can't go easy, then just go as easy as you can.

Bob Dylan: Almost Went to See Elvis. Cool Daddy Productions. Made in Egypt. The second cut: Sam Cooke's "Cupid." Recorded at the Columbia Studios, Nashville, May 1969.

St. Andrew's Hall, Detroit, July 6, 1999. Between versions of "Silvio" and "Man in the Long Black Coat," Dylan pauses and says: "This afternoon I went over to the Motown Museum. I went over the Motown Museum and went in, and I asked the man there, 'Where's the Smokey Robinson stuff?' And he says to me, 'I don't know where the Smokey Robinson stuff is.' I say, 'Say what? You don't know where the Smokey Robinson stuff is?' 'No,' he says, 'I don't know where the Smokey Robinson stuff is.' 'Well,' I say, 'That's why I'm here. That is what I am looking for, the Smokey Robinson stuff. That's what I am here looking for. I am here looking for the Smokey Robinson stuff.'"

Compiled by Aaron Proudfoot and Kara Frank

Further Reading

I. DETROIT JAZZ: PARADISE VALLEY DAYS

Bjorn, Lars, and Jim Gallert. *Before Motown: A History of Jazz in Detroit, 1920–60.* Ann Arbor: University of Michigan Press, 2001.

Borden, Ernest H. *Detroit's Paradise Valley.* Charleston, SC: Arcadia, 2003.

Boyd. Herb. *Black Detroit: A People's History of Self Determination.* New York: Harper Collins, 2017.

Chinen, Nate. *Playing Changes: Jazz for the New Century.* New York: Pantheon Books, 2018.

DeVaeaux, Scott. *The Birth of Bebop: A Social and Musical History.* Berkeley: University of California Press, 1999.

Lateef, Yusef, and Herb Boyd. *The Gentle Giant: The Autobiography of Yusef Lateef.* Irvington, NJ: Morton Press, 2006.

Levine, Philip. *My Lost Poets. A Life in Poetry.* New York: Knopf, 2018.

Milan, Jon. *Detroit Ragtime and the Jazz Age.* Charleston, SC: Arcadia, 2009.

Porter, Lewis. *John Coltrane: His Life and Music.* Ann Arbor: University of Michigan Press, 2008.

Slobin, Mark. *Motor City Music: A Detroiter Looks Back.* New York: Oxford University Press, 2018.

Szwed, John F. *Billie Holiday: The Musician and the Myth.* New York: Penguin Books, 2016.

Williams, Jeremy. *Detroit: The Black Bottom Community.* Charleston, SC: Arcadia, 2009.

II. DETROIT BLUES: HASTING STREET OPERA

Baraka, Amiri. *Blues People: Negro Music in White America.* New York: Perennial, 2002.

Beaumont, Daniel. *Preachin' the Blues: The Life and Times of Son House by Daniel Beaumont.* New York: Oxford University Press, 2011.

Davis, Angela. *Blues Legacies and Black Feminism: Gertrude 'Ma' Rainey, Bessie Smith, and Billie Holiday.* New York: Vintage, 1999.

Hooker, John Lee. *John Lee Hooker—A Blues Legend.* New York: Goodman, 1991.

Livingston, Stanley, and Michael Erlewine. *Blues in Black & White the Landmark Ann Arbor Blues Festivals.* Ann Arbor: University of Michigan Press, 2010.

III. NORTHERN SOUL: DANCING IN THE STREETS

Benjaminson, Peter. *The Lost Supreme: The Life of Dreamgirl Florence Ballard.* Chicago Review Press, 2009.

———. *Mary Wells: The Tumultuous Life of Motown's First Superstar.* Chicago Review Press, 2012.

———. *The Story of Motown.* New York: Grove, 1979.

Boland, S.R., and Marilyn Bond. *The Birth of the Detroit Sound: 1940–1964.* Charleston, SC: Arcadia, 2002.

Douglas, Tony. *Jackie Wilson: The Man, the Music, the Mob.* Edinburgh, UK: Mainstream, 2001.

Early, Gerald Lyn. *One Nation under a Groove: Motown and American Culture.* Ann Arbor: University of Michigan Press, 2009.

Edmonds, Ben. *Marvin Gaye: What's Going On and the Last Days of the Motown Sound.* Edinburgh, UK: Canongate, 2003.

Gaye, Jan, and David Ritz. *After the Dance: My Life with Marvin Gaye.* New York: Amistad, 2015.

George, Nelson. *Where Did Our Love Go?: The Rise and Fall of the Motown Sound (Music in American Life).* Champaign–Urbana: University of Illinois Press, 2007.

Hirshey, Gerri. *Nowhere to Run: The Story of Soul Music.* London, UK: Southbank, 2006.

Jordan, Herb, ed. *Motown in Love: Lyrics from the Golden Era.* New York: Pantheon, 2006.

Liebler, M.L. *Heaven Was Detroit. Detroit Music from Jazz to Hip Hop & Beyond.* Detroit: Wayne State University Press, 2016.

Maraniss, David. *Once in a Great City: A Detroit Story.* New York: Simon & Schuster, 2016.

Morgan, Pat. *Motown Artist by Artist.* G2 Entertainment, 2015.

Posner, Gerald. *Motown: Music, Money, Sex, and Power.* New York: Random House, 2005.

Reeves, Martha, and Mark Bego. *Dancing in the Street: Confessions of a Motown Diva.* New York: Hyperion, 1994.

Ribowsky, Mark. *Signed, Sealed, and Delivered: The Soulful Journey of Stevie Wonder.* Hoboken, NJ: Wiley, 2010.

Ritz, David. *Divided Soul: The Life of Marvin Gaye.* New York: Omnibus, 2005.

———. *Respect: The Life of Aretha Franklin.* New York: Little, Brown, 2016.

Ross, Diana. *Secrets of a Sparrow.* New York: Villard, 1993.

Ryan, Jack. *Recollections The Detroit Years: The Motown Sound by the People Who Made It.* Ed. Thomas J. Saunders. Whitmore Lake, MI: Glendower Media, 2011.

Smily, Tavis, and David Ritz. *Before You Judge Me: The Triumph and Tragedy of Michael Jackson's Last Days.* New York: Little, Brown, 2016.

Smith, Suzanne E. *Dancing in the Street: Motown and the Cultural Politics of Detroit.* Cambridge, MA: Harvard University Press, 2001.

Stevenson, William Mickey. *Motown's First A & R Man Presents: The A & R Man.* Los Angeles: Stevenson International Entertainment, 2015.

Szwed, John F. *Billie Holiday: The Musician and the Myth.* New York: Penguin Books, 2016.

Werner, Craig Hansen. *A Change Is Gonna Come: Music, Race and the Soul of America.* Ann Arbor: University of Michigan Press, 2006.

Whitall, Susan. *Fever: Little Willie John's Fast Life, Mysterious Death and the Birth of Soul: The Authorized Biography.* London, UK: Titan, 2011.

———. *Women of Motown: An Oral History (For the Record).* New York: Harper Perennial, 1998.

Wilson, Mary. *Dreamgirl: My Life as a Supreme.* New York: St Martin's, 1986.

IV. (PART ONE) DETROIT ROCKS: KICK OUT THE JAMS

Bartkowiak, Matthew J. *The MC5 and Social Change: A Study in Rock and Revolution.* Jefferson, NC: McFarland, 2009.

Callwood, Brett. *The Stooges: Head On, A Journey through the Michigan Underground.* Detroit: Wayne State University Press, 2011.

Carson, David A. *Grit, Noise, and Revolution: The Birth of Detroit Rock 'n' Roll.* Ann Arbor: University of Michigan Press, 2006.

Carson, David. *Rockin' Down the Dial: The Detroit Sound of Radio from Jack the Bellboy to the Big 8.* Troy, MI: Momentum Books, 2000.

Coffey. Dennis. *Guitars, Bars and Motown Stars.* Ann Arbor: University of Michigan Press, 2009.

Cosgrove, Stuart. *Detroit 67: The Year That Changed Soul.* Edinburgh, UK: Polygon, 2017.

Davis, Michael. *I Brought Down the MC5.* Los Angeles: Cleopatra Press, 2018.

Early, Leo. *The Grande Ballroom: Detroit's Rock 'n' Roll Palace.* Charleston, SC: The History Press, 2016.

Gold, Jeff, and Iggy Pop. *Total Chaos: The Story of The Stooges, as Told by Iggy Pop.* Nashville, TN: Third Man Books, 2016.

Grimshaw, Gary, and Leni Sinclair. *Detroit Rocks!* Detroit Artists Workshop Press, 2012.

Harris, Bob, and John Douglas Peters. *Motor City Rock and Roll: The 1960s and 1970s.* Charleston, SC: Arcadia, 2008.

Hasted, Nick. *Jack White: How He Built an Empire from the Blues.* New York: Overlook Omnibus, 2016.

Hilburn, Robert. *Paul Simon: The Life.* New York: Simon and Schuster, 2018.

Hoffmann, Jens. *Sonic Rebellion: Music as Resistance: Detroit 1967–2017.* Museum of Contemporary Art Detroit, 2018.

Jackson, Andrew Grant. *1965: The Most Revolutionary Year in Music.* New York: Thomas Dunne Books, 2018.

James, Billy. *An American Band: The Story of Grand Funk Railroad.* London, UK: SAF, 1999.

Kramer, Wayne. *The Hard Stuff: Dope, Crime, the MC5 and My Life of Impossibilities.* Boston: Da Capo Press, 2018.

McLeese, Don. *The MC5's Kick Out the Jams.* New York: Bloomsbury Academic, 2005.

Miller, Steve. *Detroit Rock City: The Uncensored History of Rock 'n' Roll in America's Loudest City*. Boston: Da Capo Press, 2013.

Ryder, Mitch. *Devils and Blue Dresses: My Wild Ride as a Rock and Roll Legend*. Cool Titles, 2011.

Simmons, Michael, and Cletus Nelson. *The Future Is Now!: An Illustrated History of the MC5*. London, UK: Creation, 2004.

Sinclair, John. *Guitar Army: Rock and Revolution with The MC5 and the White Panther Party*. Los Angeles: Process, 2007.

———. *It's All Good: A John Sinclair Reader*. London, UK: Headpress, 2009.

Sugrue, Thomas J. *Detroit 1967: Origins, Impacts, Legacies*. Detroit: Wayne State University Press, 2017.

IV. (PART TWO) DETROIT ROCKS INTO THE '70S AND BEYOND: FROM EVERYONE LOVES ALICE TO CASS CORRIDOR PUNK TO DEATH

Bangs, Lester. *Psychotic Reactions and Carburetor Dung*. New York: Anchor, 2003.

Clinton, George. *Brothas Be, Yo Like George, Ain't That Funkin' Kinda Hard On You?: A Memoir*. New York: Atira Books, 2017.

Delicato, Armando, and Elias Khalil. *Detroit's Cass Corridor*. Charleston, SC: Arcadia, 2012.

Derogatis, Jim. *Let It Blurt: The Life and Times of Lester Bangs, America's Greatest Rock Critic*. New York: Broadway, 2000.

DeWitt, Howard A. *Searching for Sugar Man: Sixto Rodriguez' Mythical Climb to Rock N Roll Fame and Fortune*. Scottsdale, AZ: Horizon, 2015.

Dunaway, Dennis, and Chris Hodenfield. *Snakes! Guillotines! Electric Chairs!: My Adventures in The Alice Cooper Group*. New York: Thomas Dunne, 2015.

Graff, Gary. *Travelin' Man: On the Road and Behind the Scenes with Bob Seger*. Detroit: Wayne State University Press, 2010.

Hackney, Bobby Dean. *Rock-N-Roll Victims, the Story of a Band Called Death: My Story of Growing up in Detroit, My Family, and Rock-N-Roll*. Self-published, BookBaby, 2015.

Handyside, Chris. *Fell in Love with a Band: The Story of the White Stripes*. New York: St. Martin's, 2004.

Matheu, Robert, and Brian J. Bowe. *CREEM: America's Only Rock 'N' Roll Magazine*. New York: Collins Living, 2007.

Rettman, Tony. *Why Be Something That You're Not: Detroit Hardcore 1979–1985*.

Huntington Beach, CA: Revelation Records, 2010.

Rudick, Nicole. *Return of the Repressed: Destroy All Monsters 1973–1977.* Ed. Mike Kelley and Dan Nadel. New York: PictureBox, 2011.

Simone, Alina. *Madonnaland: and Other Detours into Fame and Fandom.* Austin: University of Texas Press, 2016.

Smith, Patti. *M Train.* New York: Bloomsbury, 2016.

Strydom, Craig Bartholomew, and Stephen "Sugar" Segerman. *Sugar Man: The Life, Death and Resurrection of Sixto Rodriguez.* New York: Bantam, 2015.

Sullivan, Denise. *The White Stripes: Sweethearts of the Blues.* San Francisco: Backbeat Books, 2004.

Whitall, Susan. *Joni on Joni: Interviews and Encounters with Joni Mitchell.* London, UK: Titan, 2018.

V. HIP-HOP INTO TECHNO: LOSE YOURSELF WITH THE BELLEVILLE 3

Dawkins, Marcia Alesan. *Eminem: The Real Slim Shady.* Santa Barbara, CA: Praeger, 2013.

Eminem. *The Way I Am.* New York: Plume, 2009.

Ferguson, Jordan. *J Dilla's Donuts.* New York: Bloomsbury Academic, 2014.

George, Nelson. *Hip Hop America.* New York: Penguin, 2005.

Hanf, Mathias Kilian. *Detroit Techno: Transfer of the Soul through the Machine.* Saarbrücken, Germany: VDM Verlag Dr. Müller, 2010.

Hasted, Nick. *The Dark Story of Eminem.* New York: Omnibus, 2011.

Matos, Michaelangelo. *The Underground Is Massive: How Electronic Dance Music Conquered America.* New York: Dey Street, 2015.

Miller, Steve. *Juggalo: Insane Clown Posse and the World They Made.* Boston: Da Capo Press, 2016.

Needs, Kris. *George Clinton: The Cosmic Odyssey of the P-Funk Empire.* New York: Omnibus, 2014.

Parker, Scott F. *Eminem and Rap, Poetry, Race: Essays.* Jefferson, NC: McFarland, 2014.

Reynolds, Simon. *Energy Flash: A Journey Through Rave Music and Dance Culture.* New York: Soft Skull, 2012.

Violent J (Joseph Bruce), and Hobey Echlin. *ICP: Behind the Paint.* Royal Oak, MI: Psychopathic Records, 2003.

Contributors

Marrim Akashi participated as a student in the InsideOut Techno Poetics Project 2016 in Detroit with poet Nandi Comer.

Mark James Andrews has worked as a gravedigger, inspector at a defunct auto plant, and a librarian. He is the author of *Burning Trash*. His poems, stories, and reviews have appeared in many print and online venues, most recently or upcoming in *Short Fast and Deadly, Red Fez, Wayne Literary Review,* and *Lummox Anthology*. He lives and writes just outside the Detroit city limits most of the time.

Glen Armstrong holds an MFA in English from the University of Massachusetts, Amherst and teaches writing at Oakland University in Rochester, Michigan. He edits a poetry journal called *Cruel Garters* and has three recent chapbooks: *Set List, In Stone,* and *The Most Awkward Silence of All*. His work has appeared in *Poetry Northwest, Conduit,* and *Cloudbank*.

Hajjar Baban served as the 2017 Detroit Youth poet laureate and was a First Wave scholar at the University of Wisconsin–Madison. She is a Pakistan-born, Afghan-Kurdish writer and has recently performed at the Poetry Foundation in Chicago and the Gracie Mansion in New York City. Her debut collection of poems, *Relative to Blood,* is forthcoming from Penmanship Books. She spends most of her time avoiding running from herself. Hajjar participated in the InsideOut Techno Poetics Program in 2016.

Peter Balakian is the author of seven books of poems and four books of prose. *Ozone*

Journal won the 2016 Pulitzer Prize for poetry, and *Black Dog of Fate* won the PEN/ Albrand Prize for memoir. He teaches at Colgate University.

Jan Beatty's books include *Jackknife: New and Selected Poems, The Switching/Yard, Red Sugar, Boneshaker,* and *Mad River,* published by the University of Pittsburgh Press. Beatty worked as a waitress for fifteen years, a welfare caseworker, and as a social worker and teacher in maximum-security prisons.

Ben Blackwell is the creator and director of Cass Records, a poet and writer, one of two drummers in the Detroit-based rock band the Dirtbombs, a music writer, and a vinyl record collector. He's an employee at Third Man Records and the official archivist of the White Stripes.

David Blair (or simply **Blair** on stage) was born in Newton, New Jersey, in 1967—co-incidentally, a fateful year of urban rebellions—and he died on August 2011 in Detroit. He was a much loved member of the Detroit poetry community, and a major figure on the national and international slam poetry scene. Blair garnered many awards and performed his unique brand of poetry as far away as South Africa and Russia. He was a 2010 Callaloo Fellow, was nominated seven times for the Detroit Music Awards and won in 2007, which was also the year he earned a BENT Writing Institute Mentor Award. He churned out seven records in ten years. In 2010, he and his band, The Boyfriends, released *The Line* on Repeatable Silence Records. He led the Detroit Slam Team to its National Championship back in 2002. His first and only book of poems was *Moonwalking.*

Arthur "Blind" Blake is a figure of enormous importance in American music. Not only was he one of the greatest blues guitarists of all time, but also Blake seems to have been the primary developer of "finger-style" ragtime on the guitar, the six-string equivalent to playing ragtime on the piano. Blake mastered this form so completely that few, if any, guitarists who have learned to play in this style since Blake have been able to match his quite singular achievements in this realm. Blind Blake was the most frequently recorded blues guitarist in the Paramount Records' race catalog; indeed, Paramount waxed him as often as they could, as he was their best-selling artist. By the time the Paramount label folded in the fall of 1932, Blake had recorded an amazing seventy-nine known sides for them under his own name and had contributed accompaniments to Paramount recordings by other artists such as Gus Cannon, Papa Charlie Jackson, Irene Scruggs, Ma Rainey, and Ida Cox to name only a few.

Heather Bourbeau's fiction and poetry have been published in *100 Word Story, Cleaver, Duende, Eleven Eleven,* Francis Ford Coppola Winery's Chalkboard, *Open City,* and *The Stockholm Review of Literature.* She has been nominated for a Pushcart Prize and has worked for the UN peacekeeping mission in Liberia and UNICEF Somalia.

Melba Joyce Boyd is an award-winning poet and author of nine books of poetry. She received the Library of Michigan Award for Poetry for *Roses and Revolutions: The Selected Writings of Dudley Randall.* Other awards for her literary works include awards from the Black Caucus of the American Library Association, the NAACP Image Award Honor, the Independent Publishers Award for Poetry, and the ForeWord Honor. She is a Distinguished Professor of African American Studies at Wayne State University, and an Adjunct Professor at the University of Michigan in the Department of Afroamerican and African Studies. Her poetry has been translated into German, Italian, French, and Spanish. She is a documentary filmmaker, and has published over one hundred essays on African American culture in academic and cultural journals in the United States and Europe.

Billy Bragg is a well-known singer and songwriter from the United Kingdom. Popular for his first album, *Life's a Riot with Spy vs Spy,* he has also established himself as a left-wing activist. His music is composed of various inspirational words that help the younger generation involved in activist causes. Talented and industrious, Billy Bragg was born in Barking, Essex, England, United Kingdom. Billy is a longtime fan of Motown Music.

Charles W. Brice is the author of *Flashcuts Out of Chaos* (2016) and *Mnemosyne's Hand* (2018). His poetry has been nominated for a Pushcart Prize and has appeared in over fifty publications, including *The Atlanta Review, Chiron Review,* and *SLAB.*

L. Soul Brown is a Boston writer whose work reflects the cultural expressions and sociopolitical struggles of the African diaspora. Influenced by the Black Arts Movement, her poems can be found in *The Anthology of Liberation Poetry* and *From Totems to Hip-Hop: A Multicultural Anthology of Poetry Across the Americas, 1900–2002*. She is a graduate of Framingham State University (MPA) and Tufts University (BA).

A'leetzia Burns participated in the InsideOut Techno Poetics Program in 2016, and graduated from Wayne State University in May of 2019.

Writer L. Bush is an award-winning, internationally published poet, author, and activist. Writer L. Bush has labored in the literary field for twenty years. He won the Barrett Award for his seminal work, *The God's Eye Spider* (1998). Writer is also an essay contributor to Tonja Bagwell's anthology: *Step Into My Shoes: Expressions From The LGBTQ Community* (2011). His novels *Kill Switch* (2007) and *Shadows in the Sunlight* (2008) are featured in the Wayne State University African American Literature Special Collection. For his best-seller, *Hanna Valentine* (2013), Writer was selected as one of Detroit's Top Authors in 2013 by CBS News. Writer published *The Left Handed Boy* and *The Ugly Americans* in 2018. His website is www.wlbush.com.

Ginny Carr is the leader/founder, musical director, alto voice, and principal songwriter/arranger for the internationally acclaimed Uptown Vocal Jazz Quartet (UVJQ). She has emerged as a composer, lyricist, and vocal arranger of distinction, especially for her signature compositions on UVJQ's 2012 CD, *Hustlin' for a Gig*. Press, radio, and celebrity artists have praised Ginny's work as a standout for its creative originality and have described her delightfully literate lyrics, elegant melodies, and tight vocal harmony arrangements as "vocalese at its best" and "old school moving to new cool."

UVJQ has made the Billboard Top 25 Jazz Albums Chart, stood multiple weeks on Amazon's Top Seller list, been selected as a *Washington Post* Editor's Pick and received many other accolades of distinction. They have been interviewed twice on NPR's "Weekend Edition" and been played and profiled on countless radio programs worldwide, including Satellite Radio's Jazz Channel, Pandora Radio, and Radio Jazz Smithsonian. Ginny holds a psychology degree from the College of William and Mary and a music education degree from Virginia Commonwealth University. She works full-time as a Training Specialist at the Library of Congress and moonlights as a professional pianist and solo entertainer in the Washington, DC area, in addition to her work with Uptown Vocal Jazz Quartet.

Hayan Charara is the author of three poetry books, *The Alchemist's Diary* (2001), *The Sadness of Others* (2006), and *Something Sinister* (2016). He also edited *Inclined to Speak* (2008), an anthology of contemporary Arab American poetry, and is series editor with Fady Joudah of the Etel Adnan Poetry Prize.

Esperanza Cintrón is the author of three books of poetry. Her first, *Chocolate City Latina,* was published by Swank Books in 2005. *What Keeps Me Sane,* her second, was published by Lotus/Wayne State University Press and won the 2012 Naomi Long Madgett Award. *Visions of a Post-Apocalyptic Sunrise* was published by Stockport Flats in 2014. Her essays and fiction appear in a number of anthologies. She has a doctorate in English literature from SUNY Albany and teaches literature and writing at a college in her native Detroit.

Andrei Codrescu, born in Sibiu, Transylvania, Romania, emigrated to the United States in 1966. His first poetry book, *License to Carry a Gun,* won the 1970 Big Table Poetry award. He founded *Exquisite Corpse: a Journal of Books & Ideas* in 1983, taught literature and poetry at Johns Hopkins University, University of Baltimore, and Louisiana State University where he was MacCurdy Distinguished Professor of English. He's been a regular commentator on NPR's *All Things Considered* since 1983, and received a Peabody Award for writing and starring in the film *Road Scholar.* In 1989 he returned to his native Romania to cover the fall of the Ceausescu regime for NPR and ABC News, and wrote *The Hole in the Flag: An Exile's Story of Return and Revolution.* After his return, he reconnected with Romania and started to write again in his native language, producing a separate body of work in poetry, essay, and criticism. English remains his primary language, the site of his many books of poetry, novels, essays; the most recent are *The Art of Forgetting: New Poems* (2016), *Bibliodeath: My Archives (with Life in Footnotes)* (2012), *So Recently Rent a World: New and Selected Poems* (2012), *Whatever Gets You Through the Night: A Story of Sheherezade and The Arabian Entertainments* (2011), *The Posthuman Dada Guide: Tzara and Lenin Play Chess* (2009), and *The Poetry Lesson* (2010). His work, correspondence, notebooks, art works, and sundry related documents are at the Hill Memorial Library at LSU in Baton Rouge, the Slavic Library at the University of Illinois in Champaign-Urbana, and the collection of Twentieth-Century Avant-Garde Art at the University of Iowa in Iowa City.

Nandi Comer has received fellowships from Virginia Center for the Arts, Cave Canem, and Callaloo. Her poems and essays have appeared or are forthcoming in *To Light a Fire: 20 Years with the InsideOut Literary Arts Project* (2014), *Detroit Anthology* (2014), *Another and Another: An Anthology From the Grind Daily Writing Series* (2012), *Callaloo, Crab Orchard Review, Green Mountains Review, Prairie Schooner Review, Southern Indiana Review,* and *Sycamore Review.*

Desiree Cooper is the award-winning author of *Know the Mother* from Wayne State University's Made in Michigan Series. She is a former attorney, Pulitzer Prize–nominated journalist, and Detroit community activist whose fiction dives unflinchingly into the intersection of racism and sexism. Using the compressed medium of flash fiction, she explores intimate spaces to reveal what it means to be human. Her fiction and poetry have appeared in *Callaloo, Detroit Noir, Best African American Fiction 2010,* and *Tidal Basin Review,* among other online and print publications. Cooper was a founding board member of Cave Canem, a national residency for emerging black poets. She is currently a Kimbilio Fellow, a national residency for African American fiction writers.

David Cope: b. 1948 Detroit, raised on Thornapple River. Six books: *Quiet Lives,* foreword by Allen Ginsberg, 1983; *On The Bridge,* 1986; *Fragments from The Stars,* 1990; *Coming Home,* 1993; *Silences for Love,* 1998; *Turn the Wheel,* 2003. Seventh book, *Moonlight Rose in Blue: Selected Poems,* forthcoming. 1988 Award in Literature, American Academy and Institute of Arts and Letters. Editor and publisher, *Big Scream* poetry magazine, 1974–present, *Nada Poems,* 1988, and *Sunflowers and Locomotives: Songs for Allen, elegies for Allen Ginsberg,* 1998. Coeditor of *Demotic Fire:* the post-beat poets, still unpublished. Teaches women's studies, Shakespeare, drama, and creative writing at Grand Rapids Community College. Archive, David Cope papers, at the University of Michigan Special Collections Library. David is an avid kayaker and gardener.

Jim Daniels is the author of numerous poetry and fiction books, including the recent *Rowing Inland, Street Calligraphy,* and *The Middle Ages,* in poetry and *Eight Mile High.* and *The Perp Walk* in fiction. A native of Detroit, Daniels is the Thomas S. Baker University Professor at Carnegie Mellon University.

iBRAHIM dEATHRAY, born Roderick Herrera, October 14, 1972, in the Philippines. *Welcome to Doom Town* is his collection of poetry/rants and digital collages.

Diane DeCillis' poetry collection, *Strings Attached* (2014) has been honored as a Michigan Notable Book for 2015, won the 2015 Next Generation Indie Book Award for poetry, and was a finalist for the Forward Indie Fab Book Award for poetry. Her poems have been nominated for three Pushcart Prizes, and for Best American Poetry. Her poems and essays have appeared in *CALYX, Evansville Review, Minnesota Review, Nimrod International Journal, Connecticut Review, Gastronomica, Rattle, Slipstream, Southern Indiana Review, William and Mary Review,* and numerous other journals. She currently teaches advanced poetry for Springfed Arts in Detroit.

Toi Derricotte is the author of *The Undertaker's Daughter* (2011) and four earlier collections of poetry, including *Tender,* winner of the 1998 Paterson Poetry Prize. Her literary memoir, *The Black Notebooks* received the 1998 Anisfield-Wolf Book Award for Nonfiction and was a *New York Times* Notable Book of the Year. Her honors include, among many others, the 2012 Paterson Poetry Prize for Sustained Literary Achievement, the 2012 PEN/Voelcker Award for Poetry, the Lucille Medwick Memorial Award from the Poetry Society of America, two Pushcart Prizes, and the Distinguished Pioneering of the Arts Award from the United Black Artists. Derricotte is the cofounder of Cave Canem Foundation (with Cornelius Eady), professor emerita at the University of Pittsburgh, and was a chancellor of the Academy of American Poets.

Detroit Count (Bob White) moved to Detroit in 1938. He worked and recorded in Detroit into the late 1940s. His recordings include the (78 rpm JVB single) *Hastings Street Opera*. Very little else is known about the Count aside from his epic *Opera,* the lyrics of which have never been officially available. M. L. Liebler transcribed these from his own recording of *The Hastings Street Opera*.

Fats Domino was born in the Big Easy (New Orleans) in 1928. Pianist, singer, and songwriter, Fats Domino ultimately sold more records (65 million) than any fifties-era rocker except Elvis Presley. Between 1950 and 1963, he made Billboard's pop chart sixty-three times and its R&B chart fifty-nine times. Incredible as it may seem, Fats Domino scored more hit records than Chuck Berry, Little Richard, and Buddy Holly put together. His best-known songs include "Ain't That a Shame," "Blueberry Hill," and "I'm Walkin.'" He passed away on October 25, 2017.

Mark Donovan is a poet and songwriter who lives in the suburbs of Detroit with a passion for live music that has led him to explore the city and find a river of music that flows from simple soulful soliloquies to rampant rushing rock and roll.

Sean Thomas Dougherty is the author or editor of fifteen books including *The Second O of Sorrow* (2018) and *Double Kiss: Stories, Poems, Essays on the Art of Billiards* (2017).

Rita Dove was born in Akron, Ohio, the daughter of one of the first black chemists in the tire industry. Dove was encouraged to read widely by her parents and excelled in school. She was named a Presidential Scholar, one of the top one hundred high-school graduates in the country, and attended Miami University in Ohio as a National Merit Scholar. After graduating, Dove received a Fulbright to study at the University of Tübingen in West Germany, and later earned an MFA at the Iowa Writers' Workshop where she met her husband, the German writer Fred Viebahn. Dove made her formal literary debut in 1980 with the poetry collection *The Yellow House on the Corner,* which received praise for its sense of history combined with individual detail. The book heralded the start of long and productive career, and it also announced the distinctive style that Dove continues to develop. In works like the verse-novel *Thomas and Beulah* (1986), which won the Pulitzer Prize, *On the Bus with Rosa Parks* (1999), a finalist for the National Book Critics Circle Award, and *Sonata Mulattica* (2009), Dove treats historical events with a personal touch, addressing her grandparents' life and marriage in early twentieth-century Ohio, the battles and triumphs of the civil rights era, and the forgotten career of black violinist and friend to Beethoven, George Polgreen Bridgetower.

Donald Duprie: songwriter, firefighter, drinker, fighter, out-all-nighter. Born, raised, works and lives in the great city of River Rouge, Michigan. I'm not livin for the craft, I'm dyin for it. It is the love of my life.

Poet/Playwright/Songwriter **Cornelius Eady** was born in Rochester, New York, in 1954, and is the author of several poetry collections: *Kartunes; Victims of the Latest*

Dance Craze, winner of the 1985 Lamont Prize; *The Gathering of My Name,* nominated for the 1992 Pulitzer Prize in Poetry; *You Don't Miss Your Water; The Autobiography of a Jukebox; Brutal Imagination, Hardheaded Weather* (2008), and the anthologies *Every Shut Eye Ain't Asleep, In Search of Color Everywhere,* and *The Vintage Anthology of African American Poetry, (1750–2000).* He wrote the libretto to Diedra Murray's opera *Running Man,* which was short listed for the Pulitzer Prize in Theatre, and his verse play *Brutal Imagination* won the Oppenheimer Prize for the best first play from an American playwright in 2001. He was awarded tenure at SUNY Stony Brook in 1995, and holds a PhD in the Arts (Hon) from the University of Rochester (2010). His awards include fellowships from the NEA, the Guggenheim Foundation, and the Rockefeller Foundation, a Lila Wallace-*Reader's Digest* Traveling Scholarship, and *The Prairie Schooner* Strousse Award. He is cofounder of the Cave Canem Foundation, and was, before returning to Stony Brook, the Miller Family Endowed Chair in Literature and Writing and professor in English and theater at the University of Missouri–Columbia.

Robin Echiele was born in Santa Monica four months before Pearl Harbor. Camped out during early years in California, Delaware, and Western Pennsylvania. Product of Monteith College, Wayne State University, the London School of Film Technique, and years of autodidact mountaintops. Heavily influenced by Dickens, Whitman, and Black Mountain poets in specific, and New American poets in general. One of the founders of the Detroit Artists' Workshop Society and the Detroit Artists' Workshop Press. Read his work at the 1965 Berkeley Poetry Conference as part of the Young Poets program. Found in the archives of many small poetry publications.

W. D. Ehrhart teaches history and English at Haverford School for Boys in suburban Philadelphia. A Marine Corps veteran of the American War in Vietnam, he is the author of numerous books of poetry and prose. His newest collection of poems is *Praying at the Altar* from Adastra Press.

The Electrifying Mojo (Charles Johnson) The sparks that fired the great conflagration of techno in Detroit were in no small part provided by the Electrifying Mojo, a late '70s and early '80s DJ who made it his occupation to "save Detroit and the world from the musical blahs." Born and raised in Little Rock, Arkansas, he joined the Air Force and began to DJ at his base in the Philippines. When he returned to the United States, Mojo worked a few years in radio before deciding to enter law school at the University of Michigan. He worked as a college DJ, amazing audiences with an incredibly broad range of genres and artists. After college, he moved to Detroit and began to apply the same techniques to his off-hours shift on a local radio station, encompassing the Clash, Prince, the B-52s, Madonna, Kraftwerk, and Depeche Mode. Techno pioneers Juan Atkins and Derrick May (among many others) listened and were introduced to a broad range of music, from punk to electronic pop. The pair began working for Mojo, producing lengthy mixes that then appeared on the show.

Elizabeth Ellen is a Pushcart Prize recipient and the author of several books including *Person/a: A Novel, Fast Machine,* and *Saul Stories.*

Thomas Sayers Ellis grew up in Washington, DC, and earned his MFA from Brown University. He is the author of *Skin, Inc.* (2013) and *The Maverick Room* (2005). He cofounded the Dark Room Collective in Cambridge, Massachusetts, and received a Whiting Award in 2005. Ellis has taught at Sarah Lawrence College, Case Western Reserve University, and Lesley University. He lives in Brooklyn, New York.

Eminem (Marshall Mathers) is an American rapper, record producer, and actor, known as one of the most controversial and best-selling artists of the early twenty-first century.

Robert Fanning is the author of four full-length collections: *Severance* (2019), *Our Sudden Museum* (2017), *American Prophet* (2009), and *The Seed Thieves* (2006), as well as two chapbooks: *Sheet Music* (2015) and *Old Bright Wheel* (2001). He is a professor of English at Central Michigan University.

Bryn Fortey is a veteran UK short story writer and poet who often appears on the American jazz poetry site The Song Is . . . His work has received Rhysling, Dwarf Star, and Pushcart nominations. He recently had a poetry sequence in the Van Gogh anthology *Resurrection of a Sunflower.*

Linda Nemec Foster is the author of ten collections of poetry, including the recent Made in Michigan Series' *The Lake Michigan Mermaid, Talking Diamonds, Amber*

Necklace from Gdansk, Listen to the Landscape, and *Living in the Fire Nest.* Foster was selected to be the first poet laureate of Grand Rapids, Michigan, from 2003 to 2005. She is the founder of the Contemporary Writers Series at Aquinas College.

Stewart Francke has been a long-time writer, inspirational speaker, and musical institution in his adopted hometown of Detroit for nearly three decades, where he's enthralled thousands of fans, both onstage and via his lengthy discography, with a colorful fusion of spirited blue-eyed soul and edgy rock and roll from The Beatles and Bowie to Stevie Wonder and Marvin Gaye. Stewart has won numerous Detroit Music Awards, including Best Artist, Songwriter, and Album. Stewart and his band have opened touring dates with Bob Seger, Steve Earle, Sheryl Crow, Stevie Winwood, Hall & Oates, EWF, Chicago, Foreigner, Natalie Cole, Shawn Colvin, Warren Zevon, Eddie Money, Joan Jett, and more. He wrote and recorded "Summer Soldier," featuring a chorus sung with the legendary Bruce Springsteen. Springsteen revealed himself to be an unabashed fan of Stewart's on a Detroit radio show and comments, "he makes beautiful music."

Cal Freeman was born and raised in Detroit. He currently teaches at Oakland University.

Sasha Frere-Jones is a writer and musician from Brooklyn.

Christopher Gilbert grew up in Lansing, Michigan. He worked in General Motors assembly plants during summer vacations, where his parents and several of his siblings worked. Gilbert received a BA in psychology from the University of Michigan in 1972 and an MA in psychology from Clark University in Worcester, Massachusetts, in 1975. His first poetry collection, *Across the Mutual Landscape,* was chosen by Michael S. Harper for the Walt Whitman Award in 1983 and published by Graywolf Press the next year. *Turning into Dwelling,* a collection that includes both Gilbert's debut and a second manuscript, was posthumously published in 2015 as part of the Graywolf Poetry Re/View Series, edited by Mark Doty. Gilbert passed away in 2007.

Brian Gilmore is an award-winning poet, writer, and columnist with the Progressive Media Project. He is the author of two collections of poetry, *elvis presley is alive and well and living in harlem,* and *Jungle Nights and Soda Fountain Rags: Poem for Duke*

Ellington. His poems and writings are widely published and have appeared in *The Progressive,* the *Washington Post,* the *Baltimore Sun,* the *Sugar House Review,* and *Jubilat.* Currently, he teaches law at Michigan State University College of Law. He divides his time between Michigan and his beloved birthplace, Washington, DC.

Nikki Giovanni has been nominated for a Grammy, has been a finalist for the National Book Award, and has been awarded an unprecedented seven NAACP Image Awards. She has authored three *New York Times* and *Los Angeles Times* best sellers. Since 1987, she has been on the faculty at Virginia Tech, where she is a University Distinguished Professor.

Tino Gross, aka **Tino G,** born and raised in Detroit, right off the fabled 8 Mile Rd., has had a music presence in the Motor City since his high school days, playing drums with John Lee Hooker. Tino listened to the late-night blues and rock and roll creeping out of the living room hi-fi. Tino has performed and recorded with many of the blues giants of the day: Bo Diddley, Big Walter Horton, Johnny Shines, Otis Rush, Eddie Taylor, and others. In addition, Tino has shared stages with the J. Geils Band, George Clinton and The P-Funk, ZZ Top, Ben Harper, Tom Petty, Bob Dylan. Tino is the front man for one of the region's most popular local Detroit bands, the Howling Diablos. He opened his Funky D Studios and record label out of a basement, and he has done award-winning writing and production with R. L. Burnside (2 albums), Nathaniel Mayer, Little Freddie King, Kenny Brown, Uncle Kracker, Howling Diablos, Horse Cave Trio, The Royal Blackbirds, The Ruiners, Barrett Strong, Robert Bateman, The Original Vandellas, Jimmie Bones, and recently with deaf rapper Sean Forbes. Tino Gross has won several awards for Outstanding Producer, Outstanding Songwriter, and recently Outstanding Record Label at the 2017 Detroit Music Awards.

Jim Gustafson (1949–1986) was the author of six books of poetry and was a considerable major presence in Detroit's Cass Corridor.

Jessica Hagedorn is a poet and fiction writer. Her novels include *Toxicology, Dream Jungle, The Gangster of Love,* and *Dogeaters,* winner of the American Book Award and a finalist for the National Book Award. Hagedorn is also the author of *Danger and Beauty,* a collection of poetry and prose, and the editor of three anthologies:

Manila Noir, Charlie Chan Is Dead: An Anthology of Contemporary Asian American Fiction and *Charlie Chan Is Dead 2: At Home in the World.* Jessica's work in theatre includes the musical play *Most Wanted,* a collaboration with composer Mark Bennett and director Michael Greif at La Jolla Playhouse; *Fe in the Desert* and *Stairway to Heaven* for Campo Santo in San Francisco, and the stage adaptation of *Dogeaters,* which was presented at La Jolla Playhouse and at the NYSF/Public Theater (dir. by Michael Greif), at the Kirk Douglas Theatre in Culver City (dir. by Jon Lawrence Rivera) and in Manila (dir. by Bobby Garcia). Hagedorn wrote the screenplay for *Fresh Kill,* a feature film directed by Shu Lea Cheang. She wrote the scripts for the experimental animated series *The Pink Palace,* which was created for the first season of the Oxygen Network.

Brian "Champtown" Harmon, better known by his stage name Champtown, is an American rapper, disc jockey, film director, and teacher from Detroit, Michigan. Founder of the Straight Jacket independent record label, Champtown is known for helping establish the careers of a number of Detroit hip-hop artists, including Kid Rock and Eminem. He has also worked with Ice-T, Rev Run, Public Enemy, and Uncle Kracker. He has released a documentary film, *The Untold Story of Detroit Hip Hop,* narrated by Chuck D and featuring interviews with notable Detroit rappers.

Aurora Harris is an award-winning poet published in several anthologies and *Educational Studies: A Journal of the American Educational Studies Association.* Her book of poetry *Solitude of Five Black Moons* won a 2012 PEN Oakland Award. She was recipient of the 2014 Howard Zinn Lifetime Achievement Award.

Bill Harris is professor emeritus of English at Wayne State University and is author of numerous plays, including *Robert Johnson: Trick the Devil, Stories About the Old Days, Riffs,* and *Coda.* He is the author of three books of poetry, *Birth of a Notion; Or, the Half Ain't Never Been Told* (2009), *The Ringmaster's Array,* and *Yardbird Suite: Side One,* which won the 1997 Naomi Long Madgett Poetry Award. Harris was named the 2011 Kresge Eminent Artist by the Kresge Foundation in recognition of his professional accomplishments and community engagement. He has a forthcoming novel from the Made in Michigan Series at Wayne State University Press.

Peter J. Harris is author of *Bless the Ashes,* winner of the 2015 PEN Oakland Josephine Miles Award, His website is www.blackmanofhappiness.com

Kaleema Hasan was a wonderful Detroit poet who passed away in spring 2017. She was a published poet, short-story writer, essayist, and a performance poet. Kaleema performed and read her work locally and regionally at clubs, community centers, schools and universities, churches, and mosques. Kaleema was an important part of the Detroit Black Arts Movement. She was working on her PhD at Wayne State University at the time of her death.

Robert Hayden was born Asa Bundey Sheffey. Hayden spent his childhood in a Detroit ghetto nicknamed "Paradise Valley," shuffled between his parents' home and that of a foster family living next door. Childhood events would result in times of depression he would call "my dark nights of the soul." A nearsighted boy, he was often ostracized by his peers and was excluded from many physical pursuits. Reading, however, occupied a great deal of his time. Hayden finished high school in 1932 and through a scholarship attended Detroit City College. After graduation, he worked for the Federal Writer's Project, researching black history and folk culture. In 1941, he enrolled in a master's English literature program at the University of Michigan, where he studied under W. H. Auden—who would become a guide in the development of his writing. After finishing the degree in 1942, he taught for several years at Michigan before transferring to Fisk University; in 1969, he would return to Michigan to complete his teaching career. His first book of poems, *Heart-Shape in the Dust* was published in 1940. It was followed by an unpublished second collection, then by *The Lion and the Archer* (1948), and *The Lion and the Archer, Figures of Time: Poems* (1955). His work was internationally recognized in the '60s and *A Ballad of Remembrance* won the grand prize for poetry at the First World Festival of Negro Arts in Dakar in 1966. *Selected Poems* was published in 1966, and followed by *Words in the Mourning Time* (1970), *Night-Blooming Cereus* (1972), and *Angle of Ascent* (1975). *American Journal* was published in 1978 and 1982. In 1976, he became the first African American to be appointed Consultant in Poetry to the Library of Congress; this position was later called the Poet Laureate.

Joe Henry is a native of the Metro Detroit area, and he is a gifted songwriter and vocalist whose intimate, richly detailed songs have been shaped by his eclectic musical worldview encompassing rock, folk, country, soul, and jazz influences. Joe has authored, with his brother David Henry, the book *Furious Cool: Richard Pryor and the World That Made Him.* Joe Henry is also a well-respected producer who has helped a wide range of artists refine their songs in the studio. He produced Joan Baez's newest album in 2018.

Lolita Hernandez is the author of two collections of short stories: *Making Callaloo in Detroit,* a 2015 Michigan Notable Book, and *Autopsy of an Engine and Other Stories from the Cadillac Plant,* winner of a 2005 PEN Beyond Margins Award. She is also a 2012 Kresge Fellow. After over thirty-three years as a UAW member at General Motors, she now teaches in the Creative Writing Department of the University of Michigan Residential College.

Dennis Hinrichsen is the author of several poetry collections, including *Skin Music* (2015). He is the poet laureate of Lansing, Michigan. He teaches at Lansing Community College.

Edward Hirsch lived in Detroit and taught at Wayne State University from 1979 to 1985. He has published nine books of poems, including *The Living Fire: New and Selected Poems* (2010), which brings together thirty-five years of work, and *Gabriel: A Poem* (2014), which won the National Jewish Book Award for poetry. He has also published five books of prose, among them, *How to Read a Poem and Fall in Love with Poetry* (1999), a national best-seller, and *A Poet's Glossary* (2014), a full compendium of poetic terms. He is president of the John Simon Guggenheim Memorial Foundation.

Brooke Horvath is the author of three collections of poetry, the most recent being *The Lecture on Dust.* He is also the author of *Understanding Nelson Algren* and coeditor, with Dan Simon, of *Entrapment and Other Writings,* a selection of Nelson Algren's uncollected and unpublished work.

Lynda Hull (December 5, 1954—March 29, 1994) was a United States poet. She had published two collections of poetry when she died in a car accident in 1994. A third, *The Only World* (1995), was published posthumously by her husband, the poet David

Wojahn, and was a finalist for the 1994 National Book Critics Circle Award. *Collected Poems* by Lynda Hull was published in 2006.

Kim D. Hunter is a Detroiter employed in media relations for social justice groups. His poems appear in *What I Say, Rainbow Darkness, Abandon Automobile, HIPology,* and *Graffiti Rag.* He has published two collection of poetry, *Borne on Slow Knives* (2001) and *Edge of the Time Zone* (2009). He received a Kresge Literary Fellowship in 2012 for *The Official Report on Human Activity,* a collection of short fiction (2018).

David James, born in Detroit, has published three books and six chapbooks. He teaches at Oakland Community College.

Mark Jarman has published numerous collections of poetry, including *Bone Fires: New and Selected Poems* (2011); *Epistles* (2007); *To the Green Man* (2004); *Unholy Sonnets* (2000); *Questions for Ecclesiastes* (1997), which won the 1998 Lenore Marshall Poetry Prize and was a finalist for the National Book Critics Circle Award; *Iris* (1992); *The Black Riviera* (1990), which won the 1991 Poets' Prize; *Far and Away* (1985); *The Rote Walker* (1981); and *North Sea* (1978). Jarman served as elector for the American Poets' Corner at the Cathedral of St. John the Divine from 2009 to 2012.

John Jeffire was born in Detroit. In 2005, his novel *Motown Burning* was named Grand Prize Winner in the Mount Arrowsmith Novel Competition, and in 2007, it won a Gold Medal for Regional Fiction in the Independent Publishing Awards. About *Motown Burning,* former chair of the Pulitzer jury Philip F. O'Connor said, "It works. I don't often say that, but it has a drive and integrity that gives it credible life. . . . I find it a novel with heart." In 2009, *Motown Burning* was included on a list of "Six Savory Novels Set in Detroit" along with works by Elmore Leonard, Joyce Carol Oates, and Jeffrey Eugenides. His first book of poetry, *Stone + Fist + Brick + Bone,* was nominated for a Michigan Notable Book Award in 2009.

Robert B. Jones has more than thirty years of experience as a performer, musician, storyteller, radio producer/host, and music educator. He has opened for and played with some of the finest musicians in the world. Rev. Jones has released scores of CDs over the past many years. His website is www.revrobertjones.com.

June Jordan was born in Harlem. Her twenty-eight books include poetry, essays, and children's books. A beloved teacher and exuberant activist, she founded Poetry for the People, and was a regular columnist for *The Progressive* and a prolific writer whose articles appeared in the *Village Voice,* the *New York Times, Ms.,* and *Essence.* She died of breast cancer in 2002.

Allison Joseph lives in Carbondale, Illinois, where she directs the MFA Program in Creative Writing at Southern Illinois University. She serves as poetry editor of *Crab Orchard Review.* Her books and chapbooks include *What Keeps Us Here, Soul Train, In Every Seam, Worldly Pleasures, Imitation of Life, Voice: Poems, My Father's Kites, Trace Particles, Little Epiphanies, Mercurial, Mortal Rewards, Multitudes, The Purpose of Hands, Double Identity, Corporal Muse,* and *What Once You Loved.* She is the literary partner and wife of poet and editor Jon Tribble.

Lawrence Joseph is the author of several collections of poetry, including *So Where Are We?* (2017) and *Codes, Precepts, Biases, and Taboos: Poems 1973–1993* (2005). His debut, *Shouting at No One* (1983), won the Agnes Lynch Starrett Prize. *Bookslut* critic Nicholas Gilewicz praised *Into It* (2005), which addresses the events of September 11, as "a very intimate book, one that counterintuitively and productively sidesteps confessionalism." He has taught creative writing and law at Princeton University and is Tinnelly Professor of Law at St. John's University School of Law. He lives in downtown Manhattan.

Zilka Joseph is the author of the 2016 Made in Michigan book *Sharp Blue Search of Flame* and teaches creative writing and is an independent editor and manuscript coach. Her chapbooks, *Lands I Live In* and *What Dread,* were nominated for a PEN America and a Pushcart award, respectively. She was awarded a Zell Fellowship, a Hopwood Prize, and the Elsie Choi Lee Scholarship (Center for the Education of Women) from the University of Michigan where she earned her MFA.

George Kalamaras, former poet laureate of Indiana (2014–2016), is the author of fifteen books of poetry, eight of which are full-length, including *Kingdom of Throat-Stuck Luck,* winner of the Elixir Press Poetry Prize (2011). He is professor of English at Indiana University–Purdue University Fort Wayne, where he has taught since 1990.

Christina Kallery's poetry has appeared in *The Collagist, Gargoyle, Failbetter, Rattle,* and *Mudlark, among* other publications. She has served as submissions editor for *Absinthe: A Journal of World Literature in Translation* and poetry editor for *Failbetter.* She was born in Michigan's Upper Peninsula and recently spent seven years living in New York City. She currently lives in Detroit.

James E. Kenyon began his writing career as a reporter for *The Detroit News.* Other jobs followed, mostly in corporate America. He retired as a communications executive from what used to be simply called Chrysler Corp. He now helps manage a family-owned business, Visiting Angels of Detroit, a provider of home care to senior citizens.

Wayne Kramer is a widely respected and acclaimed American guitarist, singer, songwriter, producer, and film and television composer, originally from Detroit and now living and working in Los Angeles. Kramer came to prominence as a teenager in 1967 as a cofounder of the Detroit rock group MC5 (Motor City 5), a group known for their powerful live performances and radical left-wing political stance. The MC5 broke up amid personality conflicts and personal problems, but Wayne has moved on to many new and exciting projects in film, playing with Tom Morello of Rage Against the Machine and others. He founded Jail Guitar Doors USA with Billy Bragg and Margaret Saadi Kramer. Kramer was honored with an Artistic License Award by California Lawyers for the Arts on June 30, 2013, at the William Turner Gallery in Santa Monica, California. Since it was founded in 2009, Jail Guitar Doors has provided guitars and music lessons for inmates at more than fifty penal institutions throughout the United States.

Detroit-born **Jan Krist** is a well-established singer-songwriter and veteran of the national acoustic music scene. Jan's musical gifts have been recognized by *Billboard, Entertainment Weekly, Dirty Linen, Image Journal,* and others. In addition, Jan is a sculptor and painter currently living in Indiana.

Gerry LaFemina is the author of several books of poems including *Vanishing Horizon,* three books of prose poems, a short story collection, and *Clamor,* a novel. In 2014, Stephen F. Austin University Press released his newest poetry collection, *Little Heretic,* and a book of his essays on prosody, *Palpable Magic.* New work has recently appeared in *The Sun, APR, Gettysburg Review,* and other journals. The recipient of numerous awards and honors, he directs the Center for Creative Writing at Frostburg State University where he is an associate professor of English, and serves as a poetry mentor in the MFA program at Carlow University.

John D. Lamb is a singer-songwriter and director of Springfed Arts, a nonprofit organization that produces retreats for songwriters, poets, and writers. Lamb studied journalism at Central Michigan University. He resides in Royal Oak, Michigan.

Michael Lauchlan is the author of the poetry collections *Trumbull Ave.* (2015), *And the Business Goes to Pieces* (1981), and *Sudden Parade* (1997). His poems have appeared in many publications and have been anthologized in *Abandon Automobile* (2001) and *A Mind Apart* (2008).

A major figure in American poetry, **Philip Levine** received the Pulitzer Prize in Poetry in 1995 for *The Simple Truth.* Among his many additional honors, he was Poet Laureate of the United States in 2011. He died in 2015, and his final collection, *The Last Shift,* was published posthumously in 2016.

M. L. Liebler is an internationally known and widely published Detroit poet, university professor, literary arts activist, and arts organizer. He was named the 2017–2018 Murray E. Jackson Scholar in the Arts at Wayne State University. Liebler is the author of fifteen books and chapbooks including the 2017 award-winning *I Want to Be Once* and *Heaven Was Detroit: Essays on Detroit Music from Jazz to Hip Hop.* In 2005, he was named St. Clair Shores' (his hometown) first poet laureate. Liebler has taught at Wayne State University in Detroit since 1980, and he is the founding director of both the National Writer's Voice Project in Detroit and the Springfed Arts: Metro Detroit Writers Literary Arts Organization. In 2010, he received the Barnes & Noble, Poets & Writers, Writers for Writers Award with Maxine Hong Kingston and Junot Diaz. He is currently president of the Detroit Writers' Guild. His website is www.mlliebler.com.

Gordon Meredith Lightfoot Jr. (born November 17, 1938) is a Canadian singer-songwriter who achieved international success in folk, folk-rock, and country music.

He is credited with helping to define the folk-pop sound of the 1960s and 1970s. He is often referred to as Canada's greatest songwriter and is known internationally as a folk-rock legend.

Rachel Loden is the author of *Dick of the Dead,* which was shortlisted for the PEN USA Literary Award for Poetry and the California Book Award. Her book *Kulchur Girl: Notes from Berkeley 1965* was excerpted in the *Journal of Poetics Research* (online). Loden's poem "Memo from the Benefits Department," from her book *Hotel Imperium,* is on the curriculum for the Irish "leaving" exam in 2019.

Janice A. Lowe, composer and poet, is the author of *Leaving Cle: Poems of Nomadic Dispersal* (2016) and composer of the musical *Lil Budda,* (text by Stephanie L. Jones). Her poetry has appeared in *Best American Experimental Writing 2016.* She has composed music for plays including *12th & Clairmount* by Jenni Lamb. She is a cofounder of The Dark Room Collective and has performed with the experimental bands w/o a net, Heroes Are Gang Leaders, and Digital Diaspora.

Art Lyzak is a founding members of Detroit's iconic punk-rock band The Mutants. In the early days of punk, he managed Lilli's Bar in Hamtramck, Michigan. In addition to writing songs and lyrics, Art is a writer and blogger on all things related to music and Detroit. He is a native Detroiter living in Santa Monica, California.

Peter Markus is the author of a novel, *Bob, or Man on Boat,* as well as five other books of fiction, the most recent of which is *The Fish and the Not Fish,* a Michigan Notable Book of 2015. His fiction has appeared widely in anthologies and journals including *Chicago Review, Iowa Review, Alaska Quarterly Review, Black Warrior Review, Quarterly West, Massachusetts Review, Northwest Review,* among many others. He was awarded a Kresge Arts in Detroit Fellowship in 2012 and has taught for twenty years as a writer-in-residence with the InsideOut Literary Arts Project.

Adrian Matejka is the poet laureate of Indiana where he is the Ruth Lilly Professor / Poet-in-Residence at Indiana University in Bloomington. He has received fellowships from Cave Canem, the Guggenheim Foundation, the Lannan Foundation, and United States Artists. He is the author of *The Devil's Garden* and *Mixology.* His third collection,

The Big Smoke, is about Jack Johnson and was a finalist for the 2013 National Book Award and the 2014 Pulitzer Prize and won an Anisfield-Wolf Book Award. His newest collection, *Map to the Stars,* was published by Penguin in 2017.

Dawn McDuffie's work explores imagination, memories, and dreams that reveal hidden aspects of Detroit. She has taught creative writing in Detroit since 2000, and her chapbook, *Happenstance and Miracles,* was published in 2018.

Ray McNiece is the author of nine books of poems and monologues, most recently *Love Song for Cleveland,* a collaboration with photographer Tim Lachina. The *Orlando Sentinel,* reporting on Ray's solo show at the Fringe Festival, called him "a modern day descendant of Woody Guthrie. He has a way with words and a wry sense of humor." He toured Russia with Yevgeny Yevtushenko where he appeared on *Good Morning, Russia* and performed at the Moscow Polytech, the Russian Poets' Hall of Fame, where he was dubbed "the American Mayakovski." He toured in Italy twice with Lawrence Ferlinghetti.

Ken Meisel is a poet and psychotherapist with publications in one hundred national poetry magazines including *Midwestern Gothic, Rattle, Concho River Review, Firefly, Freshwater, Lake Effect, Cream City Review,* and *San Pedro River Review.* He is a Pushcart Prize nominee, a Liakoura Prize winner, a 2012 Kresge Arts Literary Fellow, and the author of seven poetry collections. His most recent publication is *Mortal Lullabies* (2018).

Ken Mikolowski is the author of six books of poetry. He taught at the University of Michigan for thirty-seven years before retiring in 2015. Along with his late wife, Ann, he was editor, publisher, and printer of The Alternative Press. He lives in Ann Arbor.

Ron Milner was an African American playwright from Detroit. His play *Checkmates,* starring Paul Winfield and Denzel Washington, ran on Broadway in 1988. He died in 2004.

Wardell Montgomery Jr. is known as Detroit's Urban Folk Poet. Wardell Montgomery Jr. wrote songs as a member of the original Motown Records in the late '60s. As a freelance lyric writer Montgomery had songs recorded by the Burnette Sisters and the Barrino Brothers. Wardell's song, "It Doesn't Have to Be That Way" was recorded by Holland-Dozier-Holland of Invictus Records. A few years ago Wardell Montgomery and Keith Gamble (Creative Tradition) produced a CD titled "Do I Have to Live This?" spoken word by Wardell, jazz by saxophonist Keith Gamble and pianist Mike Evans. Wardell and Keith performed at several libraries around the state of Michigan. In Detroit, New York City, and Denver, Wardell has taught and sometimes still teaches poetry workshops for children, seniors, young adults, inmates, and the substance-abuse-recovering community. The Go-Getters Circle of his church home, Plymouth United Church of Christ, selected Montgomery to receive their Community Service Award at the Fifth Annual Black History Month Service on February 20, 2005. Wardell Montgomery is an active church member, reading poetry during intermission of their First Friday Jazz and Fish Fry; member of Plymouth Players Theatre Ministry; DUPAAS writers, and Detroit Artists Workshop and Broadside Press. Wardell Montgomery is also a founding member and host of Horizons in Poetry.

K. Michelle Moran is an award-winning journalist, poet, and fiction writer who lives in Metro Detroit. She still buys music on CDs.

Cindy Hunter Morgan teaches at Michigan State University. *Harborless,* her book of poems informed by Great Lakes shipwrecks, was published by Wayne State University Press and won the 2017 Moveen Prize in Poetry. She also is the author of two chapbooks, and she writes regularly for *Murder Ballad Monday,* a blog devoted to the exploration of the murder ballad tradition in folk and popular music.

Scott Morgan is one of the major and enduring figures on the Michigan rock scene, forming his first band well before the British Invasion helped sparked the '60s garage rock explosion and still playing tough, soulful rock and roll nearly fifty years later. His first band The Rationals were signed to Capitol Records in the mid-60's, and he went on to play with Fred Smith's Sonic's Rendezvous Band, Scots Pirates, The Hydromatics, and The Solution. Scott just released a new album in 2018 with The Sights.

Terrell Morrow is a youth author and musician based out of Detroit. His early introduction to poetry started with InsideOut's Citywide Poets site at Mumford High School.

Since then he has been using his training as a poet to embark on ambassador work for iO and excel in his creative musical endeavors. He participated in the InsideOut Techno Poetics Program in 2016.

Thylias Moss has authored many poetry collections including *Wannabe Hoochie Mama Gallery of Realities' Red Dress Code: New and Selected Poems* (2016) and the novels *New Kiss Horizon, a romance* (2016) and *Aneurysm of the Firmament* (2016), *Tokyo Butter (2006), Last Chance for the Tarzan Holler* (1999), *Small Congregations: New and Selected Poems* (1993), *Rainbow Remnants in Rock Bottom Ghetto Sky* (1991), *At Redbones* (1990), *Pyramid of Bone* (1989), and *Hosiery Seams on a Bowlegged Woman* (1983). Known for expansive poems full of details ranging from art, history, and laundry detergents to ants and Disney characters, she has garnered multiple awards, including the Witter Bynner Prize, an NEA grant, and fellowships from the MacArthur and Guggenheim Foundations.

Dahveed Nelson (formerly David Nelson) is one of the founding members of The Last Poets, and his group is often referred to as The Godfathers of Hip-Hop. His poems have been used in songs by NWA, Public Enemy, and others. He splits his time between his hometown of Detroit and Ghana. Dahveed played a major role in The Last Poets' independent film of 1970 entitled *Right On*. He is also featured in the French documentary about The Last Poets entitled *Made in Amerikkka*. The Last Poets celebrated fifty years in 2018.

Richard Peabody is the founder and current editor of *Gargoyle* magazine, and editor (or coeditor) of twenty-two anthologies. He is the author of a novella, three short story collections, and seven books of poetry. A native Washingtonian, his most recent book is *The Richard Peabody Reader*.

Sonya Marie Pouncy is a Callaloo Creative Writing Workshop Fellow, and she holds an MA in Creative Writing. Her poems have appeared in *Callaloo, Temenos, Central Review, Aunt Chloe: A Journal of Artful Candor, Drum Voices Revue,* and *Seeds.* Sonya has served as a poet-in-residence with InsideOut and the Broadside Press Detroit Public Library Program.

Ashley Rae graduated from Cass Technical High School and now lives in Hawaii where she writes. She participated in the InsideOut Techno Poetics Program in 2016.

Lisa Jane Recker: Detroit born, Michigan raised. Wayne State University, met my professor and friend, M. L. Liebler. Did bands, Beatnik Party and The Vanderbilts in Detroit. Stand-up comedy and acting. Moved to San Francisco and expanded the comedy and professional acting. Stage plays, unions, cabaret gigs, the band Cathedral Dogs and many commercials later. I still write. I gig. I live. I raise my daughter. It's all too beautiful. Resist. Believe.

Eugene B. Redmond is an acclaimed American poet. His poetry is closely connected to the Black Arts Movement. In 1989, he joined the faculty at Southern Illinois University Edwardsville (SIUE), where he is currently an emeritus professor of English. Redmond has published a multitude of books and chapbooks, and his work can be found in numerous journals and anthologies. In 1976, Redmond was named poet laureate of East St. Louis.

Robbie Robertson is a founding member of The Band, a guitarist and songwriter from Toronto, Canada.

Judith Roche is a poet and the author of four collections of poetry. They are *Myrrh/My Life as a Screamer, Ghost, Wisdom of the Body* (winner of an American Book Award), and *All Fire All Water.* She is coeditor of *First Fish, First People: Salmon Tales of the North Pacific Rim,* which also won an American Book Award, and has edited a number of poetry anthologies.

John G. Rodwan Jr. is the author of *Holidays & Other Disasters* (2013) and *Fighters & Writers* (2010). His writing on music has appeared in *Jazz Research Journal, The American Interest,* and *Palimpsest* as well as *Heaven Was Detroit* (2016), edited by M. L. Liebler. He lives in Detroit.

Nancy J. Rodwan is an award-winning filmmaker, visual artist, and writer. Her art has been exhibited in many museums, festivals, and galleries. She has directed, shot, animated, and edited several short films and a feature-length documentary. Her films have been screened in numerous national and international film festivals.

Corie Rosen is a fiction writer and poet. Her work has been featured on public radio, taught in high-schools and colleges, and has been nominated for the Pushcart Prize. A Colorado resident by way of Los Angeles, Berkeley, and Phoenix, she currently lives in Denver.

Franziska Ruprecht, a German performance poet, holds a master's degree in English with an emphasis in creative writing from Wayne State University. She teaches performance poetry at Munich University. In 2015, Wolfbach published "Meer-Maid," her collection of poetry in German.

Lisa Rutledge works daily to improve the health of her community through advocacy, collaboration, and creating innovative health improvement programs. Her poetry has appeared in places like *freefall, Cellar Roots, Ostentatious Mind, Poetic Resonance Imaging,* and *Workers Write!: Tales from the Clinic.* She grew up in Detroit during a great time to be a kid in the city.

Raquel "Rok" Salaysay works at Detroit Labs. In addition to working there, she owns Sugar's (a home bakery business) and has played bass and sung in such bands as Slumber Party, The Joint Chiefs of Detroit, Jeecy and the Jungle, and M. L. Liebler's Coyote Monk Poetry Band.

Ed Sanders cofounded the Fugs, opened the Peace Eye Bookstore, and appeared on the cover of *Life* magazine. He is the author of *The Family* and lives in Woodstock, New York.

James Scully, born in New Haven, Connecticut, taught at Rutgers and the University of Connecticut, retiring in 1992 to San Francisco. He was the founding editor of Curbstone Press' Art on the Line series, has published eleven books of poetry, five works of translation, and two critical collections, including *Line Break: Poetry as Social Practice.* Jim currently lives in Vermont.

Patty Seyburn has published four books of poems: *Perfecta* (2014), *Hilarity* (2009), *Mechanical Cluster* (2002), and *Diasporadic* (1998). She is a professor at California State University, Long Beach.

During his distinguished career **Paul Simon** has been the recipient of many honors and awards including twelve Grammy Awards, three of which were albums of the year. In 2003 he was given a Grammy Lifetime Achievement Award for his work as half of the duo Simon and Garfunkel. He is a member of the Songwriters Hall of Fame, a recipient of their Johnny Mercer Award, and is in the Rock & Roll Hall of Fame.

John Sims, a Detroit native, is a multimedia artist/creator, writer and producer. He has authored essays for CNN, Al Jazeera, the Huffington Post, Guernica, The Rumpus, and The Grio. Follow him on Twitter: @JohnSimsProject.

Poet, blues and jazz historian, former manager of the MC5, radio host, and political activist all describe **John Sinclair**, but the consistent profile is one of a dedicated music enthusiast. Born in Flint, Michigan, John has authored several books of poetry starting with *We Just Change the Beat, Fattening Frogs for Snakes, Thelonious: A Book of Monk, Guitar Army,* and *The John Sinclair Reader.*

Fred "Sonic" Smith was a Detroit guitar hero known as one of the best, his musical legacy firmly established by his time spent as one half of the dual guitar arsenal that fueled the legendary MC5, and later fronting his own Sonic's Rendezvous Band and collaborating with his wife, Patti Smith. In the late '60s and early '70s, the MC5 defined the Detroit rock sound. Under the guidance of radical writer John Sinclair, the five were dangerous, using guitars as their weapons of choice in the fight to change the world.

Kevin Stein has published eleven books—poetry, scholarship, and anthologies—including the collections *Sufficiency of the Actual* and *American Ghost Roses* as well as the essays *Poetry's Afterlife: Verse in the Digital Age.*

Larry Smith is a poet, fiction writer, critic, and editor-publisher of Bottom Dog Press in Ohio. His rock and roll days were spent in the Ohio Valley listening to the Pittsburgh radio scene. He still plays guitar and likes to lead sing-alongs of the old tunes. He taught writing and film at BGSU Firelands College for thirty-five years.

Patricia Smith is the author of seven books of poetry, including *Incendiary Art* (2017), winner of an NAACP Image Award; *Shoulda Been Jimi Savannah* (2012), which won the Lenore Marshall Prize from the Academy of American Poets; *Blood Dazzler* (2008), a chronicle of the human and environmental cost of Hurricane Katrina, which was nominated for a National Book Award; and *Teahouse of the Almighty,* a 2005 National Poetry Series selection.

Carolyn Striho has been nominated for nearly sixty Detroit Music Awards. Striho has been defying musical genres and creating music in punk, folk, rock and roll, jazz, blues as a singer/songwriter musician and performer for many years. The one constant is that Carolyn pushes the boundaries—of society and herself—to make the music that she wants to. Carolyn first made a name for herself fronting the Detroit Energy, but her early days as the lead vocalist, keyboardist, and chief songwriter for The Cubes while working as a DJ at NPR/WDET-FM Radio provided a springboard. Striho went on to perform with The Ramones, The New York Dolls, Was (Not Was), Iggy Pop, Steve Earle, and Tori Amos; she played the Detroit International Jazz Festival several times as well as Lollapallooza. Striho has also worked with Patti Smith numerous times—both on stage, two tours in the U.S., Canada, and the U.K., and in the studio.

Keith Taylor has recently retired from teaching at the University of Michigan. His most recent full-length collection of poems is *The Bird-While* (2017).

Russell Thorburn is the author of *Somewhere We'll Leave the World* (2017). A National Endowment for the Arts recipient and first poet laureate of the Michigan's Upper Peninsula, he lives in Marquette with his wife. His poems have appeared in many literary journals and anthologies, including *And Here: 100 Years of Upper Peninsula Writing,* and *Poetry in Michigan.*

Rodney Torreson's recent poetry collections include *A Breathable Light* (2002) and *The Ripening of Pinstripes: Called Shots on the New York Yankees* (1998). The former poet laureate of Grand Rapids, Michigan, Torreson has won the *Seattle Review*'s

Bentley Prize, and his poems have been featured in former US poet laureate Ted Kooser's syndicated newspaper column "American Life in Poetry." Torreson lives in Grand Rapids, Michigan.

Thomas Trimble: The song "Muscle Car" appeared on Detroit-band American Mars' debut record, *Late,* released on the group's own Diamond Wine Music label in 1997. Trimble went on to write and record four more records with a different line-up of American Mars, including *No City Fun* (2001), *Western Sides* (2008), *Chasing Vapor* (2012), and *Exposure* (2016). Trimble teaches writing at Wayne State University in Detroit.

David Trinidad's latest collection of poems is *Swinging on a Star* (2017). His other books include *Notes on a Past Life* and *Descent of the Dolls: Part I,* a collaboration with Jeffery Conway and Gillian McCain, both published in 2016 by BlazeVOX [books]. Trinidad lives in Chicago, where he is a professor of creative writing/poetry at Columbia College.

Robin Tyner was an American musician and songwriter best known as lead singer for the Detroit proto-punk band MC5. His adopted surname was in tribute to the jazz pianist McCoy Tyner. It was Tyner who issued the rallying cry of "kick out the jams, motherfuckers" at the MC5's live concerts. Tyner had originally auditioned as the bass player, but the band felt his talents would be best used as a lead vocalist. He died in 1991.

Chris Tysh is poet and playwright based in Detroit. She has published several collections of poetry and drama. Her book *Hotel des Archives* was published in 2018 by
Station Hill Press in Barrytown, New York.

George Tysh teaches film studies and poetics at the College for Creative Studies in Detroit. In 2010, United Artists Books (New York) published his tenth collection of poetry, *The Imperfect,* and a new series of poems, *The Slip,* appeared from BlazeVOX (Buffalo) in 2015.

Andrew Vinstra is a huge devotee and fan of '60s British Invasion classic rock, '50s rockabilly, American blues and soul music, and the classic standards of American popular music from the '30s, '40s, and '50s as well as old country, jazz, and folk.

Barry Wallenstein is the author of eight collections of poetry, the most recent being *At the Surprise Hotel and Other Poems* (2016). He has made eight recordings of his poetry with jazz. He composed the lyrics for "I Carry Your Heart," the ballads of Pepper Adams (2012). Barry is an emeritus professor of literature and creative writing at the City University of New York and an editor of the journal, *American Book Review.*

Rayfield A. Waller is a widely published poet, fiction writer, and journalist. Waller is a contributing writer to *The Panopticon Review* and is a member of the Francis Ford Coppola ZOETROPE.COM writers' workshop. Waller teaches in the Africana Studies Department at Wayne State University. He is currently working on a degree in global studies from Harvard University and is a graduate of Wayne State University and Cornell University. He blogs at rayfieldwaller.blogspot.com.

Jack White is an American musician, singer, songwriter, record producer, and actor. Born in Detroit, he currently lives in Nashville, Tennessee. White has enjoyed consistent critical and popular success and is widely credited as one of the key artists in the garage-rock revival of the 2000s. He has won twelve Grammy Awards.

Crystal Williams is the author of four books of poetry.

Tyrone Williams is the author of five books and several chapbooks of poetry. He teaches literature at Xavier University in Cincinnati, Ohio.

Willie Williams was born in Black Bottom in Detroit the year Willie Mays became a Giant. "Poetry found me in high school and fifty years later I'm still seeing the world through that prism."

Baron Wormser is the author/coauthor of fifteen books and a poetry chapbook. His most recent book is a novel, *Tom o' Vietnam.*

Al Young is an award winning poet, memoirist, and novelist raised in Detroit. He served as the State of California's poet laureate. His volumes of poetry include *Something About the Blues: An Unlikely Collection of Poetry* (2008); *Coastal Nights and Inland Afternoons:*

Poems 2001–2006 (2006); *The Sound of Dreams Remembered: Poems 1990–2000* (2001); *Heaven: Collected Poems, 1956–90* (1992), and many others.

Michael Zadoorian was born and raised in Detroit. He is the author of two novels, *The Leisure Seeker,* which was adapted for a motion picture starring Helen Mirren and Donald Sutherland, and *Second Hand,* which was an ABA Booksense 76 selection, a Barnes & Noble Discovery Award finalist, and winner of the Great Lakes Colleges Association New Writers Award. A new novel, *Beautiful Music,* was published in 2018 by Akashic Books.

Credits

Akashi, Marrim. "A Meditation on Music." Used by kind permission of the author. © Marrim Akashi.

Andrews, Mark James. "Shot 3 Silenced the Singer: The Murder." Used by kind permission of the author. © Mark James Andrews.

Armstrong, Glen. "The Last DJ." Used by kind permission of the author. © Glen Armstrong.

Baban, Hajjar. "A Meditation on Music." Used by kind permission of the author. © Hajjar Baban.

Balakian, Peter. "Joe Louis's Fist" first appeared in *Ozone Journal,* University of Chicago Press, 2015, and in *Tikkun Magazine,* 2014. Used by kind permission of the author. © Peter Balakian.

Beatty, Jan. "Love Poem with Strat" and "Love Poem with Strat #2" both from *Red Sugar.* University of Pittsburgh Press. Used by kind permission of the author. © Jan Beatty.

Blackwell, Benjamin. "The Nain Rogue" and "Bury My Body at Elmwood." Used by kind permission of the author. © Benjamin Blackwell.

Blair, David. "Detroit: While I was Away." Used by kind permission of the author's estate. © Estate of David Blair.

Blake, Arthur "Blind." "Detroit Bound." Public Domain.

Bourbeau, Heather. "Thank You, Berry Gordy." Used by kind permission of the author. © Heather Bourbeau.

Boyd, Melba Joyce. "A Mingus Among Us and a Walden Within Us" and "Working It Out" were previously published in *Death Dance of a Butterfly* by Melba Joyce

Boyd (Ferndale, MI: Past Tents Press, 2013). "Blow Marcus Blow" and "The Bass Is Woman." Used by kind permission of the author.

Bragg, Billy. "Levi Stubbs' Tears." Words and Music by Billy Bragg © 1986, reproduced by permission of Sony/ATV Music Publishing (UK) Limited, London W1F 9LD. Used by kind permission of the author. © Billy Bragg.

Brice, Charlie. "Setting Up Soul—1968" from *Flashcuts Out of Chaos,* WordTech Editions, 2016. Used by kind permission of the author. © Charlie Brice.

Brown, Laura Soul. "Oh! Mercy Mercy Me! A Family Gathers to Marvin Gaye." Used by kind permission of the author. © Laura Brown.

Burns, A'leetzia. "Between Dexter & Linwood," "My Body as a Spaceship," and "A Meditation on Music." Used by kind permission of the author. © A'leetzia Burns.

Bush, Writer L. "A Love Supreme." Used by kind permission of the author. © Writer L. Bush.

Carr, Ginny. "He Was the Cat." Used by kind permission of the author. © Ginny Carr 2012.

Charara. Hayan. "Bob Seger's 'Night Moves' on the Radio in Winter (Leaving Henry Ford Hospital)." Used by kind permission of the author. © Hayan Charara.

Cintrón, Esperanza. "Music –3 The African World Festival." Used by kind permission of the author. © Esperanza Cintrón.

Codrescu, Andrei. "String City." Used by kind permission of the author. © Andrei Codrescu.

Comer, Nandi. "Detroit Tells Its Techno Story," "Dear Derrick," "My Body as a Spaceship," and "A Meditation on Music." Used by kind permission of the author. © Nandi Comer.

Cooper, Desiree. "Come See About Me." Used by kind permission of the author. © Desiree Cooper.

Cope, David L. "River Rouge." Used by kind permission of the author. © David L. Cope.

Daniels, Jim. "School's Out" from *Rowing Inland* (Detroit, MI: Wayne State University Press, 2017). "Detroit Hymns" from (Pittsburgh, PA: University of Pittsburgh Press, 1993). "Patti Smith at the Punch and Judy Theater," from *Red Vinyl, Black Vinyl* (Toledo, OH: Aureole Press, 2001). Reprinted by permission of the author.

deathray, ibrahim. "Dec 4 2014 m e r c y." © iBRAHIM dEATHRAY. Used by kind permission of the author. © iBRAHIM dEATHRAY.

DeCillis, Diane. "The Girl from Ipanema Visits Detroit, 1964." Used by kind permission of the author. © Diane DeCillis.

Derricotte, Toi. "Blackbottom" from *Captivity* by Toi Derricotte, © 1989. Reprinted by permission of the University of Pittsburgh.

Domino, Fats. "Detroit City Blues." Words and Music by Dave Bartholomew and Antoine Domino © 1950 (Renewed) EMI UNART Catalog, INC. All Rights Controlled by EMI UNART Catalog, INC. (Publishing) and Alfred Publishing Co., Inc. (Print). All Rights Reserved. Used by Permission of Alfred Publishing, LLC.

Donovan, Mark. "Finding Culture/Saturday Night." Used by kind permission of the author. © Mark Donovan.

Dougherty, Sean Thomas. "One Nation Under a Groove" appeared in the book *Love Song of the Young Couple,* the Dumb Job (Red Dancefloor Press, 1995). Used by kind permission of the author.

Dove, Rita. "Golden Oldie." Used by kind permission of the author. © Rita Dove.

Duprie, Don. "What Am I Supposed to Do." Used by kind permission of the author. © Donald Duprie.

Eady, Cornelius. "Aretha Franklin's Inauguration Hat" and "The Supremes." Used by kind permission of the author. © Cornelius Eady.

Eichele, Robin. "28 December 1965" and "Blues Scholars at Work." Used by kind permission of the author. © Robin Eichele.

Ehrhart, W. D. "Dancing in the Streets." Used by Permission of the author. © W. D. Ehrhart.

Ellen, Elizabeth. "Target." Used by kind permission of the author. © Elizabeth Allen.

Ellis, Thomas Sayers. "Photograph of Dr. Funkenstein." Used by kind permission of the author. © Thomas Sayers Ellis.

Eminem. "Eight Mile" and "Lose Yourself." Used by kind permission of the author. © by Marshall Mathers.

Fanning, Robert. "Memorial in Open Air." Used by kind permission of the author. © Robert Fanning.

Fortey, Bryn. "Hey There Blues." Used by kind permission of the author. © Bryn Fortey.

Foster, Linda Nemec. "History of Sweat" was published in *Living in the Fire Nest* (Ridgeway Press, 1996) and "Dancing with My Sister" was published in *Amber Necklace from Gdansk* (Louisiana State University Press, 2001). Both used by kind permission of the author and the LSU Press.

Francke, Stewart. "Motor City Serenade." Used by kind permission of the author. © Stewart Francke.

Freeman, Cal. "Visiting the Inside Outlaws in River Rouge, MI." Used by kind permission of the author. © Cal Freeman.

Frere-Jones, Sasha. "Haiku for Eminem." Used by kind permission of the author. © Sasha Frere-Jones.

Gilbert, Christopher. "Time with Stevie Wonder in It" from *Across the Mutual Landscape*. Copyright © 1984 by Christopher Gilbert. Reprinted with the permission of The Permissions Company, Inc. on behalf of Copper Canyon Press, www.coppercanyonpress.org.

Gilmore, Brian. "living for the city." Used by kind permission of the author. © Brian Gilmore.

Giovanni, Nikki. "Poem for Aretha" from *The Collected Poetry of Nikki Giovanni 1968–1998* by Nikki Giovanni. Copyright compilation © 2003 by Nikki Giovanni. Reprinted by permission of HarperCollins Publishers.

Gross, Martin. "'I Almost Played with The Stooges.'" Used by kind permission of the author. © Martin Gross.

Gustafson, Jim. "Juke Box" appeared in *Virtue and Annihilation* (Alternative Press, 1988); "Final Wish" was produced as a postcard by The Alternative Press with artwork by Ann Mikolowski and appeared in *Breath Torque* (Yondotiga, 1994); "Tales of the MC5." Used by kind permission of the author's estate.

Hagedorn, Jessica. "Motown/Smokey Robinson." Used by kind permission of the author. © Jessica Hagedorn.

Harmon, Brian ("Champtown"). "Armageddon." Used by kind permission of the author. © Brian Harmon.

Harris, Aurora. "So Beautiful." Used by kind permission of the author. © Aurora Harris.

Harris, Bill. "Ron Carter: The Pulse in Autumn." Used by kind permission of the author. © Bill Harris.

Harris, Peter J. "Some Songs Women Sing." Used by kind permission of the author. © Peter Harris.

Hasan, Kaleema. "Lost Bird: Take 2." Used by kind permission of the author. © Kaleema Hasan.

Hayden, Robert. "Homage to the Empress of Blues" and "Mourning Poem for the Queen of Sunday." Copyright © 1966–2013. Reprinted with the permission of the Robert Hayden Estate with special thanks to Frederick Glaysher.

Henry, Joe. "Written." Used by kind permission of the author. © Joseph Henry.

Hernandez, Lolita. "Silver Anniversary." Used by kind permission of the author. © Lolita Hernandez.

Hinrichsen. Dennis. "Radio Motown." Used by kind permission of the author. © Dennis Hinrichsen.

Hirsch, Edward. "Let's Get Off the Bus." Used by kind permission of the author. © Edward Hirsch.

Horvath, Brooke. "I Thought We'd Never Get Over That First Album." Used by kind permission of the author. © Brooke Horvath.

Hull, Lynda. "Chiffon" from *Collected Poems*. Copyright © 1995 Lynda Hull. Reprinted by kind permission of the Permissions Company, Inc., on behalf of Graywolf Press, Minneapolis, Minnesota, www.graywolfpress.org.

Hunter, Kim D. "the sound before." Used by kind permission of the author. © Kim Hunter.

James, David. "Floating." An earlier version of this work was published in *Peninsula Poets*. Used by kind permission of the author. © David James.

Jarman, Mark. "The Supremes." Used by kind permission of the author. © Mark Jarman.

Jeffire, John. "i luv you suzi quarto." Used by kind permission of the author. © John Jeffire.

Johnson, Charles (The Electrifying Mojo). "The Painting." Used by kind permission of the author. © Charles Johnson.

Jones, Robert B., Sr. "Arnesia" and "Poor Man's Promised Land." Used by kind permission of the author. © Robert B. Jones.

Jordan, June. "Owed to Eminem." Used by Permission of the June M. Jordan Literary Trust, 2 Fifth Avenue, Apt. 20L, New York, NY 10011. Copyright © 2005 June Jordan Literary Estate. Reprinted with the permission of the June M. Jordon Literary Estate, and Copper Canyon Press.

Joseph, Allison. "Junior High Dance" appears courtesy of Carnegie Mellon

Loden, Rachel. "Tumbling Dice" first appeared in the *Beloit Poetry Journal*. Used by permission of the author. © 1990 Rachel Loden.

Lowe, Janice A. "Whazzup Nod 2 Cybotron Cosmic Cars." Used by permission of the author. © Janice A. Lowe.

Lyzak, Art. "SO AMERICAN" and "AFRAID OF DETROIT." Used by permission of the author. © Art Lyzak.

Markus, Peter. "On Turning Fifty-Two." Used by permission of the author. © Peter Markus.

McDuffie, Dawn. "Dear Detroit Earthquake." Used by permission of the author. © Dawn McDuffie.

McNiece, Ray. "Pop Songs through the Night." Used by kind permission of the author. © Raymond McNiece.

Matejka, Adrian. "From the Edge of the World." Used by kind permission of the author. © Adrian Matejka.

Meisel, Ken. "John Lee Hooker's Boogie Chillun" was first published in *Concho River Review*. Used by kind permission of the author. © Ken Meisel.

Mikolowski, Ken. "At the Grande Ballroom 1968." Used by kind permission of the author. © Ken Mikolowksi.

Milner, Ron. "From the Porches." Used by kind permission of the author. © Ron Milner.

Montgomery, Wardell, Jr. "Michael Was Unique." Used by kind permission of the author. © Wardell Montgomery Jr.

Moran, K. Michelle. "Help Wanted." Used by kind permission of the author. © K. Michelle Moran.

Morgan, Cindy Hunter. "Incident on Grand River, 1967." Used by kind permission of the author. © Cindy Hunter Morgan.

Morgan, Scott. "16 With a Bullet" & "Detroit." Used by kind permission of the author. © Scott Morgan.

Morrow, Terrell. "My Body is a Spaceship." Used by kind permission of the author. © Terrell Morrow.

Moss, Thylias. "Vashti's First Plane Ride to Manhattan from Detroit Metro Airport." Used by kind permission of the author. © Thylias Moss.

Nelson, Dahveed. "Into the Streets." Used by kind permission of the author. © Dahveed Nelson.

Peabody, Richard. "Marvin's Voice." Used by kind permission of the author. © Richard Peabody.

Pouncy, Sonya Marie. "Musing I: Her Inspiration." Used by kind permission of the author. © Sonya Marie Pouncy.

Rae, Ashley (Carson). "My Body as a Spaceship" and "A Meditation in Music." Used by kind permission of the author. © Ashley Rae.

Recker, Lisa Jane. "I Wanna Testify." Used by kind permission of the author. © Lisa Jane Recker.

Redmond, Eugene B. "Kwansaba: Rolling Late Sixties–Style Ntu Motor City." Used by kind permission of the author. © Eugene B. Redmond.

Robertson, Robbie. "Somewhere Down the Crazy River." Used by kind permission of the author. © Robbie Robertson.

Roche, Judith. "Detroit Music." Used by kind permission of the author. © Judith Roche.

Rodwan, John G., Jr. "More than Motown." A version of this poem first appeared in *The Hoot & Hare Review,* Fall 2013. Reprinted by permission of the author. © John G. Rodwan Jr., 2013. "JC on the Set." Printed with the permission of author. © John G. Rodwan Jr., 2017.

Rodwan, Nancy J. "Night Moves" and "Waiting on the Revolution." Used by kind permission of the author. © Nancy J. Rodwan.

Rosen, Corie. "Madonna for the Damned—a 1980s Heroine." Used by kind permission of the author. © Corie Rosen.

Ruprecht, Franziska. "Detroit." Used by kind permission of the author. © Franziska Ruprecht.

Rutledge, Lisa. "New School Year." Used by kind permission of the author. © Lisa Rutledge.

Salaysay, Raquel. "Mutants and Monsters, Pillows and Truncheons: A Garage Punk Reunion." Used by kind permission of the author. © Raquel Salaysay.

Sanders, Ed. "Going to a Meeting on Bank Street" and "Ten Years for Two Joints." Used by kind permission of the author. © Ed Sanders.

Scully, James. "Motown." Originally published in *May Day* (Minnesota Review Press, 1980). Used by kind permission of the author. © James Scully.

Seyburn, Patty. "Wild One." Originally printed in *Askew,* 2009. Used by kind permission of the author. © Patty Seyburn.

Simon, Paul. "Papa Hobo" by Paul Simon, Copyright © 1971 (Renewed) by
Paul Simon (BMI) International Copyright Secured. All Rights Reserved.
Reprinted by Permission.

Sims, John. "D-City Blues." Used by kind permission of the author. © John Sims.

Sinclair, John. "bags' groove." Used by kind permission of the author. © John
Sinclair.

Smith, Fred "Sonic." "City Slang." © Stratium Music Inc., c/o 9111 Sunset Blvd., Los
Angeles, CA 90069, Used by kind permission of the licensor. "Sister Anne."
Words and Music by Fred Smith. Copyright © 1971 (Renewed) Cotillion
Music INC. (BMI) and Motor City Music (BMI) All Rights Administered by
Cotillion Music INC. All Rights Reserved. Used by permission of Alfred Music.

Smith, Larry. "Bo Diddley Died Today—Hey, Bo Diddley." Used by kind permission
of the author. © Larry Smith.

Smith, Patricia. "A Colored Girl Will Slice You If You Talk Wrong about Motown"
and "Motown Crown" from *Shoulda Been Jimi Savannah*. Copyright © 2012
by Patricia Smith. Reprinted with the permission of The Permissions Company,
Inc., on behalf of Coffee House Press. www.coffeehousepress.org

Stein, Kevin. "Upon Finding a Black Woman's Door Sprayed with Swastikas, I Tell
Her This Story of Hands," is reprinted from *Bruised Paradise* (Champaign-
Urbana, IL: University of Illinois Press, 1996). Copyright © 1996 Kevin Stein.
Used by kind permission of the author.

Striho, Carolyn. "City Music Lights." Used by kind permission of the author. ©
Carolyn Striho.

Taylor, Keith. "Detroit Dancing, 1948" appeared in *Guilty at the Rapture* (Hanging
Loose Press, 2006). Used by kind permission of the author. © Keith Taylor.

Thorburn, Russell. "Woodward Avenue on the Bus Downtown." From *Ballad in
Plain Be Flat,* unpublished manuscript. Used by kind permission of the author.
© Russell Thorburn.

Torreson, Rodney. "Since You Always Threw Yourself Out There, David Ruffin."
Used by kind permission of the author. © Rodney Torreson.

Trimble, Thomas. "Muscle Car." Used by kind permission of the author. © Thomas
Trimble.

Trinidad, David. "Meet the Supremes" from *Dear Prudence: New and Selected Poems*
(Turtle Point Press, 2011). Copyright © David Trinidad, 2011.

Tyner, Robin. "Grande Days." Used by kind permission of the author. © Robin Tyner.

Tysh, Chris. "By Any Means Necessary." An excerpt from *car men, a play in d* by Chris Tysh. (Hamtramck, MI: Past Tents Press, 1994), 68–69. Used by kind permission of the author. © Chris Tysh.

Tysh, George. "Jazz" appeared originally in *Kick Out the Jams: Detroit's Cass Corridor 1963–1977* (Detroit: Detroit Institute of Arts, 1980). "Vintage Soul" appeared originally in George Tysh's *The Imperfect* (New York: United Artists Books, 2010). Reprinted by kind permission of the author. © George Tysh.

Vinstra, Andrew. "Detroit Rock & Roll 2 a.m. Séance for Jesus." Used by kind permission of the author. © Andrew Vinstra.

Wallenstein, Barry. "Julian." Lyrics written for the recording *I Carry Your Heart: Alexis Cole Sings Pepper Adams*. Reprinted by kind permission of the author. © Barry Wallenstein.

Waller, Rayfield A. "This is Faruq Bey on His Bike." Used by kind permission of the author. © Rayfield A. Waller.

White, Bob. a.k.a, "The Detroit Count." "Hastings Street Opera." Public Domain.

White, Jack. "Courageous Dream's Concern." Used by kind permission of the author. © Jack White.

Williams, Crystal. "Homecoming" and "Parable of Divas: Aretha Franklin & Diana Ross." Used by kind permission of the author. © Crystal Williams.

Williams, Tyrone. "How Like an Angel." Used by kind permission of the author. © Tyrone Williams.

Williams, Willie. "The Baron." Used by kind permission of the author. © eilliWilliams.

Wormser, Baron. "Soul Music." from *Scattered Chapters: New & Selected Poems* (New York: Sarabande Books, 2008). Used by kind permission of the author. © Baron Wormser.

Young, Al. "Detroit 1958" and "Who Am I in the Twilight" from *Something About the Blues: A Poetry Speak Book* (Sourcebooks MediaFusion, 2007). Reprinted by kind permission of the author. © Al Young.

Zadoorian, Michael. "The Jams" is an excerpt from Michael Zadoorian's novel *Beautiful Music* (New York: Akashic Press, 2018). Used by kind permission of the author. © Michael Zadoorian.

Index of Poets